Courage to Change

to

One Day at a Time in Al-Anon II

Al-Anon Family Group Headquarters, Inc.

Library of Congress Catalogue Card No. 92-071379
ISBN 0-910034-79-6

Approved by
World Service Conference
Al-Anon Family Groups

For information, catalogue of litereature and details of your nearest
group please write to:

AL-ANON FAMILY GROUPS UK & EIRE
61 GREAT DOVER STREET
LONDON SE1 4YF
TEL: 0171 403 0888

UK A-15/B16/96   Family Groups Ltd, Registered Charity

Printed by KSC Printers, Tunbridge Wells, Kent

The Al-Anon Family Groups are a fellowship of relatives and friends of alcoholics who share their experience, strength, and hope, in order to solve their common problems. We believe alcoholism is a family illness and that changed attitudes can aid recovery.

Al-Anon is not allied with any sect, denomination, political entity, organization, or institution; does not engage in any controversy, neither endorses nor opposes any cause. There are no dues for membership. Al-Anon is self-supporting through its own voluntary contributions.

Al-Anon has but one purpose: to help families of alcoholics. We do this by practicing the Twelve Steps, by welcoming and giving comfort to families of alcoholics, and by giving understanding and encouragement to the alcoholic.

The Suggested Preamble to the Twelve Steps

&

The Serenity Prayer

God grant me the serenity
To accept the things I cannot change,
Courage to change the things I can,
And wisdom to know the difference.

PREFACE

Taking life one day at a time has proven essential in the Al-Anon program of recovery for those whose lives have been adversely affected by the problem of alcoholism in a relative or a friend. This book, like its companion volume *One Day at a Time in Al-Anon*, is designed to keep our focus on today and give us the courage to change the things we can.

The 1988 Al-Anon World Service Conference voted to produce a second daily reader to more fully reflect the variety of our fellowship, whose members are the real authors of this collection. Such collective wisdom helps us to view each day as an opportunity for happiness by focusing on the reality of today without the burdens of yesterday or the fears of tomorrow.

Because these selections are based on sharings from individuals, they contain references to gender and to specific relationships, but the thoughts are applicable to people of all walks of life.

As in *One Day at a Time in Al-Anon*, the meditations are reinforced by appropriate quotations. The use of these quotes implies no endorsement of the person or the volumes quoted. They have been selected for what was said, not who said it.

We live in a society of instant gratification: instant coffee, instant breakfast, instant money from our local ready bank machine—it's everywhere we look! No wonder so many of us arrive at Al-Anon's doors looking for the instant answer to all the problems that come from living with and loving an alcoholic.

Recovery is a process. It takes time to regain, reclaim, and recoup all that was lost while we tried on our own to cope with active drinking. Building trust takes time, change takes time, healing old wounds takes time; there are no immediate, ready-made solutions. But the tools and principles of our program—Steps, Traditions, slogans, meetings, sponsorship, service—can lead us to the answers that are right for us.

We all have dark times in our lives, but the journey to better times is often what makes us happier, stronger people. When we stop expecting instant relief, we may come to believe that where we are today is exactly where our Higher Power would have us be.

Today's reminder

Al-Anon is a "One day at a time" program. No matter what is going on around me, today I know that I am moving forward. I will trust the process of recovery. I'll let time take time.

> "If I am under pressure and setting myself deadlines, I will stop for a few minutes and think of just this one day and what I can do with it."
>
> *One Day at a Time in Al-Anon*

Turning to an alcoholic for affection and support can be like going to a hardware store for bread. Perhaps we expect a "good" parent to nurture and support our feelings, or a "loving" spouse to comfort and hold us when we are afraid, or a "caring" child to want to pitch in when we are ill or overwhelmed. While these loved ones may not meet our expectations, it is our expectations, not our loved ones, that have let us down.

Love is expressed in many ways, and those affected by alcoholism may not be able to express it the way we would like. But we can try to recognize love whenever and however it is offered. When it is not, we don't have to feel deprived; most of us find an unfailing source of love in Al-Anon. With the encouragement and support of others, we learn to treat our needs as important and appropriate, and to treat ourselves as deserving.

Today's reminder

Today the alcoholic may or may not be able to give us what we desire. And no one person will ever offer all that we require. If we stop insisting that our needs be met according to our will, we may discover that all the love and support we need is already at our fingertips.

"In Al-Anon I discover in myself the power to throw new light on a seemingly hopeless situation. I learn I must use this power, not to change the alcoholic, over whom I am powerless, but to overcome my own distorted ideas and attitudes."

One Day at a Time in Al-Anon

I am writing my life story with every single *today*. Am I moving in a positive direction? If not, perhaps I need to make some changes. I can do nothing to change the past except stop repeating it in the present. Going to Al-Anon meetings and practicing the principles of the program are some of the ways in which I am already breaking out of unhealthy and unsatisfying patterns of the past.

I believe that my life is built upon layers of little everyday accomplishments. When I think this way, setting goals and taking small risks becomes nothing more than a daily striving to make my life better. Taking some tiny action each day can be much more effective than weeks and months of inactivity followed by a frenzied attempt to make radical changes overnight. It certainly leaves me more serene. When I face a new challenge, I try to take my beginning wherever it may be and start from there.

Today's reminder

No one can make me change. No one can stop me from changing. No one really knows how I must change, not even I. Not until I start. I will remember that it only takes a slight shift in direction to begin to change my life.

> "The journey of a thousand miles begins with a single step."
>
>   Lao-tse

When I first found Al-Anon I was desperate and lonely. I yearned for the serenity that others in the meetings so obviously possessed. When members shared about the tools that had worked for them, I paid close attention.

Here is what I heard: Go to meetings and share when you can; work all the Steps, but not all at once—start with Step One; get a sponsor; read some Al-Anon literature every day; use the phone to reach out between meetings. Gradually I took each of these suggestions and began to see real changes in my life. I began to believe my life could amount to more than a string of painful days to be survived. Now I had resources that helped me to deal with even the most difficult situations. I came to see that, with the help of my Higher Power, I could handle anything that came to pass and even grow as I did so. In time, the tools and principles of the program helped me gain the serenity I had long desired.

Today's reminder

Al-Anon gives me tools I can use to achieve many goals, including serenity, sanity, and detachment with love. And Al-Anon members who share their experience, strength, and hope show me how to put these tools to work in my life.

> "Daily vigilance will turn out to be a small price to pay for my peace of mind."
>
> *The Dilemma of the Alcoholic Marriage*

I was terribly confused about the meaning of "compassion" when I came to Al-Anon. I thought it meant making excuses for the alcoholic or covering bad checks. Al-Anon helped me to find another word for this behavior: "enabling." I learned that when I cleaned up the consequences of alcoholic behavior, I enabled the alcoholic to continue drinking comfortably and acting out without having to pay the price. A more compassionate way to respond to those I love might be to allow them to face the consequences of their actions, even when it will cause them pain.

How do I know whether a particular action is enabling? While this is not always clear, I find it helpful to look carefully at my motives. Am I trying to interfere with the natural consequences of a loved one's choices? Am I trying to do for someone what they could do for themselves? Am I doing what I think is best for me? Do I resent what I am doing? If so, is it really a loving choice? Sometimes the most compassionate thing I can do is to let others take responsibility for their behavior.

Today's reminder

Today I will remember that I have choices, and so does the alcoholic. I will make the best choices I can and allow others in my life to do the same without interference.

"I must learn to give those I love the right to make their own mistakes and recognize them as theirs alone."

Al-Anon Faces Alcoholism

Between meetings, I need to keep in close touch with other Al-Anon members by telephone. Like many who have been affected by alcoholism, when I came into the program I was tremendously overburdened. Lots of patient listening at the other end of the line continues to help me get these burdens off my chest.

Sharing Al-Anon recovery by telephone allows me to reach out to someone else for support. The person I am talking to is not my counselor, confessor, or problem-solver. Nor is he or she obliged to sit and listen to all my sob stories.

Instead, this person may help me reason things out. Sometimes I'll be reminded of an Al-Anon idea or tool that will enable me to gain some perspective on my situation. I am not given advice about what I should or should not do—that is for me to decide. By the time the conversation is over, I've usually found some relief from the problem that had seemed so enormous while it stayed trapped inside my head.

Today's reminder

It is my responsibility to solve my own problems with the help of the God of my understanding. Since God often speaks through other people, when I reach out and make an Al-Anon call, I become willing to receive that help.

"We cannot climb up a rope that is attached only to our own belt."

William Ernest Hocking

"Just for today I will have a quiet half hour all by myself and relax." How simple that sounded until I tried to do it. I found it difficult to spend even a little time alone—thirty quiet minutes out of my busy schedule were far too many! So I started with five minutes. In time I was able to find ten, and then twenty, and then thirty minutes for myself.

Amazingly, these quiet half hours are restoring me to sanity. It is through these times with myself, much of which is spent in prayer and meditation, that I find the peace and power of my God.

As a result, I have learned to tolerate and even enjoy my own company. Now, no matter what is going on, I need this half hour every day to get a perspective on my life. By sitting quietly in the midst of turmoil, I find that I am not alone. If I take the time, my Higher Power sends the message.

Today's reminder

I care enough about myself to take a quiet half hour to relax. But if a half hour is more than I can manage, I can let that be all right. Whatever time I give to myself will be a step forward. If I can stop the wheels from turning for even a few moments, my Higher Power can take charge and steer me in the right direction.

"Take rest; a field that has rested gives a beautiful crop."

                                                    Ovid

I once emphatically told my family that their bickering was making our newly-sober loved one nervous and this might cause her to start drinking again. I was shocked when I was told, just as emphatically, "Well, let her!" I realized that I was still trying to make everything smooth and easy for the alcoholic, because I hadn't accepted that I was just as powerless over alcoholism in sobriety as I had been during the active years.

It was then that I truly discovered how beautifully "Letting go and letting God" can work. When I fully understood how powerless I was over the situation, I was able to trust that the alcoholic has her own Higher Power and that, together, they can work out her future. I felt like a new person because I was free of the constant need to watch over her, free to live my own life.

I care about the alcoholic in my life more than I can say. I wish her health, happiness, and sobriety, but I cannot hand these things to her. She and her Higher Power are in charge of that. I can only love her, and when I stop to think about it, that is enough.

Today's reminder

Today I choose to place my trust in that Higher Power, knowing that all is well.

"If we supply the willingness, God supplies the power."

Al-Anon Family Groups

How often I look outside myself for approval! The project at work is successful, but my good feelings depend on having that success acknowledged. The meal I fix at home is not as tasty when no one compliments the cook. I resent the favors I do for my children when they neglect to thank me.

We all need an occasional pat on the back. But when the applause of others becomes the reason for my behavior and necessary for me to feel satisfied, then I have given them power over me.

People may forget to notice the terrific things that I've done or may not be comfortable praising me. I don't have to take it personally. Self-pity and resentment are not my only options. If I can learn to evaluate my own actions and behavior and to value my own judgment, then the approval of others will be enjoyable, but no longer essential to my serenity.

Today's reminder

Just for today, I will appreciate myself. I will not look to others for approval; I will provide it for myself. I'll allow myself to recognize that I am doing the best I can. Today my best is good enough.

> "Your vision will become clear only when you can look into your own heart."
>
> Carl Jung

I suspect that if I reclaimed all the minutes, hours, and days I've sacrificed to worry and fear, I'd add years to my life. When I succumb to worry, I open a Pandora's box of terrifying pictures, paranoid voices, and relentless self-criticism. The more attention I pay to this mental static, the more I lose my foothold in reality. Then nothing useful can be accomplished.

To break the cycle of worry and fear, I'm learning to focus all my attention on this very moment. I can turn away from destructive thoughts and concentrate instead on the sights and sounds around me: light and shadows, the earth beneath my feet, the pulse of everyday living—all pieces of the here-and-now. These bits of reality help rescue me from "what-if's" and "should have's" by anchoring me in the present. Prayer and meditation, the slogans, and phone calls to Al-Anon friends are other sources of serenity that bring me back to this moment. As I shut out the noise, I am more receptive to my Higher Power's will, and therefore much more able to work my way through difficult times.

Today's reminder

This day is all I have to work with, and it is all I need. If I am tempted to worry about tomorrow's concerns, I will gently bring my mind back to today.

"The past has flown away. The coming month and year do not exist. Ours only is the present's tiny point."

Mahmud Shabistari

I feel like the luckiest person in the world because I've found a second family, and I am a very real part of it. In my new family, I am accepted just as I am. I never have to pretend, or wear a mask over my feelings. I can speak freely and know that my words won't leave the room.

In my new family, people empathize when I share my troubles. But instead of trying to solve my problems for me, they allow me the dignity to do so on my own. They do offer their experience, strength, and hope, and in this sharing I often hear just what I need to help me with a troublesome situation.

In my new family, love is not a point system. I don't have to earn love from others—it's given freely as a gift. I don't have to earn my place in the sun, I can just relax and be myself.

Today's reminder

When a loved one's alcoholism brought me to Al-Anon, I found a new, second family, a family that helped me discover the me that had been hidden for so long, a family that will always be there for me. Today I will enjoy having a place where I really belong.

> "For me, alcoholism has proven to be a bittersweet legacy—bitter, because of the pain I suffered, and sweet, because if it weren't for that pain, I wouldn't have searched for and found a better way of living."
>
> *Al-Anon Faces Alcoholism*

Early one morning I stopped to watch a colony of bees. A little intimidated by the frenzied motion and intense buzzing, I reminded myself that if I didn't poke my nose into their hive, I wouldn't get stung. If I chose to maintain a safe distance from a dangerous situation, I would be fine.

To me, that is exactly the lesson that detachment teaches. The choice is mine. When I sense that a situation is dangerous to my physical, mental, or spiritual well-being, I can put extra distance between myself and the situation. Sometimes this means that I don't get too emotionally involved in a problem; sometimes I may physically leave the room or end a conversation. And sometimes I try to put spiritual space between myself and another person's alcoholism or behavior. This doesn't mean I stop loving the person, only that I acknowledge the risks to my own well-being and make choices to take care of myself.

Today's reminder

Now I know how to end an argument by simply refusing to participate, to turn to my Higher Power for help with whatever I'm powerless to change, to say, "No," when I mean no, and to step back from insanity rather than diving into it. Detachment is a loving gift I continue to give to myself and to others.

"If a man carries his own lantern, he need not fear darkness."

Hasidic saying

Al-Anon gives me great spiritual freedom because it encourages me to find a personal understanding of God, and to allow others the same freedom. Until I could think of God in terms that were meaningful to me, I was not able to truly turn my life over to a Higher Power.

My concept of God evolves. It changes and grows as I continue to change and grow. How wonderful it is, for I now sense a Higher Power that is as alive as I am! Never in my life did I dream of finding such a source of serenity, courage, and wisdom.

There is a sense of unique purpose to my journey through life. I am the only one who can live it, and I need the help of the God *of my understanding* in order to live it fully. Grounded in faith, I can hold tight to my course and meet the future with confidence.

Today's reminder

Once upon a time I was afraid to live life for myself. This was because I did not know how to do it and thought that there was no one to show me. Now I have a resource deep within me to guide me along life's many roads. I am not alone on my journey.

"In the midst of winter, I finally learned that there was in me an invincible summer."

Albert Camus

I learned in Al-Anon that I'm bound to fail to make someone else stop drinking because I am powerless over alcoholism. Others in the fellowship had failed as well, yet they seemed almost happy to admit it. In time I understood: By letting go of this battle we were sure to lose, we became free.

Gradually I learned that nothing I did or did not do would convince my loved one to get sober. I understood intellectually, but it took time before I believed it in my heart. Frequent Al-Anon meetings, phone calls, and reading of Al-Anon literature were indispensable to this learning process.

Later, when my loved one chose sobriety, I found new ways to apply this principle of powerlessness. Although I was tempted to check up on the number of meetings attended and to protect the alcoholic from anything upsetting, I had accepted that nothing I could do would make or break another person's sobriety. After a while, I saw that my fears had little to do with the alcoholic. Instead, they indicated that I needed to work my program.

Today's reminder

When I am able to admit that I am powerless over alcohol, my life becomes more manageable. Today I will take the path to personal freedom and serenity that begins when I surrender.

> "Our spiritual growth is unlimited and our reward endless if we try to bring this program into every phase of our daily lives."
>
> *The Twelve Steps and Traditions*

Recently I learned about a crisis in the life of an alcoholic I love. Today, while trying to work, I found myself slumping in my chair, depressed and distracted. Soon, all thoughts of work had fled, and I was busy projecting a horrible outcome to my loved one's crisis and dreading the ways in which the consequences might affect me. The slogan, "One day at a time" reminds me that, in spite of my fears, I don't know what tomorrow will bring.

Why am I leaping into the future? Perhaps I've given my feelings no room to exist. Part of me gambles that by worrying in advance, bad news will be easier to face if it comes. But worrying will not protect me from the future. It will just keep me from living here and now.

Today's reminder

I needn't explore how I'll feel about something that might occur in the future. I don't actually know how I'll feel, and it may never happen. So when I feel myself leaving the present, I'll remind myself that the future is not today's problem.

"Worry never robs tomorrow of its sorrow; it only saps today of its strength."

A.J. Cronin

There was a time when, if a thought entered my mind, it automatically came out of my mouth. Even if I wasn't sure that what I was saying was true, the words poured out of me. In Al-Anon I have learned to "Think" before I speak.

When I'm tempted to respond to angry accusations with accusations of my own, I stop and "Think." When I have an urge to betray a confidence, to gossip, or to tell something extremely personal to a total stranger, I stop and "Think." And when my opinion about another person's business has not been requested, I take the time to "Think" before I get involved. That way I make a conscious choice about how I will respond.

Perhaps I will decide to say nothing, or choose a more tactful way to proceed, or question whether I really mean what I have been thinking. I may decide that this is not an appropriate place to discuss what is on my mind. Or I may choose to go right ahead and speak up in a very direct manner. Regardless of which option I select, today I am willing to accept the consequences of my actions because I have taken the time to make a choice.

Today's reminder

Today I will let my words serve my best interests. I will choose them with care.

"I don't let my mouth say nothin' my head can't stand."

                                        Louis Armstrong

Anyone who watched my interactions with the alcoholics in my life probably would have considered me the crazy one. I was the one who searched from bar to bar, made scenes in public places, and got hysterical over little things. I was also the one who agonized over the alcoholic's behavior, lied, made apologies and excuses, and resented everything I was doing. Was this sane?

Al-Anon was the first place where I ever thought to question my own sanity. I found that I couldn't overcome the effects of this disease by force of will or reason. As they say, my best thinking got me here. But Al-Anon's Second Step suggested that a Higher Power could restore me to sanity.

I knew that I felt more rational in an Al-Anon meeting than I did at any other time, and so I turned for help to the Power that seemed to flow through those meetings. From time to time I still have my irrational moments, but I no longer blame my erratic behavior on anyone else. I now know exactly where to turn when I am ready to find sanity once more.

Today's reminder

Today I will focus on my own behavior. If it could stand some improvement, I will ask a Power greater than myself for help.

> "If we do not change our direction, we are likely to end up where we are headed."
>
> Ancient Chinese proverb

When I first heard that the best way to help an alcoholic was to focus on myself, I thought Al-Anon was a heartless place where I would be forced to stop caring about my loved ones. I had decided never to return, but someone shared a thought that changed my mind. He said that although the desire to help another person can be well-motivated and compassionate, our old ways of "helping" don't necessarily help. Al-Anon offers a new way to help.

I examined my version of helping the alcoholic. I saw that when I covered her bad checks or made excuses for her, I kept her from facing the consequences of her actions. I actually was depriving her of opportunities to want to change.

I also had to consider why I felt so desperate unless I was helping. When I took a look at my motives, I found that it was *my* anxiety I didn't want to face.

Today's reminder

Is the help I offer truly loving or do I have other motives? Am I trying to change another person or get them to do what I want? Talking it over with my sponsor can offer perspective. My best hope for helping those I love really does begin when I focus on myself.

> "In Al-Anon we learn:
> –Not to create a crisis;
> –Not to prevent a crisis if it is in the natural course of events."
>
> *Detachment*

Today I seek to become a little more accepting of myself, a little more comfortable in my own skin. Although it is important to recognize and admit my limitations and flaws, only my Higher Power can remove them.

Condemning my imperfections has never enhanced my appreciation of life or helped me to love myself more. Perhaps I can let go of all condemnation for this one day. I will recognize that I am on a spiritual path of self-improvement. Every tiny step I take on that path moves me closer to wholeness, health, and serenity.

If I become impatient with myself, I can examine my expectations. Perhaps I expect recovery to happen overnight. I will take time today to acknowledge my efforts and to trust the process of the Al-Anon program.

Today's reminder

Al-Anon is a gentle, healing program. I will remember to be gentle with myself today, trusting that the healing will come.

> "Today I can accept myself for what I am because I know that whatever happens, I have a Higher Power and a group of people who will love me anyway."
>
> *. . . In All Our Affairs*

"Anonymity is the spiritual foundation of all our Traditions." Anonymity makes it possible to leave not only our surnames, but all the labels and expectations with which we have been burdened, outside the Al-Anon rooms. Through our commitment to anonymity we can put aside *what* we are and begin to know *who* we are.

As I began to recognize how valuable this spiritual principle already was in my life, I understood why it was so important to protect the anonymity of others, including the alcoholic. If I want the benefits the program has to offer, I have an obligation to extend to others the same respect and courtesy that keep me feeling safe, free from labels, and free to be myself.

Today's reminder

In taking my place among the thousands of anonymous individuals who make up the Al-Anon Family Groups, I know that I never again have to be alone. I won't jeopardize this valuable resource by violating its most fundamental spiritual principle.

> "Each person should be able to leave an Al-Anon meeting secure in the knowledge that what he, or she, has shared will not be repeated."
>
> *Why Is Al-Anon Anonymous?*

Before Al-Anon, I could never tell the difference between what was and was not my business. I felt I had to take care of everyone around me until I couldn't stand it any more. I usually kept this up until I became physically ill. My body tried to tell me to pay attention to my own needs, but I simply wasn't ready to listen.

Al-Anon helps me to "Listen and learn" from my body, my soul, and my Higher Power. How do I do it? I try to check in with myself on a regular basis. Am I hungry, angry, lonely, or tired? If so, I can make a point of stopping what I'm doing long enough to attend to my needs.

When I pay attention to the messages I'm being given, I have a better chance of detaching from other people and situations, should that be appropriate. For me, this is the foundation of serenity.

Today's reminder

I no longer have to wait until my health, my financial situation, or my emotional state collapses before paying attention to my needs. Today I can practice becoming more aware of what my inner voice is trying to teach me. I can "Listen and learn."

"Don't listen to friends when the Friend inside you says 'Do this!'"

Mahatma Gandhi

I tried so hard to learn detachment. Living with active alcoholism was confusing, and the idea of detachment seemed vague. The alcoholic in my life was a restless sleeper who fell out of bed almost every night. Feeling it my duty, I would always help him back into bed. One night, after attending Al-Anon meetings for a while, I stepped over his body and got into bed, leaving him on the floor. Triumphantly, I went to my next Al-Anon meeting and told them, "I finally learned detachment!" "Well," they said, "that's not exactly what we meant. We meant detachment *with love*."

I left that meeting with a new understanding that I put into practice the very next time my loved one fell out of bed. When I found him on the floor, I still didn't help him into bed. But I did put a blanket over him before stepping over his body and going to bed myself. This, to me, was detachment with love.

Today's reminder

With my Higher Power's help, I will keep a loving blanket of detachment with me. I will cover my loved ones with it, whether or not they struggle with a disease, keeping in mind that when I am dealing with other human beings, I am dealing with children of God.

> "Detachment is not isolation, nor should it remain focused on not enabling the sick behavior of the past. Detachment is not a wall; it is a bridge across which the Al-Anon may begin a new approach to life and relationships generally."

> *Al-Anon: Family Treatment Tool in Alcoholism*

In Step Three we "Made a decision to turn our will and our lives over to the care of God *as we understood Him.*" This is a big decision for those of us who have a tough time making even small decisions. Until I found Al-Anon, I tended to let others decide how I should live, where I should go, and what I should do. The paradox is that, though I took little responsibility for my own life, I saw myself as an expert on everyone else's life and felt accountable for all that happened.

The order in which the first three Steps are written helps me to overcome these attitude problems. First, I accept my inability to control the disease of alcoholism and admit that my life is unmanageable. Next, I come to believe that a Power greater than myself can help. After taking these two Steps, it becomes possible, desirable, and even logical, to make the enormous decision to trust my life to a Higher Power's care.

Today's reminder

At the start of each day I can make the decision to turn my will and my life over to the care of God. This way I begin my day with a strong assertion that I choose to accept the reality of my life. I am moving in a healthy direction, growing ever more able to live a good life and to love those I meet along the way.

"Decision is a risk rooted in the courage of being free."

Paul Tillich

I will dare to be myself. I may be tempted to paste a smile on my face even though I am angry, in order to please another person. When turning down an invitation, I may want to make excuses so that nobody will be hurt. I may be inclined to cancel plans that I care about, without protest, because a loved one prefers to stay home and I don't want to make waves. These may be perfectly acceptable choices, and I may opt for any or all of them. But today I will be honest with myself as I do so—I will not pretend to feel what I do not feel or to want what I do not want.

Al-Anon does not tell me how to behave. It doesn't legislate right or wrong choices. But Al-Anon does encourage me to look searchingly and fearlessly at myself, my feelings, motives, and actions. I can only learn to love myself if I am willing to learn who I am.

Today's reminder

I have a right to want what I want and to feel the way I feel. I may not choose to act on those feelings or desires, but I won't hide them from myself. They are part of me.

"This above all: to thine own self be true."

William Shakespeare

Before I discovered Al-Anon I often used other people's problems as an excuse to avoid my obligations. I loved the drama of another's crisis and talked about it at every opportunity. My own life seemed increasingly trivial, and my problems felt silly.

It was therefore very difficult for me to focus on myself when I came to Al-Anon. I wanted to talk about the alcoholic when I came to meetings, but no one seemed interested. They all kept asking about me—how *I* felt, what *I* did, what *I* wanted.

I found that I was overly interested in others because I had such a low opinion of myself. My sponsor helped me to see that when I acted as if someone else's life was more important than mine, I was harming myself. This had to stop if I wanted to learn to value my own experience. Focusing on myself was the beginning of building self-esteem. It took practice, but with the support I got in meetings, I grew more comfortable. I learned to talk about myself and to view my feelings, achievements, and concerns as valid and important.

Today's reminder

Today, if I'm tempted to gossip or to create a drama around someone else's life, I will ask myself, "What is going on with me?"

"We talk about the part we played in our problems and how we change our attitudes and actions by applying the Al-Anon program to our lives."

Al-Anon Spoken Here

I'd read the Twelfth Step many times before I saw it. But *there* it was: "Having had a spiritual awakening as a result of these Steps . . ." What a promise! If I worked these Steps, I'd have a spiritual awakening! There was hope, even for me!

Now that's not why I first came to Al-Anon. Like many, I came to find out how to make someone stop drinking. It was much later when I realized that my life was missing a sense of direction only a Higher Power could provide.

Those wonderful Twelfth Step words gave me the encouragement I needed to begin at the beginning. Slowly, sometimes painfully, I worked my way through the Steps. In time, something amazing happened. I was filled with a sense of my God and His love for me. I felt whole. I knew I'd never be the same again.

Today's reminder

The Steps offer me a road map for living that leads to a spiritual awakening and beyond. I can't skip ahead to the end of the journey—which can at times be a hard one—but I can put one foot in front of the other and follow the directions I've been given, knowing that others who have gone before me have received more along the way than they had ever dreamed.

"The first time I ever heard the Twelve Steps read at a meeting, I became very still. I felt I was not breathing . . . I was just listening with my whole being . . . I knew deep within me that I was home."

As We Understood . . .

I knew I was in trouble: I was ready to throw someone I loved very deeply out of my life forever because he had left unwashed dishes in the sink. I was obviously overreacting, yet I couldn't calm down. I picked up the phone and called an Al-Anon friend.

After hearing me out, she mentioned that I seemed angry about more than dirty dishes. I certainly was. To me, those dishes were evidence of a whole pattern of disrespect. She said that she too grew annoyed and played martyr when faced with the same situation again and again, but whenever she tried to mend all the problems of a relationship in a single day, she failed—it just isn't possible to do so. Instead, she tried to deal with one situation at a time.

I still don't like dirty dishes, but I don't have to interpret them as having a deeper meaning. I am learning to take things at face value. Sometimes dirty dishes are just dirty dishes.

Today's reminder

Why do I allow myself to suffer, to blow small things out of proportion? I can break a situation down to a more manageable size by taking it "One day at a time."

"The whole purpose of Al-Anon is to help us iron out the rough spots in our living, and that can be done only one day at a time."

One Day at a Time in Al-Anon

Newcomers are often surprised at the number of years long-time members have been attending Al-Anon meetings. They may be even more surprised that some of us have sobriety in our homes, or no longer have any alcoholics in our lives. Why do we keep coming back? For many of us the answer is "serenity."

Sometimes I get impatient, or rebellious, or bored. I go through periods where I see little change in myself, and I begin to doubt. But even after many years of Al-Anon recovery, if I miss too many meetings, things seem to become unmanageable all over again. I have been affected by someone else's drinking. I don't want to underestimate the lasting impact that alcoholism has had on me. So I keep coming back.

I came to Al-Anon for a quick fix for my pain, but I stay because of the consistency, security, and friendship I find each day. Because of my commitment to my own growth, I am able to handle very difficult situations with a great deal of peace, and the delight in my life continues to exceed my wildest dreams.

Today's reminder

I see my recovery as a healthy way of life that I can gladly share with others. Today I am actively pursuing a better life because I am working on myself.

"Just for today I will have a program. I may not follow it exactly, but I will have it."

Just For Today

Many of us learn the value of self-expression in Al-Anon. We discover how we feel and benefit from giving voice to those feelings when it seems appropriate. But there's a difference between expressing ourselves and using words to control others.

Sometimes the only way I can determine whether I'm trying to control someone else or whether I'm simply expressing my feelings is by noticing how many times I say the same thing. If I mention something that is on my mind and then let it go no matter what response I get, I am speaking sincerely. If I repeatedly make similar suggestions or ask prodding questions again and again, I am probably trying to control. If I am satisfied only when the other person responds in a way I consider desirable—agrees with what I've said or takes my advice—then I know I've lost my focus.

Today's reminder

I am learning to be honest with myself. I will not use my recovery as an excuse to justify my efforts to change other people's thinking. Trying to control other people only gets me in trouble. Instead, I will promptly admit such mistakes and put my energy back where it belongs by focusing on myself.

"We should have much peace if we would not busy ourselves with the sayings and doings of others."

                                        Thomas à Kempis

Living with alcoholism, I learned that plans could change at any moment and that rules varied accordingly. I developed a deep mistrust of everyone and everything, because I could count on nothing.

As a result, I have often found myself jumping at any opportunity without thinking it through. Behind my action was a sense of desperation: "I'd better grab this now—this may be my only chance." Al-Anon shows me a different approach: I can live "One day at a time." I can base my choices on what I feel is right for me today, rather than on what I fear I might lose sometime in the future. I can "Think" before I react to my fears, and remember that "Easy does it."

If I feel unable to do something today, I trust that there will be another opportunity if it is something I am meant to do. It doesn't have to be now or never, all or nothing.

Today's reminder

Today I don't have to be limited by my old fears. Instead, I can do what seems right. I do not have to follow every suggestion or take every offer I receive. I can consider my options and pray for the guidance to choose what is best for me.

"There is a guidance for each of us, and by lowly listening we shall hear the right word . . . Place yourself in the middle of the stream of power and wisdom which flows into your life. Then, without effort, you are impelled to truth and to perfect contentment."

Ralph Waldo Emerson

After working Al-Anon's Twelve Steps zealously for over a year, I was despondent over my continuing lapses into self-pity and resentment over the alcoholic's inability to give me the emotional support I wanted. One evening during a meditation on the Sixth and Seventh Steps, three words seemed to flash in my mind: We were entirely ready to have *God* remove all these defects of character, and we *humbly* asked *Him* to remove our shortcomings.

I suddenly realized that much of my zealous working of the program had been the exercise of my own limited power. With a new and sincere humility, I asked God to remove my shortcomings. When I saw the alcoholic the next morning, it was as if a veil had been lifted from my eyes. I saw her suffering, struggling to stay sober, and I had compassion for my own struggle as well. My self-pity and resentment were gone.

Today's reminder

I want to be ready for shortcomings to be removed, and I will do what I can to prepare. I can develop a non-judgmental awareness of myself, accept what I discover, and be fully willing to change. But I lack the power to heal myself. Only my Higher Power can do that.

"I accept the fact that I need help in being restored to sanity, and that I cannot achieve this without help."

The Dilemma of the Alcoholic Marriage

I thought that if I stopped enabling the alcoholic in my life, the drinking would stop. When the drinking seemed to get worse instead of better, once again I thought I had done something wrong. I was still trying to control alcoholism and its symptoms. Al-Anon helped me to learn that I am powerless. I cannot stop an alcoholic from drinking. If I choose to stop contributing to the problem, I do so because it seems to be the right thing to do, something that will help me to feel better about myself.

When I change my behavior, the behavior of those around me may also change, but there is no guarantee that it will change to my liking. Today I am learning to make choices because they are good for me, not because of the effect they might have on others.

Today's reminder

It is hard to stop acting as I have in the past. But with Al-Anon's support, I can be the one to break the pattern. I can choose to do what I think is right—for me.

> "You have to count on living every single day in a way you believe will make you feel good about your life . . ."
>
> Jane Seymour

I used to live my life as if I were on a ladder. Everyone was either above me—to be feared and envied—or below me—to be pitied. God was way, way at the top, beyond my view. That was a hard, lonely way to live, because no two people can stand comfortably on the same rung for very long.

When I came to Al-Anon, I found a lot of people who had decided to climb down from their ladders into the circle of fellowship. In the circle we were all on equal terms, and God was right in the center, easily accessible. When newcomers arrived we didn't worry about rearranging everyone's position, we simply widened the circle.

Today I no longer look up to some people and down on others. I can look each person in the eye, squarely and honestly. Today, being humble means climbing down from the ladder of judgment of myself and others, and taking my rightful place in a worldwide circle of love and support.

Today's reminder

My thoughts are my teachers. Are they teaching me to love and appreciate myself and others, or are they teaching me to practice isolation? Today I will choose my teachers with greater care.

> "'Live and let live' sets us free from the compulsion to criticize, judge, condemn, and retaliate . . . which can damage us far more than those against whom we use such weapons. Al-Anon teaches us tolerance rooted in love."
>
> *This Is Al-Anon*

As a newcomer to Al-Anon, I heard that the principles of the program could lead to serenity. I'd have preferred to hear that the program would cure the alcoholic, undo the damage of the past, or at least pay the gas bill. My idea of serenity was sitting on a mountaintop with a silly grin on my face, not caring very much about anything. I was more interested in passion!

Eventually I realized that serenity didn't have to strip me of my passion. Instead, it offered me a sense of inner security that freed me to live my life as fully and passionately as I pleased, because it tapped into an unlimited source of energy and wisdom: a Higher Power. I could make strong choices and take risks because, with this help, I was better able to deal with anything that happened.

Nothing can compare to the drama of exploring my full potential as a human being. Once I had a taste of the rich life that could be mine with the help of Al-Anon and my Higher Power, I discovered that serenity was a great treasure.

Today's reminder

Today I seek serenity, knowing that when I am serene, I am capable of becoming more fully, and more passionately, myself.

> "Without this program I could not have appreciated how truly wonderful my life can be in spite of difficult situations."
>
> . . . *In All Our Affairs*

Sometimes when I'm unhappy with my situation, I feel that God is punishing me. Once again I've lost my image of a loving God and need to recover it.

It helps to call my sponsor, who reminds me that God is not a terrorist. I read Al-Anon literature and go to extra meetings. Mostly I walk beside the river and talk with God about how afraid I am. I watch the water and thank God for the good things in my life: Al-Anon recovery, the gift of the Twelve Steps, creativity and the joy I have in expressing it, my loving Al-Anon family. After I've talked it through, I sit and wait until I feel God's healing touch reassuring me, drying my tears.

The funny thing is that, after I'm through those hard times, I never truly remember the pain. What I remember is the sunshine on the water, the peace of the moment, the love of my Higher Power wrapping around me as tangibly as the sunshine. The pain is gone, but the increased trust in my Higher Power remains.

Today's reminder

When faced with difficult or painful situations, I can remember that a loving God is always here for me, always available as a source of comfort, guidance, and peace.

"No one is alone if they've come to believe in a Power greater than themselves."

Sponsorship—What It's All About

"When the student is ready, the teacher appears," say the Zen Buddhists. Or, as an Al-Anon speaker put it, "We each get here right on time." To me, this is an important reason to have a public relations policy based on attraction rather than promotion, as the Eleventh Tradition suggests.

My own arrival in Al-Anon was right on schedule. I first heard about the program when I was a teenager; I attended my first meeting twenty years later. I don't regret that lapse of time because I don't think I would have been ready to come to Al-Anon any sooner—I spent those twenty years resenting any implication from well-meaning family members that I had been affected by alcoholism. Only after many years of living with the effects of the disease did I really become ready to get help. No amount of nagging would have hurried me along any faster.

Today's reminder

There is no magic wand that can make others ready for Al-Anon. And it is presumptuous to assume that I have a better idea of their true path than they do. Let me help those who want help. When my life improves as a result of working the program myself, I do more to carry the message than I ever could by forcing it on others.

> "Let me not dilute the effectiveness of the help I can give by letting it take the form of giving advice. I know I will never have enough insight into another's life to tell that person what is best to do."

The Dilemma of the Alcoholic Marriage

By the time I reached Al-Anon I was desperate to do something about my relationship with an alcoholic. I hoped that you would tell me to "throw the bum out," so I was dismayed when a member suggested that I make no major changes for six months after coming to Al-Anon. By the end of the six months, my thinking had changed dramatically and I was grateful to have waited.

At that point, something inside told me to continue to wait, to learn, to recover, before deciding about this relationship. But I hate to wait. I struggled, prayed for guidance, weighed the pros and cons. The answer was always the same: "Wait. Do nothing yet. The time will come." That wasn't the answer I was looking for. So I ignored it. I forced a "solution" and walked out.

I was immediately consumed with guilt and self-doubt. Had I made the worst mistake of my life? I still loved this person so much, and though I was deeply troubled, I wasn't convinced that leaving was the answer. I had to admit that I had acted prematurely. Only with more time was I eventually able to come to a decision that I knew I could live with.

Today's reminder

When my thinking becomes distorted by trying to force solutions, I probably won't get the results I seek. As the saying goes, "When in doubt, don't."

> "Guide me in all I do to remember that waiting is the answer to some of my prayers."

> *As We Understood . . .*

Today I have a chance to make a contribution to my sense of well-being. I can take some small action that will strengthen a relationship, pursue a goal, or help me to feel better about myself. I don't expect to dramatically alter my life. My goal is simply to move in a positive direction, knowing that major strides often begin with very small steps.

Perhaps I will ask someone to become my sponsor, reach out to a newcomer, or try a different Al-Anon meeting. I might get some exercise, make an appointment for a check-up, listen to music, or clean a closet. I could write a letter to a friend I've neglected or spend some time alone enjoying a few minutes of peace and quiet. Perhaps I'll do something I'm afraid to do, just for the exercise. I might pick up groceries for a sick friend, fix a wobbling table, read a book to stimulate my mind. Maybe I'll meditate on one of the Twelve Steps or share my experience, strength, and hope with someone who wants to hear it.

Today's reminder

There are so many ways in which I can improve the quality of my life. Instead of fretting about what I can't have or can't do, I'll take action to create something positive in my life today.

"To improve the golden moment of opportunity, and catch the good that is within our reach, is the great art of life."

Samuel Johnson

I like people, and at one time I wanted everyone to be my friend. With the best of intentions, I tried to encourage friendships with certain individuals, although my attempts were repeatedly, discreetly rebuffed.

I was comforted by the words I heard at the close of each Al-Anon meeting: ". . . though you may not like all of us, you'll love us in a very special way—the same way we already love you." It was an important lesson that, while I can't have everyone's friendship, I can offer and receive respect, support, and understanding. Patience and humility soothed my wounded pride.

Today's reminder

It is unrealistic to expect everyone to like me. With such an expectation, I set myself up to fail and give myself an excuse to blame that failure on others. I can't change other people, but I can change my own attitudes. I can let go of my rules about how others should feel about me. When I am disappointed in another's response, I can make an extra effort to be kind, warm, and loving to myself. I am loveable just the way I am.

"To love oneself is the beginning of a lifelong romance."

Oscar Wilde

There was nothing simple about my life before I came to Al-Anon. My work was highly stressful, my time was always short, and my attention was intensely focused on the alcoholic, but I didn't realize I was under a strain. During the early days in Al-Anon, I shifted my intense focus to the program. As my denial broke, I became aware that I was exhausted all the time. The topic at an Al-Anon meeting, "Keep it simple," was just what I needed to hear!

I decided that the top priority for my unmanageable life was to recover from the effects of alcoholism. I had responsibilities and couldn't eliminate all the stress from my life, but I tried to simplify it wherever possible. In my case, this meant letting go of some social activities, temporarily switching to a lower paying but less stressful job, and leaving some household chores undone. It wasn't a permanent change, just a way to give myself the time I needed for my emotional and spiritual health.

It was such a relief! By the time I returned to my normal schedule, I had a better grasp on keeping it simple, so I was able to handle it more serenely.

Today's reminder

If I am overwhelmed, I may be trying to do too much. Today I will try to "Keep it simple."

> "The ability to simplify means to eliminate the unnecessary so that the necessary may speak."
>
> Hans Hofmann

One of the effects of alcoholism is that many of us have denied or devalued our talents, feelings, achievements, and desires. In Al-Anon we learn to know, appreciate, and express our true selves. Creativity is a powerful way to celebrate who we are. It is spiritual energy that nourishes our vitality. It is a way to replace negative thinking with positive action.

Every one of us is brimming with imagination, but it often takes practice to find it and put it to use. Yet anything we do in a new way can be creative—building a bookcase, trying a new seasoning on a vegetable, taking a new approach to handling finances, finger painting, problem-solving, tapping out a rhythm on a tabletop. Creative energy is within us and all around us, whether we are writing a masterpiece or folding the laundry.

Every original act asserts our commitment to living. Our program encourages us to acknowledge our achievements and to live each day fully. When we create, we plant ourselves firmly in the moment and teach ourselves that what we do matters.

Today's reminder

Today I will make use of the precious gift of imagination. Thus I will turn away from negativity, self-doubt, and fear, and celebrate life instead.

> "Do what you can, with what you have, where you are."
>
>   Theodore Roosevelt

Tradition Five helps me to set three goals: to work the Steps for myself; to have compassion for alcoholics; and to have compassion for those who come to Al-Anon. What strikes me is the amount of love to be found in these three goals. First, I love myself enough to try to heal and grow by working the Twelve Steps. Next, I call upon this strength to love those people I once thought were my enemies, recognizing that they too were struggling to cope with this terrible disease. Finally, I draw upon these experiences and extend love to those who are following a similar journey—the families and friends of alcoholics.

I know that I was pulled from despair by the love of strangers who quickly became friends. Now I have enough love and wholeness within myself to share it with others who suffer from the effects of alcoholism.

Today's reminder

I needed love before I even knew what it was. Now that I understand something about it, I need it even more. By loving myself, I not only take care of my own needs, but I lay a foundation for loving others. By loving others, I learn to treat myself well.

"Each Al-Anon Family Group has but one purpose: to help families of alcoholics. We do this by practicing the Twelve Steps of AA *ourselves*, by encouraging and understanding our alcoholic relatives, and by welcoming and giving comfort to families of alcoholics."

Tradition Five

For me, detachment is relatively easy with casual friends, where I'm not very emotionally involved. I've noticed that when I am detached, I can listen to other people being critical or grumpy without being affected. But if members of my family act the same way, I often take on their negative frame of mind. My own behavior shows me that I have a choice about my response to other people's moods and attitudes.

What I have learned by comparing these two situations is that detachment involves paying attention to my own mood before I have a chance to take on someone else's. Then I can simply see and hear negativity or anger, without becoming negative or angry. I don't have to have a bad day just because someone I love is struggling. This knowledge allows me to let everyone, including myself, feel whatever they feel without interference.

Today's reminder

If I pause for a moment before focusing on someone else's mood, I may find out that I have feelings of my own that deserve attention. I will look for those moments to check in with myself today.

> "We let go of our obsession with another's behavior and begin to lead happier and more manageable lives, lives with dignity and rights, lives guided by a Power greater than ourselves."

> *Detachment*

Every snowflake is different. Every thumbprint is different. Every person in Al-Anon is different despite the common problem that brings us together.

Comparing myself to others was a defect of character that plagued me all my life and continued during my early years in Al-Anon. I focused on how others seemed to be grasping the program more quickly than I, had the "right" things to say when they shared, seemed more popular. I didn't like myself because I wasn't living up to what I believed to be true about others.

Today, just like the snowflake and the thumbprint, I realize that I too have special qualities. I know that my growth in Al-Anon can't be compared with anyone else's. I have learned that I can't judge my insides by other people's outsides. We're all doing the best we can. Like every other member of the fellowship, I offer an important contribution to the Al-Anon family groups simply by participating and being myself.

Today's reminder

A sponsor or trusted Al-Anon friend can help me see that I have value just as I am.

"It is the chiefest point of happiness that a man is willing to be what he is."

Desiderius Erasmus

Confusion can be a gift from God. Looking back on instances when I felt desperately in need of an immediate solution, I can see that often I wasn't ready to act. When I became fully ready, the information I needed was there for the taking.

When I know too much about my options before the time is right to exercise those options, I tend to use the information only to drive myself crazy. That's why today, when I am feeling confused, I try to consider it grace. It may not yet be time for me to act.

I think that dealing with confusion can be like cooking. If the bread isn't done, I don't take it out of the oven and insist that it's time to eat. I let it finish baking. If a clear solution to a problem hasn't shown itself yet, I can trust that it will appear when the time is right.

Today's reminder

I will thank my Higher Power for whatever I experience today, even if I feel troubled or confused. I know that every experience can offer me a gift. All I have to do is be willing to look at my situation in the light of gratitude.

> "Everything has its wonders, even darkness and silence, and I learn, whatever state I may be in, therein to be content."
>
> Helen Keller

We talk a great deal about *working* the program. Actually what we do is to practice what we're learning. It's like studying a second language. A student reads books and attends classes, but this only gives him technical knowledge. To be able to *use* the language he must be around those who speak and understand it. He practices listening and speaking while continuing to read. If he stays with it, in time it will become a lifelong skill.

So it is with many of us. We begin with little knowledge and many misconceptions. We go to meetings, learn about alcoholism, and study Al-Anon literature. But to actually be able to use this knowledge takes time, patience, and effort. We spend time around people who speak the Al-Anon language, especially those who are making a strong commitment to practicing Al-Anon's principles in their own lives. We continue to listen, to read, to learn. In this way the Al-Anon way of life sinks in until it becomes second nature. Then, because we are constantly changing, we have opportunities to learn and practice some more.

Today's reminder

If I want to become skillful at applying the Al-Anon program to my life, I need to do more than go to an occasional meeting. I must make a commitment and practice, practice, practice.

"We are what we repeatedly do. Excellence, then, is not an act, but a habit."

Aristotle

In a tornado, you not only have to look out for the tremendous winds, but also whatever the winds pick up and hurl in your direction. Like a tornado, alcoholism often brings along additional problems, including verbal, physical, and sexual abuse, illness, debt, prison, infidelity, and even death. Some of these problems can be so embarrassing that we don't dare to talk about them. But in Al-Anon, we learn that we are only as sick as our secrets. Until we let them out into the light, they keep us trapped.

Most of us find it best to share our secrets with someone we can trust, someone who understands the disease of alcoholism. No matter how hopeless, different, or ashamed we may feel, there are Al-Anon members who have been through similar crises and are willing to listen and help.

Today's reminder

The times I most want to hide out with my secrets are probably the times I most need to reach out and share them with others. When facing a difficult situation, let me remember that my Higher Power speaks through other people. I don't have to face it alone.

> "We move from being at the mercy of any problem that comes along to an inner certainty that no matter what happens in our lives, we will be able to face it, deal with it, and learn from it with the help of our Higher Power."
>
> . . . *In All Our Affairs*

My vision can be so limited. I often think that the only possible outcomes are those that I can imagine. Fortunately, my Higher Power is not restricted by such logic. In fact, some of the most wondrous events grow out of what appear to be disasters.

But faith takes practice. Fears can loom large, and I can get lost in my limited thinking. When I can't see any way out and I doubt that even a Higher Power can help me, that's when I most need to pray. When I do, my actions demonstrate my willingness to be helped. And time after time, the help I need is given to me.

Today I know that even when my situation looks bleak and I can't see any way out, miracles can happen if I turn my will and my life over to God.

Today's reminder

I have an important part to play in my relationship with my Higher Power—I have to be willing to receive help, and I have to ask for it. If I develop the habit of turning to my Higher Power for help with small, everyday matters, I'll know what to do when faced with more difficult challenges.

"In the hour of adversity be not without hope
For crystal rain falls from black clouds."

                                              Persian poem

Daily practice of the Al-Anon program is helping me to become more tolerant of other people. For example, when I take my own inventory and examine my motives, I recognize the same shortcomings I once eagerly pointed out in others. It is easier to accept the limitations of others when I acknowledge my own.

I see now that my thinking has often been distorted, my behavior inconsistent. If my perceptions of myself have been so inaccurate, how reliable can my perceptions of others be? I really don't know what anyone else should think, feel, or do. Therefore, I can no longer justify intolerance.

Regular, dedicated practice of the principles of the program keeps me feeling good about myself. This permits me to be increasingly open-minded and considerate toward everyone in my life.

Today's reminder

Al-Anon meetings, fellowship, Steps, Traditions, and literature all help me to improve my ability to relate to others. I will renew my commitment to recovery today.

"An earnest and concentrated study of the Al-Anon program, in depth, will help us to become more tolerant, confident, and loving, teaching us to accept the faults of others as we seek to correct shortcomings in ourselves."

The Dilemma of the Alcoholic Marriage

When I wrote my Fourth Step inventory, I carried a notebook around with me day and night. I didn't want to leave anything out. I discovered my first defect—obsession. I was still writing fifteen minutes before I shared my Fifth Step.

As I took this Step and read my words out loud, some of my patterns became clear for the first time. My behavior paralleled that of the alcoholic. The only difference was that I did it sober—insane, but sober. I saw how much I blamed other people for the events in my life, how I took everything personally, and how my reactions to the alcoholic were based on my fears.

I expected to feel differently the next day, but nothing much happened except that I felt very tired and a little fragile. But change had begun. As time went by, when I found myself in situations similar to those I had described in my Fourth Step, I noticed that my reactions were less extreme. Some things that had bothered me terribly no longer mattered. That's when I knew I'd begun to change.

Today's reminder

I am learning the "nature of my nature" through the Twelve Steps. I trust that I will uncover what I need to know for now, and leave the rest for another time. I am worth learning about.

"When we take Step Five . . . we demonstrate a willingness to change."

                                    . . . *In All Our Affairs*

One of the first things I heard in Al-Anon was that we didn't have to accept unacceptable behavior. This idea helped me to see that I need not tolerate violence or abuse, and that I had choices I hadn't even recognized before. I set some limits, not to control others, but to offer myself guidelines so that I would know what was and was not acceptable and what to do about it.

A few years later I was congratulating myself on how I no longer had such problems, when I suddenly realized that there was still one person from whom I regularly accepted unacceptable behavior—me! I was continually berating myself and blaming myself when things went wrong. I never gave myself credit for my efforts. I told myself I was homely, thoughtless, lazy, stupid. I would never say those things to a friend. I realized that until I started treating myself like a valued friend, I would be standing in the way of my own recovery.

Today's reminder

I have been affected by a disease of attitudes. When I treat myself with love and approval, I know that I am recovering.

"Let one therefore keep the mind pure, for what a man thinks, that he becomes."

The Upanishads

Thanks to Al-Anon's Traditions, I am able to have a sponsor whose politics are abhorrent to me. Although we totally disagree on other issues, this person has helped me learn valuable lessons about serenity, courage, and wisdom. If I had insisted on a sponsor with political views exactly like my own, I would have missed out on an extraordinarily rich and beneficial relationship.

I think that the spirit of the Tenth Tradition has made this possible. It states that "The Al-Anon Family Groups have no opinion on outside issues; hence our name ought never be drawn into public controversy." At the group level, this means that I can go to a meeting and know that I won't be recruited for any particular cause. As a group, we have a single purpose—to support one another as we recover from the effects of alcoholism. But on a personal level, this Tradition allows me to establish a valuable relationship with a person who, under less supportive conditions, I might have been hard pressed to treat with civility.

Today's reminder

Today I can be more tolerant of other views as I learn to take what I like and leave the rest. I don't have to let outside issues distract me from my primary spiritual goal. I'll keep the doors open, for I never know where I might find help.

> "Within the fellowship, the one thing that has brought us together must remain our sole concern."
>
> *Al-Anon's Twelve Steps & Twelve Traditions*

I had problems making decisions because my standards were impossible to achieve. I wanted to make decisions that would get me exactly what I wanted, or I didn't want to make them at all. I learned in Al-Anon that no one can know in advance all the consequences of any decision. We can only take the information at hand and do our best in choosing thoughtfully.

I don't have to make decisions alone. I can turn to God and ask for help. Over time I have come to realize that this help takes many different forms—a meeting topic that offered perspective, a tug at my stomach, a "coincidence." And sometimes God speaks through others. When members share their experience, strength, and hope, I listen carefully to how they handled similar situations.

In the grand scheme of things, no single decision is ever really that important. I can do my best to make decisions wisely, but the results are in the hands of a Higher Power.

Today's reminder

With the help of a Higher Power, decision-making can be one of life's great adventures. Each crossroad brings a new challenge, and I am capable of dealing with whatever comes my way.

"When I used to make specific requests [of God], I was so busy waiting for them to be granted that I didn't realize the answers were staring me in the face."

As We Understood . . .

Even as a child, I had grown-up responsibilities, so it is no wonder that I grew up to be a caretaker. It seemed so comfortable, so automatic to think of others first and to give myself completely to whatever crisis was at hand without a thought for myself. When I became aware that this was not one of my most admirable traits but was instead a form of self-destructiveness, I was horrified. I set out to wipe out all such behavior and attitudes. I was determined to become as self-involved and uncaring as possible.

Fortunately, I failed to make such a radical change. Today, years later, I am still a caretaker, and I probably always will be. But now I consider it a valued characteristic, a gift of my upbringing that can greatly enhance my life *if I don't carry it to the extreme.* Although I no longer do things for others that they could do for themselves, I still try to be nurturing to them as well as myself. Al-Anon helps me to find some balance.

Today's reminder

Today I will try not to condemn parts of myself while accepting other parts. I am a composite, and I love myself best when I embrace all that I am.

> "My imperfections and failures are as much a blessing from God as my successes and my talents, and I lay them both at His feet."
>
> Mahatma Gandhi

Isn't it exasperating to go to the grocery for an item, only to find the shelf empty? Fortunately, grocers can correct that situation by taking inventory to learn which shelves need replenishment.

The same is true for me. A Fourth Step inventory illuminates my own empty spaces, my shortcomings. This doesn't have to be a painful or scary experience. I don't have to pass judgment on an empty shelf, but unless I take the time to become aware of it, I won't do anything to fill it, and the problem will continue. By taking inventory, my empty spots can be filled with the help of the remaining Steps. I experience the healing power of these Steps whenever the formerly hurtful circumstances recur while the pain that I once felt does not.

Today's reminder

When I can't find a solution to a problem, when I have nagging doubts, fears, or frustrations, when I feel lost or confused, a searching and fearless moral inventory of myself can make a tremendous difference. Whenever I work the Steps, I tell my Higher Power that I am willing to heal, to find a solution, to feel better. The energy that would have been dumped into worry, tears, and obsession can be turned into positive action.

> "We all wish good things to happen to us, but we cannot just pray and then sit down and expect miracles to happen. We must back up our prayers with action."
>
> *Freedom From Despair*

Alcoholism in a family tends to promote neglect of self. Consequently, I never learned how to take care of myself when I didn't feel well. Even with a high fever, I went about my business just as I would any other day. Anything else seemed self-indulgent and weak.

In Al-Anon I've had a chance to discover a different way to take care of myself. I see others giving themselves extra attention when they are sick. They rest when they feel tired. They sometimes take the day off. They eat balanced diets. They see doctors when it seems appropriate.

By following the examples of other Al-Anon members, I am learning to accept that I can't always feel on top of the world and to respond more lovingly. It's just one more area where I am letting go of my unrealistic expectations. Maybe illness is something my Higher Power uses to tell me to be good to myself.

Today's reminder

I am not a robot. Sometimes I get sick, or tired, or preoccupied. I will make an effort to learn what I can do to help myself feel better.

"... It is crucial to be diligent about taking care of ourselves, especially during stressful periods."

... In All Our Affairs

We all make mistakes. But hopefully, as we apply the Al-Anon program and continue to grow in self-awareness, we will learn from those mistakes. Amends can be made for any harm we've done, and we can change our behavior and attitudes so that we won't repeat the same errors. Thus, even painful past experiences can help us learn to create a better future.

The greatest obstacle to this learning process is shame. Shame is an excuse to hate ourselves today for something we did or didn't do in the past. There is no room in a shame-filled mind for the fact that we did our best at the time, no room to accept that as human beings we are bound to make mistakes.

If I feel ashamed, I need a reality check because my thinking is probably distorted. Even though it may take great courage, if I share about it with an Al-Anon friend, I will interrupt the self-destructive thoughts and make room for a more loving and nurturing point of view. With a little help, I may discover that even my most embarrassing moments can bless my life by teaching me to turn in a more positive direction.

Today's reminder

Today I will love myself enough to recognize shame as an error in judgment.

> "The ultimate lesson all of us have to learn is *unconditional love,* which includes not only others but ourselves as well."
>
> Elizabeth Kubler-Ross

It is not necessary for me to map out a master plan for my recovery—my Higher Power has already done that. It is only necessary to humbly ask for God's guidance and for the willingness to follow that guidance today. I know that I am not alone: I will receive all the help I need along the way. After praying for recovery, I can let go, knowing I will walk serenely in the right direction.

But I can make some choices that will help to speed up my progress. I can take good care of myself more consistently. I can attend Al-Anon meetings, call my sponsor, try some new kind of service work. I can relax, meditate, exercise, read Al-Anon literature, play, eat a healthy meal. I find that when I put forth the effort to do what I can each day, I gradually get stronger.

Today's reminder

I can't control my recovery. I can't force myself to let go any faster, nor insist upon serenity. But I can take small actions to remind myself that I am a willing participant in this process. I have every reason to be hopeful, for each step I take is a step toward living life more fully. Today I will do something nice for myself that I haven't made time for until now.

> "If one advances confidently in the direction of his dreams, and endeavors to live the life which he has imagined, he will meet with a success unexpected in common hours."
>
> Henry David Thoreau

Turning over my will and my life to the care of a Higher Power (the Third Step) is an ongoing process. At first I surrendered only the big problems. I felt I had no choice—I was clearly powerless, and my best efforts had let me down. There was nowhere left to turn except to a Power greater than myself who could accomplish what I could not.

As my recovery progressed, I came to trust this Higher Power. Today I am pursuing a deeper relationship by improving my conscious contact with my Higher Power. When I face a decision, whether it involves dealing with an alcoholic, accepting a job offer, or making plans for the evening, I ask for guidance. When I pick up the phone to speak with an Al-Anon friend, I ask that I might serve as a channel for my Higher Power. I can't always know my Higher Power's will, but I can seek greater spiritual awareness every day by becoming willing to receive guidance.

Today's reminder

Faith takes practice. I will include my Higher Power in more of my actions and decisions today.

> "Step Three suggests I teach myself, from this moment on, to be receptive, to open myself to help from my Higher Power."
>
> *Al-Anon's Twelve Steps & Twelve Traditions*

I am told that the automatic pilot in an airplane does not work by locking onto a course and sticking to it. Instead, it steers back and forth over the path of an assigned course and makes the necessary corrections when it senses that it has strayed.

In reality, the auto pilot is on course only 5 or 10 percent of the time. The other 90 or 95 percent of the time, it is off course and correcting for its deviation.

I, too, must make continuous adjustments. I am much more willing to do so today because I have stopped expecting myself to be perfectly on course. I am bound to make plenty of mistakes, but with the help of the Al-Anon program, I am learning to accept mistakes as an inevitable part of the adventure of living.

Today's reminder

I can learn to steer the course my Higher Power sets by relying on a process of trial and error that includes a willingness to continually make adjustments.

"A man who makes no mistakes usually does not make anything."

Alcoholism, The Family Disease

Sometimes knowledge isn't all it's cracked up to be. Naturally it can be helpful to look at past experiences for information about ourselves and our relationships. There is much to be learned from inventories, memories, and reasoning things out with others. But waiting for insight can become an excuse to avoid action.

For example, some of us fall into the trap of trying to analyze alcoholism. We don't want to accept the reality of our circumstances because we haven't yet figured out the rhyme and reason of it. The fact is that alcoholism is an illogical disease; we may never fully comprehend it. Nevertheless we have an obligation to ourselves to accept the reality in which we live and to act accordingly.

Others want to ignore the spiritual nature of the Al-Anon program, waiting for a clear and comfortable understanding of a Higher Power. Many of us never attain that clarity, yet we manage to develop rewarding relationships with a Power greater than ourselves by taking the action and praying anyway.

Today's reminder

Information can be wonderfully enlightening, but it is not the answer to every problem. I will be honest about my motives today.

> "If you understand, things are just as they are; if you do not understand, things are just as they are."
>
> Zen proverb

One of the most helpful tools I've found in Al-Anon is Conference-Approved Literature (CAL). It took me a long time to be willing to open up to other people, but from my first meeting, this wonderful literature has helped me learn to replace a long-established, negative way of thinking with a new, healthier, more positive approach to life and to love.

At first I used it only when I was in pain. Now I start every day off on a positive note by reading some piece of CAL with breakfast.

It has been especially helpful to me to "Think" about what I read and condense it into a sentence or two. I write this sentence on a 3 x 5 card and carry it with me throughout the day. Whenever I remember, I take out my card and read it. You wouldn't believe how many times it has brought a difficult situation into perspective, or offered me a different approach to a project or conversation I'm about to begin.

Today's reminder

I have a wealth of information available to me which can help me grow ever freer from the effects of alcoholism on my thinking. Today I will make CAL a part of my routine by listening to a tape or by reading a pamphlet or chapter of a book.

> "The Al-Anon books and pamphlets, read each day, have opened our minds to the certainty of a better and more rewarding way of life."
>
> *This Is Al-Anon*

A recent searching and fearless moral inventory of myself (Step Four) gave me a clear message: Much of my behavior was extremely immature. But what is mature behavior? Obviously the answer is different for each of us, but exploring the question can help me to identify my goals and apply the Al-Anon program as I seek to change this behavior. To me, maturity includes:

Knowing myself.

Asking for help when I need it and acting on my own when I don't.

Admitting when I'm wrong and making amends.

Accepting love from others, even if I'm having a tough time loving myself.

Recognizing that I always have choices, and taking responsibility for the ones I make.

Seeing that life is a blessing.

Having an opinion without insisting that others share it.

Forgiving myself and others.

Recognizing my shortcomings and my strengths.

Having the courage to live one day at a time.

Acknowledging that my needs are my responsibility.

Caring for people without having to take care of them.

Accepting that I'll never be finished—I'll always be a work-in-progress.

The slogan, "Think" always puzzled me. Wasn't it my "stinking thinking" that got me into trouble? The meaning of this slogan remained a mystery until I heard a neighbor's child reciting some safety rules he'd learned in school: Stop, Look, and Listen.

Before I get into trouble, before I open my mouth to react, or get lost in obsessive analysis of another person's behavior, or worrying about the future, I can Stop. Then I can Look at what is going on and my role in it. Then I can Listen for spiritual guidance that will remind me of my options and help me find healthy words and actions.

So when something unkind is said to me, I don't automatically have to get into a loud and vicious argument. Instead, I can take a moment to "Think." I can Stop, Look, and Listen. Then I might be able to engage calmly in discussion or simply walk away. If I do choose to enter the argument, at least I am now making this decision consciously, rather than letting life decide for me.

Today's reminder

This day is a beautiful room that's never been seen before. Let me cherish the seconds, minutes, and hours I spend here. Help me to "Think" before I speak and pray before I act.

> "The program helps me gain the freedom to make wise choices that are good for me. I choose to put that freedom to work in my life today."
>
> *Alateen—A Day at a Time*

When I first started working the Steps, the thought of having my character defects removed made me very nervous. I thought I would end up like a chunk of Swiss cheese, full of holes. But I wanted to get better and I was continually assured that the Steps were the key to my recovery, so I went forward in spite of my fears. I had to take the risk and act on faith before I could receive the gifts my Higher Power held out to me.

Nowhere in Steps Four through Seven do we ask God to add anything, but rather to take away the things we do not need. I found that every single defect that was removed had been hiding an asset. I didn't lose myself at all. Instead, as I let go of the things I didn't need, I made room for my strengths, skills, and feelings to become more fully a part of my life. I take comfort in this, because it reminds me that everything I need is already present. But I couldn't be sure until I worked the Steps and found some relief from my shortcomings.

Today's reminder

God knows exactly what I need and has already given it to me. My job is to "Keep it simple" and ask for God's help in relieving me of the extra stuff—the shortcomings that keep me tied down.

"Before sunlight can shine through a window, the blinds must be raised."

American Proverb

Al-Anon has helped me realize that no one readily knows what is in my heart, mind, and soul. I can't expect my needs to be met unless I first explain what those needs are. Nor can I expect any one person to meet all those needs, even if I make them clear. If the first person I ask for help is unable to provide it, I can ask someone else. This takes the pressure off all of us.

Before I began my Al-Anon recovery, I expected those closest to me to know what I was feeling without my telling them. When I was angry and wanted to argue, I silently fumed. When I was hurt and wanted comfort, I pouted. When I wanted attention, I talked non-stop. I couldn't understand why I rarely got the responses I expected!

I no longer expect anyone to read my mind. I also accept that I can't read the mind of a loved one. Today I treat the people in my life with more respect because I am learning to ask for what I need and to encourage others to do the same.

Today's reminder

Help, comfort, and support are available to me. I am willing to reach out for what I need today.

> "I cannot expect anyone to help me unless I am willing to share that I *need* help."
>
> . . . *In All Our Affairs*

In Al-Anon I discovered that I needed to make changes in myself. After a lifetime of living with a disease of attitudes—alcoholism—I didn't think very highly of myself, so I didn't have much faith that anything good could come out of my efforts.

I learned better by watching my son's silkworms. Silkworms are fat and greedy creatures, but out of their own substance, they create something beautiful. They have no choice in the matter. They were born to express this beauty.

I, too, can transform something negative into something positive; by changing my self-defeating attitudes, I become a more beautiful human being. I was born with this beauty inside me, and if I will only allow myself, I can express it freely. Al-Anon helps me learn to put love first in my life. And gratitude, a cornerstone of my Al-Anon recovery, brings hidden loveliness clearly into view.

Today's reminder

Today I can spin a little silk and let it grace everything I touch. I don't have to look back to past ugliness except to learn from it, to enhance the present, and to release whatever beauty is trapped behind old secrets and self-defeating attitudes. One day at a time I can delight in the splendid person I am becoming.

"Sometimes it is necessary to reteach a thing its loveliness . . . until it flowers again from within..."

Galway Kinnell

One of the wonderful benefits I receive by going to Al-Anon meetings is that I find new ways to work my program. The chairperson at one of my favorite meetings passed around a basket full of Al-Anon slogans and suggested that we each take one and try to apply it to this day. It was remarkable how many of us seemed to get the perfect slogan!

The very next day I found myself in a stressful situation. I was struggling to solve a tough problem, growing frustrated and upset but no closer to a solution. I asked my Higher Power for help and suddenly remembered that basket. In my mind, I imagined myself reaching once more into a basket full of slogans. Again I got exactly what I needed: The slip of paper I pictured reminded me that "Easy does it." I stopped trying to force a solution and waited until I could approach the problem more gently. I felt much better, my thinking was clearer, and in time a solution appeared.

Today's reminder

It is not always easy to know which Al-Anon tool to apply, especially in the middle of a crisis. I am grateful for a Higher Power who knows my needs, and for meetings that help me to find new ways to put these tools to work in my life.

"As we learn to depend upon our Higher Power through applying the Al-Anon program to our lives, fear and uncertainty are replaced by faith and confidence."

One Day at a Time in Al-Anon

I often struggle to know what is my will and what is God's. I feel serenity slipping from me while a war is waged within my mind and loud voices urge me to take one path or another.

Doubt is an unavoidable companion of spiritual seeking. I don't have an instruction book, so I must continue to explore and challenge my perceptions. I know that when I feel a desperate urge to act, it is usually my will that is pushing, and when I feel a calm certainty, it is usually God's. But much of the time, I don't have such a clear indication. What then? Sometimes I wait for clarity or try to listen more closely for guidance; I may share my confusion and ask for the wisdom of others; or I may just make a choice, take an action, and see what happens. More will be revealed when the time is right, no matter what choice I make. Since I have turned my will and my life over to God, any choice I make can be used to carry out His will.

Today's reminder

Today I will remember that uncertainty is not a fault but an opportunity. Everything I do and everything that crosses my path—people, situations, ideas—all have the potential to contribute to my growth and understanding. Just for today, I don't have to know what that contribution will be.

"There lives more faith in honest doubt,
Believe me, than in half the creeds."

Alfred, Lord Tennyson

Part of my recovery has involved reversing some old ways of thinking. It had been my habit to avoid painful feelings and situations, to play it safe and keep away from risk. But life involves one risk after another, and some pain is unavoidable. Al-Anon helps me to accept what is.

Instead of running away, I am learning to look at the source of my distress. As a result, I find that pain passes much more quickly, and what I gain is freedom from fear. Al-Anon gives me tools, such as the Fourth Step inventory, with which I can take an honest look at myself and my situation. A supportive sponsor, my Higher Power, the Serenity Prayer, and many Al-Anon meetings help me to find the courage to deal with fear, pain, and risk.

When I was avoiding taking risks, fear was always with me, just over my shoulder. Now I go through it and come out the other side, often unscathed. I no longer have to keep a constant watch for potential dangers. Instead, I can occupy myself with living.

Today's reminder

Wonderful things can happen today because I welcome the thrill of participating in my own life.

"Avoiding danger is no safer in the long run than outright exposure. Life is either a daring adventure or nothing."

Helen Keller

"I've chosen my epitaph," says an Al-Anon friend. "I want it to read, 'He's finally minding his own business.'"

We laugh, enjoying some relief in contemplating the lighter side of a serious subject, those defects of character that seem so hard to shake. Laughter makes our frailties seem easier to bear, and we can forgive ourselves for our imperfections. What a change from the days when we hid in shame from our flaws or used them to beat ourselves over the head!

My friend and I resolve that in the future we will try less, accept more, and let go of our impatience, self-criticism, and self-hatred. We take a deep breath and say, "Help me, Higher Power. Help me remember that the purpose of making mistakes is to prepare myself to make more; help me remember that when I'm no longer making mistakes I'll be out of this world."

Today's reminder

In a way, I will always be a beginner. There will always be some new challenge to face because life is ever-changing and so am I. Because of this constant change, every tiny little action I take involves some risk of making a mistake. It takes courage to participate in life. Today I can applaud myself for trying. I'm doing a terrific job.

"My Higher Power is the confidence within me that makes me unafraid, even unafraid to make mistakes."

As We Understood . . .

What does another person's mood, tone of voice, or state of inebriation have to do with my course of action? Nothing, unless I decide otherwise.

For example, I have learned that arguing with someone who is intoxicated is like beating my head against a brick wall. Yet, until recently, I would always dive right into the arguments, because that was what the other person seemed to want. In Al-Anon I discovered that I don't have to react just because I have been provoked, and I don't have to take harsh words to heart. I can remember that they are coming from someone who may be in pain, and try to show a little compassion. I certainly don't have to allow them to provoke me into doing anything I don't want to do.

Today's reminder

Detachment with love means that I stop depending upon what others do, say, or feel to determine my own well-being or to make my decisions. When faced with other people's destructive attitudes and behavior, I can love their best, and never fear their worst.

> "Detachment is not caring less, it's caring more for my own serenity."

                                    . . . In All Our Affairs

I'm apt to think of Step Seven— "Humbly asked Him to remove our shortcomings"—as a Step I take tearfully and on my knees. I've had that experience, but I want to entertain the possibility that Step Seven might be taken with joy—and even humor.

Sometimes the sign that I have actually gotten humble enough to ask my Higher Power to remove a shortcoming is that I can laugh about it. Suddenly a past action or decision of mine seems ludicrous and I can stop taking myself so seriously. When this happens, I realize that my Higher Power has lessened the impact of another shortcoming. Real change often announces itself to me in the form of a belly laugh.

So the next time I want to tear my hair out because I haven't gotten rid of some nagging shortcoming, I'll try to lighten up and see how silly my intensity can be. When I'm willing to step back and see humor even in the areas that fall short of my expectations, I get out of the way and give my Higher Power room to work.

Today's reminder

Desperation and pain can certainly lead me to humility, but in Al-Anon I'm cultivating a new and eager willingness to follow my Higher Power's guidance. Because I am willing, I am freer to learn from all of life's lessons, not just the ones that hurt.

"'Humbly' . . . means seeing myself in true relation to my fellow man and to God."

Lois' Story

One beautiful day, a man sat down under a tree, not noticing it was full of pigeons. Shortly, the pigeons did what pigeons do best. The man shouted at the pigeons as he stormed away, resenting the pigeons as well as the offending material. But then he realized that the pigeons were merely doing what pigeons do, just because they're pigeons and not because he was there. The man learned to check the trees for pigeons before sitting down.

Active alcoholics are people who drink. They don't drink because of you or me, but because they are alcoholics. No matter what I do, I will not change this fact, not with guilt, shouting, begging, distracting, hiding money or bottles or keys, lying, threatening, or reasoning. I didn't cause alcoholism. I can't control it. And I can't cure it. I can continue to struggle and lose. Or I can accept that I am powerless over alcohol and alcoholism, and let Al-Anon help me to redirect the energy I've spent on fighting this disease into recovering from its effects.

Today's reminder

It's not easy to watch someone I love continue to drink, but I can do nothing to stop them. If I see how unmanageable my life has become, I can admit that I am powerless over this disease. Then I can really begin to make my life better.

"It stands to reason that a change in us will be a force for good that will help the entire family."

How Can I Help My Children?

Before Al-Anon, forgiveness meant power to me. I could judge the offender—the person who wasn't doing what I wanted—and then exercise my power by showing that I could rise above the offense and magnanimously bestow forgiveness. But I would never forget what had been done.

Today I know that forgiveness has nothing to do with power. It does not give me control. Forgiveness is simply a reminder that I am on equal footing with every other child of God. We all do good and noble things at times; on other occasions we may offend. I have no right to judge, punish, or absolve anyone. When I behave self-righteously, I'm the one who suffers—I separate myself from my fellow human beings, focus on others, and keep busy with hateful and negative thoughts. By taking this attitude I tell myself that I am a victim, so I remain a victim. The most forgiving thing I can do is to remember that my job is not to judge others, but to think and behave in a way that lets me feel good.

Today's reminder

I don't know the motives or circumstances that cause another's behavior. I do know that when I hold onto resentment and blame, I occupy my spirit with bitterness. Today I will find a more nurturing way to fill myself up.

"You can't hold a man down without staying down with him."

Booker T. Washington

Progress can be hard to recognize, especially if our expectations are unrealistically high. If we expect our negative attitudes or unhealthy behavior to change quickly and completely, we are likely to be disappointed—progress is hard to see when we measure ourselves against idealized standards. Perhaps it would be better to compare our present circumstances only to where we had been in the past.

For example, a Fourth Step inventory led me to realize that I hold grudges and that they hurt me. I try to let go of resentments and I despair when these attitudes persist. Fortunately, Al-Anon has taught me to focus on progress, not perfection. Although sometimes I still hold on to resentments, I know I'm making progress because I don't do it as often as I used to or for as long a time.

Today I am no longer seeking perfection; the only thing that matters is the direction in which I'm moving.

Today's reminder

As a result of hard work in Al-Anon and a willingness to change, I am moving in a positive direction. I will celebrate my progress today. I know that the process of recovery will continue to help me grow toward a better way of living.

"Keep adding little by little and you will soon have a big hoard."

Latin proverb

No problem lasts forever. No matter how permanently fixed in the center of our lives it may seem, whatever we experience in this ever-changing life is sure to pass. Even pain.

Difficult situations often bring out qualities in us that otherwise might not have risen to the surface, such as courage, faith, and our need for one another. All of our experiences can help us to grow.

But we may need patience. Some wounds cannot be healed quickly. They must be given time. In the meantime, we can appreciate the new capabilities we are developing, such as the capacity to mourn and the willingness to accept. Let us share our losses and triumphs with each other, for that is how we gather courage.

Today's reminder

Remembering that this too shall pass can make it easier to get through a difficult day. I will be very gentle with myself during this time. Some extra loving care and attention to myself can make everything a little easier.

"I am equal to what life presents when I use the Twelve Steps and Twelve Traditions, the slogans, literature, sponsorship, conventions, and most importantly, meetings."

. . . In All Our Affairs

Our Eighth Tradition suggests that our Twelfth Step work should remain forever nonprofessional. This means that as Al-Anon members, our own experience, strength, and hope is all we need to help one another recover from the devastating impact of alcoholism. If our program were run by professionals, I would not have been free to carry the Al-Anon message to so many others.

This Tradition encourages me to help those who really want help. I've spent so much time and energy trying to help those who *didn't* want it, that the opportunity to make a welcome contribution to someone else's well-being is precious to me. Today, because of my experience with alcoholism, I am better able to understand and empathize with other people. I'm grateful that something positive has come from the more difficult times in my life.

I am learning to give and receive without guilt. I need not feel a debt to those members who have helped me, except to pass along to others what has served me so well. And as I give, I receive.

Today's reminder

I find that sharing my experience, strength, and hope with others, as an equal, is one of Al-Anon's greatest gifts.

"The only ones among you who will be really happy are those who will have sought and found how to serve."

Albert Schweitzer

I came to Al-Anon with a compulsion to focus on other people. I had a clear idea of how everyone should behave in every situation and felt very self-righteous when they didn't follow my rules of conduct. When I realized that my own life was being neglected because all my attention was elsewhere, I had to make some major changes.

Today I still have to be vigilant about minding my own business. I know that when my thoughts begin with "He should" or "She shouldn't" I am probably in trouble. I don't have the answers for other people. I don't make the rules for appropriate behavior, good business conduct, driver courtesy, or common sense. I don't know what is best for others because I don't know the lessons their Higher Power is offering them. I only know that if I'm caught up in what they should or should not do, I have lost my humility. I have also ceased to pay attention to myself. Nine times out of ten, I am focusing on someone else to avoid looking at something in my own life.

Today's reminder

I grow in my ability to relate to others when I allow them to be exactly as they are. The greatest gift I can give to myself is my own attention.

"Clean your finger before you point at my spots."
                                        Benjamin Franklin

One of the topics in our Fourth Step guide, the *Blueprint for Progress*, is self-worth. As I worked through this Step, taking a searching and fearless moral inventory of myself, I found that I have always judged my value on the basis of my accomplishments, or on what other people said about me. This meant I had to work all the time, or constantly make myself the center of attention. At best my sense of satisfaction was fleeting.

With Step Four, I realized that part of my self-worth can be based on my ability to love other people. Saying a kind word, writing a considerate note, or just taking time out from my other thoughts to appreciate another human being, enriches my entire day. I have the power to feel good about myself, regardless of my achievements, whether or not other people validate my worthiness.

Today's reminder

Let me look for appropriate opportunities to share my love with people around me. In this way I celebrate one of my most positive traits without expecting anything in return. Paying someone a compliment that comes from the heart, or thanking them sincerely for their kindness, may be the nicest thing I can do for myself today.

"It is difficult to make a man miserable while he feels worthy of himself and claims kindred to the great God who made him."

Abraham Lincoln

A jogger was nearing the end of a run. Sand dunes on the left blocked his view of the beach beyond. Crossing the dunes would require extra effort after a long, tiring workout. Instead, he could opt to remain on the flat road that veered off to the right. Although the scenery was less appealing, the easier route was enticing. Past experience had taught him to avoid pushing himself too hard. Yet he loved the sight of the ocean.

The jogger hesitated. An inner nudge urged him toward the dunes, and he chose to respond to it. As the beach appeared, a spectacular sunset hovered above the crashing waves. Humility overwhelmed the runner when he realized that in his moment of hesitation, he had listened to a Power greater than himself, one who could see around blind corners.

Today's reminder

Logic may dictate a certain course of action while my inner voice urges me in a different direction. I may have an easier time when I follow the dictates of logic, convenience, or past experience, but am I cheating myself out of something much better? Today I will pause at a crossroad and listen for my Higher Power's voice.

> "The intellect has little to do on the road to discovery. There comes a leap in consciousness, call it intuition or what you will, and the solution comes to you and you don't know how or why."
>
> Albert Einstein

In order to survive in the contradictory and explosive world of alcoholism, many of us learned to ignore our feelings. We lost touch with ourselves without even knowing it.

For example, although I pointed an accusing finger at the alcoholics in my life for deserting me in times of need, I wasn't a very good friend to myself. In my fear and confusion, I walked away from the little child in me who lived simply, who cried when the cat died and then let it go, who could appreciate a sunset and not want to own it, and who lived one day at a time.

Recovery does not mean that I have to become a different person. It means I need to start being myself again. The lessons I'm learning in Al-Anon are lessons I already know. I just need to remember.

Today's reminder

There is an innocence within me that already knows how to trust my Higher Power, to cherish life while holding it lightly, to live fully and simply in the present moment. I will allow that part of myself to come forward and nourish me as I continue on this journey.

"It takes one a long time to become young."

Pablo Picasso

Alcoholism has contributed to many dashed hopes, broken dreams, and considerable pain in my life. I do not wish to dwell on these feelings, but neither do I wish to turn my back on them. Al-Anon is helping me to face even the most unpleasant aspects of my past. By taking hold of the hands of those in the fellowship, I am able to feel the pain and mourn the losses, and to move on.

These feelings are a deep part of me; when they come knocking at the door of my awareness, I wish to open it and let them in. I need to treat myself with the same care and respect that I would an Al-Anon member sharing pain, confusion, and turmoil at a meeting. Only in this way can I become whole and at peace.

Today's reminder

They say that pain is inevitable but suffering is optional. If I learn to accept that pain is part of life, I will be better able to endure the difficult times and then move on, leaving the pain behind me.

"... When we long for life without ... difficulties, remind us that oaks grow strong in contrary winds and diamonds are made under pressure."

Peter Marshall

I had a very difficult time believing that alcoholism was a disease. I was convinced that if they really wanted to, alcoholics could stop drinking. After all, I quit smoking. Wasn't it the same thing?

Then one day an Al-Anon member likened active alcoholism to Alzheimer's disease. We see our loved ones slip away without their being aware of what's happening or being able to stop it. They look perfectly normal on the outside, but the sickness is progressing, and they become more and more irrational and difficult to be around. When they have lucid moments and once again seem to be themselves, we want to believe that they are well, but these moments pass, and we despair. Before long we find ourselves resenting the very people we once loved.

I'll always be grateful to my friend because her explanation helped me to accept the reality of my situation. Once I did, it was much easier for me to separate the disease from the person.

Today's reminder

When I accept that alcoholism is a disease, I am forced to face the fact that I am powerless over it. Only then can I gain the freedom to focus on my own spiritual growth.

> "A family member has no more right to state, 'If you loved me you would not drink,' than the right to say, 'If you loved me you would not have tuberculosis . . .' Illness is a condition, not an act."
>
> *A Guide for the Family of the Alcoholic*

I came to Al-Anon confused about what was and was not my responsibility. Today, after lots of Step work, I believe I am responsible for the following: to be loyal to my values; to please myself first; to keep an open mind; to detach with love; to rid myself of anger and resentment; to express my ideas and feelings instead of stuffing them; to attend Al-Anon meetings and keep in touch with friends in the fellowship; to be realistic in my expectations; to make healthy choices; and to be grateful for my blessings.

I also have certain responsibilities to others: to extend a welcome to newcomers; to be of service; to recognize that others have a right to live their own lives; to listen, not just with my ears, but also with my heart; and to share my joy as well as my sorrow.

I am *not* responsible for my alcoholic loved one's drinking, sobriety, job, cleanliness, diet, dental hygiene, or other choices. It is my responsibility to treat this person with courtesy, gentleness, and love. In this way we both can grow.

Today's reminder

Today, if I am tempted to interfere with something that is none of my business, I can turn my attention instead to some way in which I can take care of myself.

"I have a primary responsibility to myself: to make myself into the best person I can possibly be. Then, and only then, will I have something worthwhile to share."

Living With Sobriety

"Anything worth doing," goes a slightly cock-eyed version of the old saying, "is worth doing badly." Perfectionism, procrastination, and paralysis are three of the worst effects of alcoholism upon my life.

I have a tendency to spend my life waiting for the past to change. I want to spend the first hundred years of my life getting all the kinks ironed out and the next hundred years actually living. Such an inclination to avoid taking risks, to avoid doing anything badly, has prevented me from doing some of the things I enjoy the most, and it has kept me from the regular practice that produces progress.

If I'm unwilling to perform a task badly, I can't expect to make progress toward learning to do it well. The only task that I can pretend to perform perfectly is the one that I have left entirely undone.

Today's reminder

Al-Anon encourages me to take risks and to think of life not as a command performance but as a continuing series of experiments from which I learn more about living.

"All the beautiful sentiments in the world weigh less than a single lovely action."

James Russell Lowell

I used to think that living meant surviving from crisis to crisis. I continued to function this way as an adult because it was the only way I knew.

Since that time, the Al-Anon fellowship has become like family to me. Our Twelve Traditions help me learn how a healthy family group functions. Today, when a problem involving other people arises, I turn to the Traditions for guidance.

They have made it possible for me to be part of a group that encourages my growth. They have led me to learn to detach, to respect other people's privacy, and to find some release from my need to dominate and control. Because of the Twelve Traditions, I have discovered that I am an important member of any group in which I take part. I have a sense of my own value, as well as my limitations. As a result, I am developing "the wisdom to know the difference" between what I can change and what I must accept.

Today's reminder

Because the Traditions are based on spiritual principles, they often apply to personal matters as well as group concerns. When I get tangled up in problems with other people, the Traditions can offer guidance and perspective.

"The Twelve Steps and Twelve Traditions embody principles that lead to recovery and personal growth, helping each of us to discover and become the person we want to be."

Al-Anon Spoken Here

What happens when I physically hold on tightly to something? I turn my head away. I squeeze my eyes shut. My knuckles ache as my fists clench. Fingernails bite into my palms. I exhaust myself. I hurt!

On the other hand, when I trust God to give me what I need, I let go. I face forward. My hands are free for healthy, loving, and enjoyable activities. I find unexpected reserves of energy. My eyes open to see fresh opportunities, many of which have been there all along.

Before I complain about my suffering, I might do well to examine myself. I may be surprised by the amount of pain I can release by simply letting go.

Today's reminder

How much can God give me if I am not open to receive? When I hold onto a problem, a fear, or a resentment, I shut myself off to the help that is available to me. I will loosen my grip on something today. I will "Let go and let God."

"All I had to do was become the least bit willing to open my clutched fist a tiny, grudging bit and miracles happened. That's God as I understand Him today."

As We Understood . . .

It's time I started being nicer to myself. The voices in my head that tell me I'm not good enough do not speak the truth; they merely reflect the damaged self-esteem that results from living with alcoholism. When I recognize that fact, I can tell them to be quiet! I will no longer listen!

Al-Anon recovery has given me gentler, loving thoughts. These remind me that I am loveable and I can learn to love myself. When I open my mind enough to hear that message, I can begin to hear all the other wonderful sounds of life, and the abusive thoughts vanish.

Today's reminder

Treating myself with kindness and respect helps me to challenge my own self-criticism. Today I will pay particular attention to any voice that speaks lovingly.

"We need to learn to live, to focus on something good or useful to our lives and let the rest of the world go about its business."

How Can I Help My Children?

When I heard that Al-Anon was a program in which we learn to keep the focus on ourselves, I wondered what others would think of me if I acted on that principle? Surely they would think me inconsiderate, thoughtless, and uncaring. Those were my complaints about the alcoholics in my life! I didn't want to be that way. Instead, I tried to do things for others that seemed loving and generous, even when I didn't want to do them. I couldn't understand why I so often grew resentful after such actions.

My efforts to be selfless by trying to please everyone but myself weren't working. The focus was on their response rather than on what seemed right for me to do. There was nothing unconditional about this kind of giving. My sponsor helped me to see that if I paid more attention to myself and to doing what I thought was best, I would be free to give without strings attached. Then I could truly be generous.

Today's reminder

The Al-Anon program works when I keep the focus on myself, attend lots of Al-Anon meetings, and make recovery my top priority. As I become more fully myself, I am better able to treat others with love and respect.

"We are best able to help others when we ourselves have learned the way to achieve serenity."

The Twelve Steps and Traditions

Al-Anon is where many of us who have lived with alcoholism begin to grow up for the first time. We learn to face the world as it really is and to take responsibility for our actions. We deal with our feelings and share honestly about our experiences. We learn about ourselves and nurture our spiritual growth and our physical and mental well-being. We become responsible adults.

An important part of the serious business of recovery involves recognizing our need to have fun—to take a trip, fly a kite, attend a concert, make noise, race down the street, or blow bubbles. Light-heartedness can put troublesome situations into perspective. It reminds us that there is more to life than the problem at hand.

Taking ourselves too seriously won't solve a problem any quicker. In fact, taking a break may help more than continuing to struggle—even Jello must be left alone in order to form as it should. A good laugh may be the best tool available to help us let go, and we'll come back to our task refreshed.

Today's reminder

A well-developed sense of humor helps me detach from my personal struggles and triumphs. I will avoid taking myself too seriously today.

"One inch of joy surmounts of grief a span,
Because to laugh is proper to the man."

François Rabelais

I've heard acceptance mentioned at meetings as one part of the "Three A's"—Awareness, Acceptance, and Action. However, I am inclined to try to jump from awareness to action without even pausing for acceptance. My thinking goes like this: "Something's wrong! Quick, let me fix it before I have to feel any discomfort."

The problem is that until I accept the situation, defect, or memory that has come to my awareness, I can rarely take effective action or live serenely with the consequences. The action doesn't work or it makes things worse, and I feel helpless and hopeless. Even if it does work, I am usually too full of self-doubt to realize it. Most of the time, I still have to go back, sit still, feel the feelings, and come to some acceptance. It helps to be reminded that my Higher Power already accepts me and my situation—and loves me on the bad days as well as the good.

Today's reminder

Moving from awareness to acceptance to action takes time, but the benefits are worth the wait. As I learn to accept my defects, circumstances, and feelings, I learn that I am a worthwhile human being just as I am. With that kind of self-acceptance, I begin to see my options, and slowly I can begin to take action, to change.

> ". . . someone suggested I stop concentrating on changing myself and think first about accepting myself. That gave me the boost I needed."
>
> *Alateen—A Day at a Time*

I have heard that the time to be especially gentle with myself is not when I'm doing well, but when I'm doing poorly. I may be able to push myself hard when things are going my way, but I invite trouble if I try this when I'm already struggling to manage the basic activities of my life. I used to worry that if I didn't push myself all the time, I would turn into a slug and nothing would get done. But my Fourth Step inventory showed me that the opposite is true. I tend to be very hard on myself, so hard at times that I make my own life unmanageable. As a result, I often accomplish less than I would if I took a more gentle approach. For me, the best antidote is the slogan, "Easy does it."

When I notice that I'm having trouble with my day, I try to slow down. And instead of automatically assuming I am wrong, I try to consider the possibility that I might be right on schedule.

Today's reminder

"Easy does it" suggests not only that I learn to slow down, but also that I learn to lighten up. Today I will strive to take a more accepting attitude toward myself and to enjoy the day, regardless of what I achieve.

"Improving our own attitudes and our own state of mind takes time. Haste and impatience can only defeat our purposes."

This Is Al-Anon

Many of us resisted coming to Al-Anon because we didn't want anyone to know about our problems. We feared that our boss or our friends would find out, or that it would get back to the alcoholic.

These fears accompanied me to my first Al-Anon meeting. To my horror, just as I sat down one of my neighbors walked into the room and sat down across from me. What could I do now? Run?

In the midst of my panic, I noticed a sign on the table that said, "Whom you see here, what you hear here, when you leave here, let it stay here." And on the wall I saw a banner with the Traditions, one of which said that anonymity is Al-Anon's spiritual foundation! I stayed for the meeting, but I still worried.

My neighbor never said a word to anyone. In time I began to trust that it was safe to get the help I so desperately needed, because the only one who would ever mention my membership in Al-Anon was me. To this day, I am confident that my anonymity was and always will be protected, and my gratitude is beyond measure.

Today's reminder

Unless I protect the anonymity of all members, Al-Anon will not be a safe place for any of us.

"Our free expression—so important to our recovery—rests on our sense of security, knowing that what we share at our meetings will be held in strict confidence."

Al-Anon Spoken Here

I used to love the stillness of early morning, but over years of living with an alcoholic, I stopped noticing it. Instead, I woke up the same way I went to sleep—frantic. Before I was out of bed I already had a long list of crises that needed my attention. So no matter how early I got up, I was already late. Sometimes I was so overwhelmed, I couldn't get up at all.

My life has changed. I heard someone in Al-Anon say that when they open their eyes in the morning, they also open their ears. Now as I awaken, I listen for the birds. I choose not to review my plans for the day until I've had my breakfast. I prefer to take time to appreciate my favorite part of the day.

Al-Anon is helping me to clear my mind of my burdens so that I am able to enjoy the wonder of the moment. I am beginning to enjoy a childlike awe about the splendor of nature, to see the beauty all around me, to let my face break into a smile spontaneously, to laugh, to love, to live again. Today I can say, "Good morning, God," instead of "Good God, it's morning."

Today's reminder

Today I'll be keenly aware of my senses. I will think about what I am experiencing at this moment. I won't let the beauty of this day slip by unnoticed.

"Real generosity toward the future consists in giving all to what is present."

Albert Camus

As wonderful as it is to see a loved one find sobriety, it often presents a whole new set of challenges. After all the years of waiting, many of us are dismayed when sobriety does not bring the happily-ever-after ending we've awaited. We once knew exactly what to expect, and now everything suddenly seems different. The homebody is never home; the life of the party is always sleeping; communication, intimacy, sex, responsibilities, and decision-making all change. At the same time, problems that we always attributed to drinking may persist even though the drinking has stopped. This stirs up some very strong feelings within many of us.

Even long-time Al-Anon members may find it more important than ever to go back to the basics of our program and learn once more to focus on ourselves. It's all right to feel disappointed, skeptical, resentful, joyous, excited, or confused about our changing circumstances. By accepting whatever we feel and sharing about it with other Al-Anon members, we are better able to take care of ourselves.

Today's reminder

I will allow myself the dignity to discover exactly how I feel about the changes that are happening today, and I will share those feelings with an Al-Anon friend.

"Al-Anon gave me the awareness that what I felt did matter."

. . . In All Our Affairs

Just as the common cold has symptoms such as a runny nose and sneezing, alcoholism also has symptoms such as blackouts and mood changes. I have to accept that I, too, display symptoms similar to those of the alcoholic, among them obsession, anxiety, anger, denial, and feelings of guilt. These reactions to alcoholism affect my relationships and the quality of my life, but as I learn to recognize them and to accept that I have been affected by a disease, I begin to heal. In time, I discover feelings of self-worth, love, and spiritual connectedness that help me to counteract the old responses. No matter how severely I have been affected, Al-Anon can help restore me to sanity.

Alcoholism is stronger than good intentions or genuine desires. I didn't choose this family disease; neither did the alcoholic. So I try to behave with compassion for us both.

Today's reminder
My acceptance of this family disease allows me to stop wasting energy fighting a hopeless battle, and to turn instead to sources of genuine help and hope—Al-Anon and my Higher Power.

"Once you have accepted the idea that alcoholism is a sickness from which compulsive drinkers and those who care about them *can* find release, you will have no reason to be ashamed of alcoholism—no reason to fear it."

So You Love an Alcoholic

Could it be that God has a sense of humor? I attended a new meeting recently at which I had been invited to speak. I had conjured up in my imagination a large group of serious-minded Al-Anon members sitting in the perfect location with the perfect format while I uttered a daunting barrage of wise words.

What I found instead was a small group perching in a temporary meeting place with a substitute secretary who had misplaced the perfectly-scripted format. Everything that could go wrong did go wrong.

In short, I soon felt right at home. My Higher Power had substituted enough familiar, spontaneous elements so that I could feel completely comfortable.

My concept of this "important" meeting and the "important" words I'd be speaking and hearing had quickly disappeared. We were just a group of members in the fellowship doing our best to muddle through and lend each other a helping hand.

Today's reminder

I give thanks for the ways my Higher Power finds to cut my pretensions down to size. When I can laugh a little, I feel less afraid.

> "I want to remember, every time I'm tempted to take a heavy, somber view of a happening, that it may not be so bad after all . . . I'll cultivate a knack for recognizing and enjoying humorous moments."
>
> *One Day at a Time in Al-Anon*

There can be great value in examining the past. It can offer information about the present, as well as clues that might help us make changes for a better future. For those of us who denied, distorted, or lost touch with painful memories, facing the reality of our past can be a critical part of our Al-Anon recovery. Fond memories must also be recognized if we hope to look back in a realistic way.

Still, it is important to remember that the past is over. We are powerless over what has gone before. Although we can take steps to make amends, we cannot change the fact that we have harmed others. And we cannot change the fact that others have harmed us. We have only the power to change this present day.

The best use we can make of the past is to face it and then move on. We can certainly learn from all that we have experienced, but we mustn't let it hold us back from living here and now.

Today's reminder

I will not get so bogged down in dealing with old wounds that I forget about new growth.

"The past is but the beginning of a beginning."
                                                    H.G. Wells

After years of denying my feelings in order to protect myself, detachment (emotionally separating myself from the disease of alcoholism) was fairly easy for me. But it was with indifference. Detachment with love was out of the question!

A major change of attitude began when my sponsor repeated a line from a play that had helped her understand the need to detach with love: "The worst sin toward our fellow creatures is not to hate them, but to be indifferent to them." I realized that by detaching with indifference, I might be taking the easy way out.

In Al-Anon I've come to feel safe enough to feel my feelings. I no longer need to shut out the love I feel for myself or for the alcoholic in my life. I can see myself as more than my feelings, and I can see the alcoholic as more than his or her disease.

Today's reminder

The unconditional love I receive in Al-Anon helps me to rediscover what love is. As I learn that I am consistently loveable regardless of my strengths or limitations, I begin to see something consistently loveable in others, even those who suffer from an unloveable disease.

"With a change of attitude . . . past actions can be put into proper perspective; love and respect can become a part of family life."

Youth and the Alcoholic Parent

Having lived with alcoholism, many of us have come to think of ourselves as innocent victims of other people's abuse. It can be shocking to discover that we too have harmed others. Listing those we have harmed (Step Eight) becomes a discovery process in which a more realistic sense of responsibility can begin to develop.

In my case, however, the problem was not in recognizing the harm I'd done, but in letting go of my exaggerated sense of responsibility. I thought that everyone I ever knew belonged on my list, especially those who were disappointed in me. For example, my parents are unhappy with the partner I have chosen. My sister wants me to pay off her debts. My kids wish I'd let them stay out all night without calling. As I thought about this Step, I realized that I am not responsible for their unfulfilled desires. So when I revised my Eighth Step list, I needed to take names off.

Today's reminder

Certainly I make choices that harm others and call for making amends. But sometimes a choice that is right for me may be uncomfortable or even unacceptable to others. Other people's expectations are not my responsibility unless I have helped to create them. I can remind myself that conflict is part of life.

"With this Step we sort out our part, taking responsibility for our actions but also releasing ourselves . . . from the burden of falsely-held responsibilities."

. . . In All Our Affairs

Why continue to come to Al-Anon? Because without spiritual help, living or having lived with an alcoholic is too much for me. I often need help to maintain a rational perspective. I long for a closer relationship with my Higher Power. The people in my meetings are so warm and loving that I would feel deprived if they were not a regular part of my life. The Steps, Traditions, and Concepts all serve to put structure and goals in my life. Al-Anon is the light that helps me find my way in the dark.

As a long-time member, I am very familiar with Al-Anon, but I am no more of an authority than any other member. I try not to present myself as a paragon of Al-Anon wisdom, and I discourage newcomers from putting me on a pedestal from which I am bound to fall.

I retain the right to have problems, to cry, to make mistakes, to not know all the answers. I still have and use a sponsor. I continue to give service to Al-Anon, but I don't have to be in charge.

Today's reminder

The amount of time I've spent in Al-Anon is less important than what I am doing with that time today.

> "I don't resort to Al-Anon only to learn to live with the active drinking problems. It is my way of life, an increasingly rich and rewarding life, as I learn to use the program in depth."
>
> *One Day at a Time in Al-Anon*

It's only natural to want a quick fix or an immediate solution to a difficult situation. As one member jokingly puts it: "Grant me patience, Lord—and hurry!" My sentiments exactly! Do I have some discomfort or a problem in my life? Let me fix it, or be rid of it now. Is it a situation I've lived with for twenty years? Fine, I'll give it fifteen minutes. Perhaps I've lived with it all my life—well then, an hour, maybe even two. Is it connected with alcoholism? Do its roots run really deep in the ground of my being? In that case, I'll make a few program calls and share at a meeting.

Is it still hanging on? Very well, I'll launch a major campaign of self-criticism. What's *wrong* with me? Why do I have all these feelings about something that isn't important? I'm sure I caused all this myself; somehow I'm to blame.

Heaven forbid I should surrender, accept my discomfort, and pray for guidance.

Today's reminder

Will power cannot eliminate in a day troubles that have taken root and flourished in my life for decades. Things take time.

> "You cannot create a statue by smashing the marble with a hammer, and you cannot by force of arms release the spirit or the soul of man."
>
> Confucius

If I don't know how to respond to a situation today, why not try responding with kindness? Whether I accept or turn down a request, agree or disagree with someone's point of view, I can still treat the other person with respect and courtesy. I can say, "No," as gently and lovingly as I can say, "Yes."

Today I can honor my decisions without being defensive because I respect my right to make the best decisions I can. Even when others are not happy with those decisions, I can behave in a way that feels good for me. Others have a right to disagree, to feel differently, to be disappointed. I can respect that right and still stick to my principles.

Relationships are complicated because people are complicated. We each have our own ideas, values, and hopes, and they can't always coincide with the desires of those we love. Disagreements can be healthy and enlightening if we view them as a way to develop and deepen our relationships. Kindness and respect for everyone concerned will go a long way toward making this possible.

Today's reminder

Today I will try to view every conflict as an opportunity to heal. I will honor myself by responding with courtesy.

"The highest form of wisdom is kindness."

The Talmud

Many of us develop a heightened awareness of our thoughts as we recover in Al-Anon. After a while, we are able to notice the change when our thinking becomes distorted. But if we wish to put a stop to negative thoughts, awareness is just the beginning.

When "stinking thinking" takes hold of me, I must do more than just dismiss the negative thoughts. I must replace them with something positive or I am likely to slide right back into my negative thinking.

Our group ordered a collection of Al-Anon Conference-Approved Literature (CAL) on audio-cassettes that I have gotten into the habit of listening to in my car when I'm driving around town. Even though I had read these CAL pamphlets many times before, hearing them spoken out loud is a different and very powerful experience. If my attitude is not good, adjusting it by listening to Al-Anon wisdom on a tape, at a meeting, or one-to-one can get me back on track.

Today's reminder

Today I'm going to pay close attention to what I tell myself. If necessary, I'll stop in mid-thought, start over, and replace negative illusions with positive truths.

> "What we teach ourselves with our thoughts and attitudes is up to us."
>
>   . . . *In All Our Affairs*

Many of us come to Al-Anon hoping to find answers to the questions that plague us. Should I leave the alcoholic? What about the financial, sexual, medical, legal, and emotional problems? How can I stop abusive behavior? There are as many legitimate options as there are members, and Al-Anon's position is that we must each find answers that are right for us.

The one exception is a life-threatening or violent situation. In this case, Al-Anon suggests putting "First things first": ensuring the safety of ourselves and our children. Perhaps this means leaving money and keys in a safe place so that we can get out in an emergency, or calling the police, or arranging to stay with a friend, if only for today. We learn that we deserve to be safe.

Today's reminder

In Al-Anon we don't make anyone's choices for them, but we do offer advice of a different kind. We suggest attending Al-Anon meetings, finding a sponsor, and reaching out by phone. We advise our members to practice the Steps, slogans, and Traditions, and to incorporate these principles into every aspect of our lives. This kind of advice helps us to find answers that we can live with.

> "When I concentrate on my personal progress, the difficulties over which I have no control will iron themselves out."
>
> *The Dilemma of the Alcoholic Marriage*

I came to Al-Anon in so much pain that I quickly opened my arms and my heart to whatever the program and its members were willing to show me. What I discovered is that what I go through in life is not as important as how I interpret the experience. In other words, I have a choice about my attitude.

For instance, I always expected my happiness to come through others, especially my alcoholic parents. I spent most of my life waiting for them to show their love and approval in a way I could understand. They didn't, and I felt deprived and unloveable as a result.

Al-Anon has helped me to interpret my situation differently. Through working the Steps, I have learned that I am loveable, regardless of what a parent or anyone else thinks. I can either feel sorry for what I have missed or I can appreciate the chance to learn to love and appreciate myself. I do some of both, but today I know I have a choice.

Today's reminder

It's time to stop waiting for others to take care of me. The only person who can love me the way I want to be loved is me.

"Gradually I accepted the fact that my 'if only' wishes were not about to come true. But I also learned that I could be happy even if they didn't."

Al-Anon Faces Alcoholism

Many of us have had anxious moments at work and around our families when it came to making decisions affecting others as a group. We'd worry, "Will everyone be happy with the decision?" Surely there was one perfect way to do things, and it was our responsibility to find it.

Al-Anon has helped me to develop a simple policy about group decisions, as suggested by Al-Anon's First Tradition: "Our common welfare should come first." This Tradition applies to the conduct of our Al-Anon groups, but I find it useful in other situations, too. If the group's plans seem designed to benefit the greatest number of people, I can usually support them. I don't mean that I ignore my own needs and feelings—I express them. But others have needs too, and I must respect them. Such choices may not bring immediate happiness to me or to others, but ultimately we will all benefit. As the First Tradition says, "Personal progress for the greatest number depends upon unity."

Today's reminder

Do I try to force my will on others in group situations, or am I learning to respect their rights as well as my own? I can feel secure in my opinions if I keep the group's best interest at heart.

> "Unity presents not only the necessary climate for the growth of Al-Anon as a whole but also the atmosphere in which each member within the group may acquire peace of mind."
>
> *The Twelve Steps and Traditions*

I had spent a lot of time yearning for things I wasn't getting from the alcoholic in my life. As a part of my Al-Anon recovery, I was encouraged to put those needs on paper. Courtesy, respect, attention, affection, communication—my list of the areas in which I felt my loved one had let me down went on and on.

My sponsor applauded my honesty and then suggested that *I* could bring all the things on my list into my life. The catch: I had to give what I wanted to receive and become what I wanted to attract. Did I present a shining example of courtesy and all the rest? If not, I had a wonderful list of goals already on paper.

I have often heard that we get back what we give, and now I know that it's true. As I grew kinder and more loving, other people responded to the change. I also felt much better about myself. Today I can honestly say that all the qualities on my list exist in my life at least some of the time. I hadn't expected these results—or any others, for that matter. I was too busy focusing on myself. I think that's why it worked.

Today's reminder

Today I can take an active role in fulfilling my needs. I can choose to become someone I would want to have in my life.

> "Many of us find that as we practice treating others fairly, with love and respect, we ourselves become magnets for love and respect."
>
> *. . . In All Our Affairs*

Learning about alcoholism has helped me to find serenity after years of struggling. I see now that alcoholics have a disease: They are ill, not bad. By attending Al-Anon meetings on a regular basis, reading Al-Anon Conference-Approved Literature (CAL), and sitting in on open AA meetings, I have gained some insight into what is and is not reasonable to expect when dealing with an alcoholic.

I've learned that I have the ability to adjust my expectations so that I no longer set myself up for constant disappointment. For instance, I have stopped expecting a drinking alcoholic to keep every promise. This makes my life more manageable.

The knowledge I gain in Al-Anon has dispersed many of my fears and made room for a new-found compassion. I see that I am not the only one with good ideas, valid criticisms, and noble motives.

Today's reminder

Learning about the disease of alcoholism can help me become more realistic about a loved one's illness—and thus to make better choices for myself.

"I have learned techniques for dealing with the alcoholic, so that I can develop a relationship with the person behind the disease."

Al-Anon Faces Alcoholism

In Al-Anon I'm learning that it is safe to be myself. Today I share with Al-Anon friends embarrassing secrets I once would have buried from sight. Sometimes I have to fight the old urge to keep quiet at all costs, but I have found that sharing is the key to healing.

For example, I was embarrassed about my physical appearance, especially about my smile. Years of humiliating criticisms from alcoholic relatives had left me feeling very insecure. It seemed best to reveal as little about myself as possible, and I avoided smiling altogether. Unfortunately, I continued to believe the criticisms, so I thought very badly of myself.

By sharing honestly with people I can trust, I challenge the old, negative ideas. My Al-Anon friends assure me that the criticisms were exaggerated. Nobody seems to find me unworthy because of my smile. In Al-Anon I can come out of hiding. I'm even free to break into a grin.

Today's reminder

Even when I feel ashamed, someone in the fellowship can help me see my situation in a different light. With their help, if I'm willing to permit it, the truth will set me free.

> "You get to the point where your demons, which are terrifying, get smaller and smaller and you get bigger and bigger."

> August Wilson

Something I've come to appreciate in Al-Anon is our unity in diversity. Tradition Four says that each group is autonomous, free to conduct meetings in a way that suits its members as long as it abides by the Traditions and doesn't harm the overall unity of Al-Anon. Some groups stick to the suggested meeting format; others use a slightly different structure.

Why should I get my nose bent out of shape because another Al-Anon group chooses to follow a meeting format different from one familiar to me? Why should I assume that *my* way is the *right* way? When I remember to "Keep an open mind," I find that the principles of the Al-Anon program remain exactly the same, no matter which group or which city I visit.

Each of us plays an essential part in this remarkable fellowship, supporting one another as we recover from the effects of alcoholism. With this solid foundation of love and support, our individual differences can only make us richer as a whole.

Today's reminder

In the perfect order of my Higher Power's world, all things are beautiful. I will pray to let go of my own rigidity, that I might see the beauty of unity in diversity.

"A foolish consistency is the hobgoblin of little minds."

                                    Ralph Waldo Emerson

At first, the idea of searching for defects of character, wrongs, shortcomings, and harm I have done can seem like just another excuse to be hard on myself. That's why it's so important to concentrate on the first three Steps long enough to develop a strong spiritual foundation.

In these early Steps, we admit the areas over which we are powerless—such as alcoholism and other people—and learn that a Power greater than ourselves has no such limitations. We decide to place our will and our life in the hands of this Higher Power. We let go of burdens that were never ours to carry. And we begin to treat ourselves more kindly and more realistically.

When we move on to later Steps, we do so for our well-being. We begin a process that is immensely rewarding, and we go forward under the guidance of a Higher Power. This enables us to be much more gentle with our recovery.

Today's reminder

The first three Steps are the cornerstone on which my progress is built. No matter how long I have been in this program, I won't hesitate to touch base with the foundation of my spiritual health.

> "I now have a goal I can see clearly and the program with which to work toward it. It is my guide to self-improvement, comfort, and a better way of life."

> *The Dilemma of the Alcoholic Marriage*

When I came to Al-Anon I didn't feel. When I lost a job, I said, "No problem, I can take it." When we had a child, I said, "No big deal, it's just another day." Nothing moved me at all. It was like being dead.

My Al-Anon friends assured me that I did have feelings, but I had lost touch with them through years of living with alcoholism and denying every hint of anger, joy, or sorrow. As I began to recover, I began to feel, and it was very confusing. For a while I thought I might be getting sicker than ever because the feelings were so uncomfortable, but my Al-Anon friends assured me that this was just part of the process. I was ready to experience feelings, and the discomfort did pass. Slowly I became more whole.

As long as I kept them trapped inside me, my feelings were painful and poisonous secrets. When I let them out, they became expressions of my vitality.

Today's reminder

Today I will stop from time to time to see how I feel. Perhaps the day will bring joy or perhaps sadness, but either will remind me that I am very much alive.

> "I would not exchange the laughter of my heart for the fortunes of the multitudes; nor would I be content with converting my tears . . . into calm. It is my fervent hope that my whole life on this earth will ever be tears and laughter."
>
> Kahlil Gibran

When something isn't working the way I think it should, I can think about the slogan, "Easy does it." Instead of redoubling my effort, I can slow down and reassess the situation. The answer I seek may be staring me in the face, but sometimes I have to let go of what I'm doing before I can see it.

I was trying to zip a removable lining back into my coat, but it wasn't working. I pushed as hard as I could, trying to force it to slide, but it wouldn't budge. Finally I saw that I had been trying to fit the lining's zipper into the coat's front zipper. No wonder I couldn't make it work!

How many times in my life have I done the same thing: forced a solution? I've tried to "zip" myself to people and situations that didn't "fit" me, becoming frustrated and disheartened in the process. But I've learned that "Easy does it." I can take the time to see if I "match" what I think I want before I jump in and start "zipping." My life is more serene because I'm not pushing to make myself fit somewhere I don't belong.

Today's reminder

If my plans hit a snag today, I will step back for a moment and take a calm look at the situation before moving ahead.

> "Easy does it . . . Think about it when you're in a hurry to do something and everything seems to go wrong . . . You'll be surprised how much this one little idea can do for you."
>
> *Youth and the Alcoholic Parent*

Many of us have discovered that the telephone can be a life line between meetings. At first we may be reluctant to call someone we barely know, but most members are grateful to receive such calls because both parties benefit. It is often as helpful for a long-time member to review the Al-Anon "basics" as it is for the newcomer to hear them. Our strength lies in the fact that we learn from each other.

A particularly useful time for Al-Anon phone calls is when we are preparing to do something new or frightening. Many of us "bookend" these actions: We make an Al-Anon call before taking the action, and we follow the action with a second call. For those of us who have always acted alone, this is a way to share our risks and our courage with others who will love and support us, no matter what happens. When we talk about what we are doing and how we feel before taking a difficult step, it becomes possible to act with confidence and serenity.

Today's reminder

I will reach out to another Al-Anon member today. If that person is busy or unavailable, I'll make another call.

> "We must learn to lean on others, and sometimes accept others' leaning on us . . . We can't do it alone."
>
> *Alateen—Hope for Children of Alcoholics*

The most important words many of us hear when we first come to Al-Anon are, "Take what you like, and leave the rest." Everything about our program is suggested, not required. This gives us the freedom to pick and choose. If we disagree with something, we don't have to use it. If we are not ready to use a Step, slogan, or tool, we are free to wait.

Many of us need time to come to terms with the spiritual nature of the Al-Anon program. If we were required to believe in a Higher Power in order to participate in Al-Anon, we might never have continued to attend meetings. Eventually, many of us do come to believe in a Higher Power because we are free to come to our own understanding in our own time. That way, whatever we learn will have meaning for us.

When we take what we like and leave the rest, we give ourselves permission to challenge new ideas, to make decisions for ourselves, and even to change our minds.

Today's reminder

Because I am able to use whatever I find helpful and leave the rest, I can benefit from the experience, strength, and hope of others and still follow my own heart.

"With the help of this program and my Higher Power, I take charge of fashioning, shaping, choosing what kind of life I will have."

. . . In All Our Affairs

Self-esteem grows when I love and accept myself as I am. I block my own well-being each time I base my self-worth on what I do or what others think of me. If I could please all the people on the earth, if I could "straighten everyone out" and remedy all the difficulties they face, if I could make the world a perfect place—even then, I probably still would not feel good about myself. Indeed, I would have had to give up all of my "self" to accomplish this impossible task.

I cannot be perfect. I cannot make others perfect. Yet I am worthy of love, respect, and joy. Let me remind myself each day that I am the child of a perfect Higher Power. That, in itself, commands respect—my respect—for the miraculous "self" I have been given. When I hold this at the forefront of my mind, I will not give up my "self" in the course of any endeavor.

Today's reminder

Today, when faced with choices, I will opt for the path that enhances my self-esteem.

"I am learning to live a full life, one in which I like and care for the person I am."

Al-Anon Faces Alcoholism

Sometimes the things we consider our greatest weaknesses prove to be our greatest strengths. They provide us with opportunities for growth that we would never have had otherwise. All my life I prayed for courage, but it was through my shyness that I learned that courage was already available to me.

I was hesitant about sharing in meetings, afraid I would be ridiculed. I sat in the back and kept my secrets to myself. Still, I heard my own story so often that I began to lose my fear. Calling upon a reserve of courage I didn't know existed, I managed to approach some members who seemed to have similar experiences. In time, I had spoken with so many people one-on-one that sharing in the group became possible, even comfortable.

If my fear had simply been removed, I might never have known that I am capable of acting on my own behalf. I didn't need enough strength to get up in front of a roomful of strangers; I only needed enough to keep me taking tiny steps. I had exactly enough strength and courage to reach my goal.

Today's reminder

Anything and everything about me can be used for my good. If I feel insecure or frightened today, I will remember that my fear is a signal that there is something for me to learn.

> "It may not be the answer I *want*, but I have to remember that it may be what I *need*."

> *As We Understood . . .*

I grew up with guilt and blame, amidst harsh criticism and constant fear. Even now, after years of Al-Anon recovery, when past mistakes come to mind I tend to react with guilt, exaggerating the significance of my errors and thinking very badly of myself.

In Al-Anon I'm learning to see myself more realistically. Sure, I have wrestled with alcoholism and taken a fall or two. I've made plenty of mistakes that had nothing to do with alcoholism. But I'm not evil. It's time I stop treating myself as if I were.

There was a time when the only power I felt I had was the power to mess things up. Today, because I am learning to believe in myself and my ability to make a positive contribution to my own life, I am free to look at my mistakes without blowing them out of proportion. I can learn to stop repeating those errors, and I can make amends for the harm I have done.

Today's reminder

I will not chain myself to the past with self-defeating guilt, or by inflating the importance of my errors. Instead, I want to face my past and heal old wounds so that I may move forward into a richer, fuller, and more joyous life today.

"You don't have to suffer continual chaos in order to grow."

John C. Lilly

I have no idea why the faucet in my bathroom started dripping. Handling the situation with great patience, I watched it drip. And drip and drip. Sometimes I tried adjusting the knob, but I really expected it to stop dripping by itself. Naturally it didn't work out that way. The problem got worse and eventually did extensive damage. Finally I had to call for help.

I can't tell you how many problems I've handled in this very way, with just as little success. Thanks to Al-Anon, I no longer have to wait for a situation to explode before I face it. One of the most useful tools has been sharing in meetings and with members of the fellowship. When I put my experiences into words, they seem more real and I am less likely to push them aside. As a result, I can often face problems when they are still only slight irritations and deal with them before they grow and take over. Today I am not so interested in high drama; I'd rather have a real life.

Today's reminder

Today I will share honestly about something that has been nagging at me. My life deserves my attention.

"One of the most helpful aspects of the Al-Anon/ Alateen fellowship is the opportunity we have to voice our dilemmas, confident that we won't be condemned for speaking frankly."

Living With Sobriety

At a recent Al-Anon meeting we were asked to fill in the blank in this statement: "If only _____ would happen, I would be happy." Many of us were tempted to answer that we would be happy if our loved ones got sober or handled sobriety differently. But other "if only's" also kept us feeling deprived: If only my boss, family, job, government, finances, would change in the way that I want, I would be happy. It became clear that many of us have put our happiness on hold for things beyond our control.

So we applied the First Step, and admitted that we were powerless over these people, places, and things. These "if only's" made our lives unmanageable, but a Power greater than ourselves could restore us to sanity. Many of us decided to surrender our "if only's" to a Higher Power. When we did, we stopped acting like victims, waiting for things to change. We chose to take a more active role in seeking happiness in the here and now.

Today's reminder

There are many areas of my life that I cannot change. What I can change is my attitude. Today I can accept my life as it is. I can be grateful and happy, here and now, with what I have.

> "Life holds so much—so much to be so happy about always. Most people ask for happiness on condition. Happiness can be felt only if you don't set conditions."
>
>   Artur Rubinstein

Sometimes I become so busy staring at my problems that I miss the guidance I'm being given. When I become willing to let go of the need to do it by myself, I can listen to others and receive direction from my Higher Power. I become better able to move beyond my problems and start solving them.

This became clear to me when I was caught in a sudden, blinding snowstorm. Visibility was so bad that I couldn't see the sides of the road; I couldn't tell where my driving lane began and ended. I struggled to find my way, but finally surrendered and began to pull off the road to sit out the storm. Then I realized that I could make it home if I allowed the trees that lined the road to help me to gauge my position.

When I accept that help often comes in unexpected forms, I can release my hold on the problem and become willing to receive help.

Today's reminder

I must do many things for myself, but I am not wholly self-sufficient. I need the help, support, and guidance I receive from my Higher Power and my Al-Anon friends. When I catch myself struggling with a problem today, I will let go of it long enough to reach out for help.

> "Once we learn to let go of the problem . . . the loving concern and help of the other members will provide strong support to help us understand what the Al-Anon program can do for us."

> *This Is Al-Anon*

Detachment. At first it may sound cold and rejecting, not loving at all. But I have come to believe that detachment is actually a wonderful gift: I am allowing my loved ones the privilege and opportunity of being themselves.

I do not wish to interfere with anyone's opportunities to discover the joy and self-confidence that can accompany personal achievements. If I am constantly intervening to protect them from painful experiences, I also do them a great disservice. As Mark Twain said, "A man who carries a cat by the tail learns something he can learn in no other way."

I find it painful to watch another person suffer or head down a road I believe leads to pain. Many of my attempts to rescue others have been prompted by my desire to avoid this pain. Today I'm learning to experience my own fear, grief, and anguish. This helps me to be willing to trust the same growth process in others, because I know first-hand about the gifts it can bring.

Today's reminder

Sometimes it is more loving to allow someone else to experience the natural consequences of their actions, even when it is painful for us both. In the long run, both of us will benefit. Today I will put love first in my life.

"All I have to do is keep my hands off and turn my heart on."

. . . In All Our Affairs

Who am I? When I came to Al-Anon, I thought I knew the answer to that question, but I discovered that my answers were all out-of-date because I had long ago stopped asking myself who I was. I could tell you about the alcoholics and everyone else in my life—their likes and dislikes, opinions, feelings—but I had no such answers for myself.

Al-Anon gave me Twelve Steps with which to rediscover myself. Making a searching and fearless moral inventory of myself and sharing it with a trusted friend (Steps Four and Five) were especially helpful. It was the first time in a long time I had paid so much attention to myself! I also learned about myself by listening in meetings—when I identified with others, I gained insight into my own thoughts and feelings.

Today I know that I am a passionate, generous, opinionated, moody, honest, tactful, stubborn person. I know how I feel and what I think on an assortment of topics, and I am aware when these thoughts and feelings change. Al-Anon has given me back the only thing that was ever really mine to keep: myself.

Today's reminder

Recovery is a wonderful word. It means getting something back. Today I will try to remember that that something is me.

> "If a man happens to find himself . . . he has a mansion which he can inhabit with dignity all the days of his life."
>
> James Michener

Humility was a tough concept for me to comprehend. Taught from childhood to place the wants and needs of others always above my own, I equated humility with taking care of others and ignoring my own feelings and needs. In Al-Anon I have learned that true humility is not degrading; it doesn't require that I neglect my own needs. In fact, humility is not measured by how much I do for other people, but by my willingness to do my part in my relationship with the God of my understanding.

I begin to learn humility when I take the First Step. By admitting I am powerless, I make room for the possibility that a Power greater than myself can do all those things that are beyond my reach. In other words, I begin to learn about what is, and is not, my responsibility. As this becomes clear, I am better able to do my part, for myself and for others, and better able to ask God to do the rest.

Today's reminder

Part of learning humility is learning to contribute to my own well-being. Today I will do something loving for myself that I'd normally do for someone else.

"We cannot tell what may happen to us in the strange medley of life. But we can decide what happens in us—how we can take it, what we do with it—and that is what really counts in the end."

Joseph Fort Newton

I was intimidated by Step Five, because it meant revealing my darkest secrets to another person. Afraid that I would be rejected for being less than perfect, I put so much energy into hiding the truth that, although no one rejected me, I was as isolated and lonely as if they had.

When I realized how painful it was to continue living that way, I found a sponsor and asked for help. We worked the Fifth Step, and I shared some of my characteristics and attitudes that I found particularly shameful. My sponsor began to laugh. "You see," he quickly explained, "I'm laughing because five years ago I said the same things to my sponsor, almost word for word!"

I would never have imagined the universality of my experiences. I would never have guessed that, in sharing what I felt made me different from other people, I would discover how alike we all really are.

Today's reminder

Many have known shame and fear and many have known joy. Sharing mine with others today will make my ride through life a smoother one.

"Deep down I had the nagging knowledge that there would be no real relief from myself until I could bring my problem out in the open and talk to somebody else about it . . ."

As We Understood . . .

Why do I find it so hard to accept that alcoholism is a disease? Would I blame a diabetic or a cancer patient for their symptoms? Of course not. I know that will power alone is not enough to defeat a disease. If alcoholics could simply stop drinking whenever they wanted, many would have stopped long ago. It would do me no good to plead, berate, or reason with tuberculosis; I will not waste my time pleading, berating, or reasoning with alcoholism.

I therefore resolve to stop blaming the alcoholic for what is beyond his or her control—including the compulsion to drink. Instead, I'll direct my efforts where they can do some good: I will commit myself to my own recovery. I know that improved health in one family member can have a profound effect on the rest of the family. In this way, I can make a much stronger contribution to the well-being of those I love than I ever could by trying to combat a disease that can't be controlled.

Today's reminder

When I accept that alcoholism is a disease, it becomes easier to recognize that I, too, have been affected by something beyond my control, and to begin to recover from those effects.

> "Whether or not the alcoholic achieves sobriety, the time for the family members to begin working out their own emotional recovery is now."
>
> *A Guide for the Family of the Alcoholic*

"Yes, but . . ." These two words have become a signal to me that I am refusing to accept something over which I am powerless. My world is rich with wonderful gifts: beauty, a loving fellowship, and challenges that strengthen and prepare me for a better life. Is it worth it to deny these gifts by wishing things were different? Will it make them change? No! I prefer to accept them gladly, enjoy them thoroughly, and humbly accept the reality my Higher Power offers without any "yes, but's."

The harsh tone, the unkind word, the apparent indifference of another is usually over in a few minutes. What price am I paying by holding on to those few minutes? I don't have to like reality, only to accept it for what it is. This day is too precious to waste by resenting things I can't change. When I accept everything as it is, I tend to be reasonably serene. When I spend my time wishing things were different, I know that serenity has lost its priority.

Today's reminder

While I am responsible for changing what I can, I have to let go of the rest if I want peace of mind. Just for today I will love myself enough to give up a struggle over something that is out of my hands.

"By yielding you may obtain victory."

Ovid

One evening, I was taken by surprise when another member complimented me. I was very uncomfortable with this gesture of kindness, feeling inside that I didn't deserve it. When I tried to talk her out of her kind words, she refused to take them back. She insisted that I deserved her compliment, and others as well. I began to realize how far down my feelings of self-worth had sunk while living with an alcoholic. I couldn't even consider that there might be something nice about me!

My sponsor suggested that I make a list of the things I liked about myself. It was awkward and embarrassing, and my list was very short, but it was a start. When I shared it with my sponsor, she agreed with every nice thing I said about myself, refusing to let me negate them when I tried instead to focus on my shortcomings. As a result, I am learning to like myself and to see that I have many qualities that are worthy of compliments.

Today's reminder

One way to learn to love myself is to accept the love of others. Even if I don't feel deserving, I can be grateful for another's kindness. And if I appreciate something about someone else, I can tell them so. A small gesture can go a long way toward healing a hurting soul.

> "I've heard people in Al-Anon say they got back their self-worth. I never had any in my life, so it was a whole new feeling to like the person called 'me.'"
>
> *As We Understood . . .*

I am so grateful to belong to a fellowship where everyone speaks for himself or herself. Al-Anon has no spokesperson, no authority who tells what "our" experience has been. I am the only one who can tell my story.

I find it very comforting to be part of a group of people who share some of my problems and feelings. Although we have much in common, each Al-Anon member has unique wisdom to offer. Through the interchange of experience, strength, and hope, we learn specific ways in which fellow members have applied the Al-Anon program to their situations. Taking what we like and leaving the rest, each of us is free to benefit from this individual approach to our common purpose—recovery from the effects of alcoholism. So when I share in a meeting, I try to avoid phrases such as, "This is a problem for us" or "We tend to do that." Instead, I look at sharing as an opportunity to see myself more clearly.

Today's reminder

Today I will speak for myself, secure in the fact that I am supported by a fellowship of men and women who "understand as perhaps few others can."

"Our recovery depends on our ability to *tell our own story*—not that of an alcoholic or another Al-Anon or Alateen member."

Why Is Al-Anon Anonymous?

I spend more time with myself than with anyone else. Wouldn't it make sense to put some energy into making that relationship as fulfilling as possible? Another person cannot prevent me from feeling lonely, but my inner emptiness *can* be satisfied. I can come to value my own company. I am a worthwhile companion.

One of the illusions shared by many of us who have been affected by alcoholism is that only another person, usually the alcoholic, can fill that empty place within us. If only he were more attentive, if only she got sober, if only they were with me now, I wouldn't be lonely. But many of us remain just as lonely even after those conditions are met.

Today, when I'm by myself, I will know that I am in good company. When I stop expecting others to meet all of my needs, I find new and exciting ways to enjoy my own friendship. And when I do get lonely, I have the comfort and support of a Higher Power who never leaves me.

Today's reminder

Today I will spend some time exploring the most intimate human relationship I will ever have—my relationship with myself.

"What a lovely surprise to discover how un-lonely being alone can be."

Ellen Burstyn

There are many times when I doubt the existence of anything that cares about what goes on in this world, let alone in my life. Being agnostic, doubt comes easily to me; belief is difficult.

But then I think of how someone guided me to Al-Anon when my life was at its darkest. I reflect on times when the words and music of certain songs have given me courage to go on with life when it might have been easier to give up. I remember that I am encouraged by the honesty of people who share their innermost thoughts in Al-Anon meetings week after week, year after year. I am aware that, deep down, there is a part of me that wants what is good for me, that pushes me to seek peace, happiness, direction, and wholeness in my life.

And I doubt my doubts.

Today's reminder

When I feel far away from a Higher Power, I have to listen very carefully. I listen at meetings, I listen to music, I listen to the wisdom that comes through our literature, and I try to be open to what I hear. I never know from where a message will come.

"Every now and again take a good look at something not made with hands—a mountain, a star, the turn of a stream. There will come to you wisdom and patience and solace and, above all, the assurance that you are not alone in the world."

　　　　　　　　　　　　　　　Sidney Lovett

I find it much easier to risk making decisions when I stop thinking about suffering the consequences and remember that I have the option to enjoy the consequences. Since coming to Al-Anon, I make my choices more conscientiously. I do whatever footwork seems appropriate and then turn the results over to God. The results are often quite favorable. Even when they aren't, I can still celebrate the fact that I have done my part.

For a long time I avoided decisions because I was sure that there was some magical "right" choice that would get me what I wanted, yet I never seemed to know which choice that was. I waited until the last minute to decide and never felt good about my choices. Today I know that choosing not to decide *is* to decide.

It can be very liberating to make a decision. Once the choice is made, I can trust that the consequences will unfold as they should. With a slight change of attitude, perhaps I can await them with excitement and hope instead of fear and dread.

Today's reminder

Today I will have faith in my ability to act. When the time seems right, I will make the best choice I can and allow myself to enjoy the results.

"Sometimes our enthusiasm for change depends on our willingness to take a chance on tomorrow by risking what we have today."

Living With Sobriety

Al-Anon recovery is a discipline that requires diligence, patience, and consistency for the best results. Regular attendance at meetings, working the Steps, and applying the Al-Anon principles to every part of the day lead to a fuller and more enjoyable life.

At times we see obvious results from our efforts, while at other times we reach plateaus and feel stuck. If we go on putting one foot in front of the other and continue to work the program, we find that all plateaus eventually come to an end. Just when we reach the end of our patience, a doorway seems to open and we suddenly take a huge leap forward. We see that none of the time that passed was wasted; although we didn't know it, we were quietly absorbing the program. Most of us find that the results were worth the wait.

Today's reminder

Whether or not I see immediate benefits, today I choose to "Keep coming back."

"Patience is the key to paradise."

Turkish proverb

When I first came to Al-Anon, I was leery about all the hugs I saw exchanged. I would scurry out the door after a meeting to avoid them. I couldn't imagine why all those seemingly respectable people were behaving this way. There had been no such displays of affection in my childhood, and none in my adult home either. The only kinds of touch I knew were negative.

The people in Al-Anon were patient with me even though I refused their hugs. They invited me to keep coming back. They respected my boundaries and didn't judge or question my need for space. Individual members sat with me as I cried, and rejoiced when I laughed. Complete strangers offered their experience, strength, and hope to me as if I were an intimate friend.

In this safe and nurturing atmosphere, I have come to appreciate that there are many different expressions of unconditional love. Whether or not I express affection in a physical way, I can find reassurance, comfort, and strength whenever Al-Anon members offer me their support. Today I am finding ways to express my love for others as well.

Today's reminder

I will not let old fears keep me away from the support that is available to me. I am worthy of love and respect.

"Love is not consolation, it is light."

                                        Simone Weil

Tradition Eight states that "Al-Anon Twelfth Step work should remain forever nonprofessional . . ." We come together as a fellowship of equals, where no one is in charge and no one is an expert. Every member can contribute to the healing power of our program simply by sharing his or her personal story of experience, strength, and hope. No special training or qualification other than membership is necessary, or even desired.

Because the help we exchange is strictly nonprofessional and has a specific goal, Al-Anon does not presume to solve every problem or cure every illness. Our program is a remarkably effective approach to recovery from the effects of someone else's drinking. Sometimes, however, we grapple with problems that Al-Anon doesn't address. At such times, many of us have found it useful to seek help from other sources in addition to working our Al-Anon program.

Today's reminder

A wonderfully nurturing atmosphere is created when people help other people by being themselves and sharing their own experiences. I will contribute to this interchange today.

"... We meet as equals and help one another, not because some are experts and others are learners, but because we all have needs and strengths."

The Twelve Steps and Traditions

"When we talk of tomorrow," says a Chinese proverb, "the gods laugh." They laugh, I believe, not because they find us ridiculous, but because they know the future is not predictable. Thus we have no choice but to live "One day at a time."

I can make plans, but I cannot determine the results. No amount of scheming about next week can control what will happen then. Circumstances will be different, and I myself will be different as well.

I can further compress the focus of this slogan to address one hour at a time, or even one minute at a time. In such small increments, life begins to feel not only bearable but precious. At any given moment, no matter what is going on, if I concentrate on being right here, right now, I know that I am fine.

Today's reminder

My worst fears about tomorrow need not affect this day. By letting them go, I am free to grow. What bad habit can I change today? What fear can I face? What joy can I acknowledge? What good fortune, no matter how modest, can I celebrate? All I have is today. Let me make today the most fully alive day I have ever experienced.

"Do not be anxious about tomorrow; tomorrow will look after itself."

The Bible

Life doesn't always go smoothly or peacefully, even though I might wish it would. In the past, when something bothered me, I'd say nothing rather than face an argument. It seemed better for me to be upset than to risk upsetting someone else. The results were usually disastrous. I would become irritable and unreasonable as I let resentment fester.

Today I suspect that adversity has value I hadn't previously recognized. When I face adversity and deal with my problems or express my feelings, things have a chance to improve. Even if they don't, I release some of the pressure I feel. I'm new at this, and I don't do it very gracefully yet: sometimes it is scary, and sometimes my words are not exactly welcomed. Nevertheless, I feel better when I realize that I have finally begun living life on life's terms.

Looking back, I see how much I've grown. I wouldn't have chosen any of the crises in my life, but since coming to Al-Anon, I've learned that every problem can help me to change for the better, deepen my faith, and add to my self-esteem.

Today's reminder

The Chinese word for crisis is written with two brush strokes. The first stands for danger, and the second for opportunity. I will look for the good hidden within everything I encounter.

"There is no such thing as a problem without a gift for you in its hands."

Richard Bach

In the past, whenever anyone disagreed with me I took it as a personal failure. If only I had found the right words, clothes, opinions, school, job, home, friends, or lover, I could have belonged.

And how did others appear to me? Happy and self-confident—they seemed to have all the answers. But because of the front I put on, people thought *I* was easy-going and happy, too. If they could be so mistaken about the way I really felt, couldn't I have a few wrong ideas about their feelings? After all, I couldn't be the only one who put on a good act. Wasn't I comparing my insides to other people's outsides?

In Al-Anon I am learning that someone can disagree with me without either of us being wrong. When no one has to be wrong, we can all fit in, just as we are.

Today's reminder

If I compare, I lose. Maybe I'll come out feeling better than somebody this time, but next time I'm bound to feel worse. The best way to stop feeling that I'm not good enough is to stop comparing altogether.

"Little by little, we come to realize at our meetings that much of our discomfort comes from our attitudes."

Understanding Ourselves and Alcoholism

Like alcoholism, obsessive thinking can be too much to handle. My best hope in battling it is not to begin, because once started, it gains steam and becomes harder to interrupt.

Before obsessive thinking takes hold, there is usually a point at which I have to make a choice. I can opt to mentally toy with a subject that has held my mind hostage in the past and is therefore dangerous. Or I can recognize the danger and try to drop any thought of the topic from my mind, praying for my Higher Power's help. I can reach out to an Al-Anon member for support before tackling a topic to which I am vulnerable, so that my thoughts won't have a chance to get locked inside my head.

I will exercise the power of choice by refusing the invitation of obsessive thoughts. If I don't pick them up, I won't have to let them go.

Today's reminder

I am learning to pay attention to my thinking. If there is something I cannot contemplate without becoming obsessed, I will respect that fact and act accordingly. I will gather the strength and support of my Al-Anon program, my friends, and my Higher Power before I try to reason it out. And if it is none of my business, I won't pick it up at all.

"If you work on your mind with your mind,
How can you avoid an immense confusion?"

                                        Seng-ts'an

When I take the Seventh Step ("Humbly asked Him to remove our shortcomings"), I calmly ask for help. I don't beg or demand; I neither grovel nor puff myself up. I needn't demean myself, and I have no one to impress. I am simply accepting my place in my relationship with my Higher Power, no more, no less. True humility should never be humiliating. Instead, I can feel honored to take my rightful place in the wonderful partnership I am developing with the God of my understanding.

Humility is said to be perpetual quietness of heart. It means that I do my part and trust God to take care of the rest. Although I may not know how my help will come, I can remain serene. All I have to do is to ask my Higher Power for healing.

Today's reminder

Today, when I ask my Higher Power to remove my shortcomings, I will try to do so with a peaceful heart.

"Humility will help us see ourselves in true perspective and keep our minds open to the truth."

Alcoholism, The Family Disease

I used to think that if I ever looked carefully at myself, my secret fears would be confirmed: I'd see that I am hopelessly flawed and unworthy. Al-Anon has shown me that if I face the effects of alcoholism by working the Steps, this belief will fade away. I'll see that the truth I've avoided is my own inner beauty.

I am powerless to change the fact that alcoholism has affected my life. Only a Power greater than myself can overcome the effects of this disease. I call upon that Power for help with the Second and Third Steps. These Steps help me to trust that, although the ground on which I stand may quiver, I will not fall, for I am held firmly by One whose will is not so easily overturned. Regardless of how shaky I may feel, I am safe.

Such a spiritual foundation makes a truly searching and fearless moral inventory possible. Only when I risk taking a close look at myself can my fears give way to the truth: As a child of God, I am all I need to be—loving, loveable, and splendid.

Today's reminder

Today I will take some time to strengthen my relationship with my Higher Power. This will bring me closer to seeing the truth as my ally and recognizing my own inner loveliness.

> "I now choose to rise above my personality problems to recognize the magnificence of my being. I am totally willing to learn to love myself."
>
> Louise L. Hay

Sometimes the healthiest thing I can do for myself is to admit that I'm not perfect. I am human. I make mistakes.

But it isn't always easy to admit this to someone else, especially when my mistake affects them. Pretending that something never happened, or that it doesn't matter, or justifying the action seems so much more inviting to me. But there is a price to pay if I refuse to own up when I've been wrong—guilt.

For years I dragged guilt behind me like a heavy duffel bag. Al-Anon offers me an alternative—the Tenth Step. I continue taking personal inventory and when I am wrong, I promptly admit it. When I admit the error, I take responsibility for my actions. I free myself from the burden of an embarrassing secret, and I move closer to accepting my imperfection. It becomes much easier to love myself if I accept myself as I truly am, mistakes and all.

Today's reminder

Today I will have the courage to look the truth in the face, admit my errors and my achievements, appreciate my growth, and make amends where I have done harm.

"I care about truth not for truth's sake but for my own."

Samuel Butler

In the words of Socrates, "Life contains but two tragedies. One is not to get your heart's desire; the other is to get it."

Translation: My will gets me into trouble. I aim for some goal or other, but even when I get it, I am rarely satisfied. It doesn't make my life complete, so I raise the ante, set a new goal, and push even harder. Or I don't get what I want and feel inadequate or deprived. Maybe that is why not one of the Twelve Steps talks about carrying out *my* will.

The only times I have ever found lasting satisfaction were when I let go of self-will and committed myself to seeking the will of my Higher Power. Prayer and meditation are two means by which I seek to discover what God's will holds for me, and they help me to gain access to the power to carry it out.

Sometimes my hopes and desires *are* forms of guidance. When I am willing to place God's will above my own, those dreams have a chance of becoming a wonderful reality.

Today's reminder

The path to my true heart's desire is to surrender to the will of my Higher Power.

> "We know that God can and will do anything that is for our ultimate good, if we are ready to receive His help."
>
> *The Twelve Steps and Traditions*

An Al-Anon meeting is where I am most likely to get an honest answer to the question, "How are you?" This is refreshing to me, because for a long time my only possible answer to this question was, "I'm fine, how are you?"—even when I wasn't fine at all.

Denial is a symptom of the effects of alcoholism. Just as alcoholics often deny their drinking problems, many of us who have been affected by this disease deny our problems as well. Although we may have been living in chaos, worried about our families, full of self-doubt, and spiritually, emotionally, and physically depleted, many of us learned to pretend that everything was just fine.

Today it is important for me to be in an environment in which honesty is practiced. I don't necessarily launch into a detailed description of my woes or my joys—that isn't always desirable or appropriate—but when asked how I'm doing, I try to ask myself what the real answer is. This frees me from the habit of denial and gives me choices.

Today's reminder

How do I feel today? How am I doing? If I can answer those questions truthfully, I am more likely to pursue the help I need and to share the happy times with others as well.

> "We can say what we mean only if we have the courage to be honest with ourselves and with others."
>
> *The Dilemma of the Alcoholic Marriage*

I have often tried to avoid repeating mistakes by making strict rules for my behavior. Although I can learn from experience, I can't plan for every situation that might happen in the future. Trying to do so only limits my options. When I get lost in such limited thinking, Al-Anon reminds me to "Keep an open mind."

I'm glad it does, because I am constantly changing. I continually need to let go of old ideas when they no longer work for me. If I don't get too attached to any one way to approach life, I adjust to change with a lot less stress and strain.

As I practice keeping an open mind, I tend to cross paths with people who are also flexible in their thinking, and we help each other to see more clearly. As a friend says, "We don't see the world as it is. We see the world as we are."

Today's reminder

As I grow, I continue to learn and to unlearn, replacing old ideas with new ones and reclaiming others that had been cast aside. Today I welcome this flow of information that will nourish and replenish me as I become more fully myself.

> "To keep our faces toward change and behave like free spirits in the presence of fate is strength undefeatable."
>
> Helen Keller

There have been days when many of us felt that good times would never come again. After so many disappointments, it seemed too painful to continue to hope. We shut our hearts and minds to our dreams and stopped expecting to find happiness. We weren't happy, but at least we wouldn't be let down any more.

Caring, hoping, wanting—these are risky. But as we recover from the effects of alcoholism, we may find that the risks are worth taking. In time, it may not be enough to simply avoid disappointment; we want more; we want rich, full, exciting lives with joy as well as sorrow. Just finding the willingness to believe that joy can exist in our lives today can be very challenging, but until we make room in our hearts for good times, we may not recognize them when they arrive.

Nobody is happy all the time, but all of us are capable of feeling good. We deserve to allow ourselves to experience every bit of joy life has to offer.

Today's reminder

I will not let fear of disappointment prevent me from enjoying this day. I have a great capacity for happiness.

"I want to grow in my willingness to make room in my life for good times, having faith in their arrival and patience in my anticipation."

Living With Sobriety

I have heard it said that the only valid comparisons are between myself as I am and myself as I used to be. When I think of Step Two and of being restored to sanity, such a comparison comes to mind.

I remember an incident some twenty years ago in which I was riding my motorcycle to a meditation class. I was late and in a big hurry to arrive on time. Right outside the meeting place I crashed my bike. My attempt to force solutions, to rush to an encounter with serenity, had failed. Did I feel contrite? Not exactly. Even then, I felt the irony of rushing to meditation, but mainly I felt angry that the town had failed to maintain the road on which I was riding. Rather than taking responsibility for my own haste and carelessness, I blamed others and saw myself as a victim. I did not feel thankful to have survived; I felt angry that I had been roughed up and thrown off schedule.

Today's reminder

Looking back, I see many examples of the grace of a Power greater than myself at work in my life. I see progress in being restored to sanity, and I am increasingly confident that my progress will continue.

"Our business in life is not to get ahead of other people, but to get ahead of ourselves."

                                                    Maltbie D. Babcock

Worry and fear can alter our perceptions until we lose all sense of reality, twisting neutral situations into nightmares. Because most worry focuses on the future, if we can learn to stay in the present, living one day or one moment at a time, we take positive steps toward warding off the effects of fear.

In the past, many of us tried to anticipate all possible disastrous outcomes so that we would be prepared to protect ourselves. But today, our program, our fellowship, and a Higher Power allow us to view this self-protectiveness more objectively. When we anticipate doom, we lose touch with what is happening now and see the world as a threatening place against which we must be on constant alert.

Most of our fears will never come to pass, and if they do, foreknowledge probably won't make us any better prepared. But as we grow in faith, self-esteem, and trust in our Higher Power, we become capable of doing for ourselves what our anticipations could never achieve: taking appropriate action in any situation.

Today's reminder

Today I will recognize that worries can be potent and mind-altering. I choose not to indulge in them at all.

"I am not afraid of storms for I am learning how to sail my ship."

Louisa May Alcott

As a result of living in a household where alcohol was abused, the concept of being gentle with myself was foreign. What was familiar was striving for perfection and hating myself whenever I fell short of my goals.

I first heard, "Be gentle with yourself," at an Al-Anon meeting. I had a hard time with the idea until I put my imagination to work. I pictured myself finding a kitten and holding it in my cupped hands. I imagined the feelings I might have toward this sweet creature—tenderness, patience, compassion, wonder, and love. I quickly put myself in the kitten's place and focused all of those gentle feelings in my own direction. It worked!

As I have grown in Al-Anon, I have come to see that my Higher Power holds me in the same gentle way—protecting me, guiding me, and loving me every day.

Today's reminder

If I am being hard on myself, I can stop and remember that I deserve gentleness and understanding from myself. Being human is not a character defect! Today I will be gentle with my humanness.

> "The question is not what a man can scorn, or disparage, or find fault with, but what he can love, and value, and appreciate."
>
> John Ruskin

Legends have often told of spiritual journeys in which the hero must face great challenges before gaining treasure at the journey's end. As the heroes of our own stories, we in Al-Anon have also embarked upon a spiritual journey—one of self-discovery.

With the help of our program and the support of our fellowship, we explore our hidden motives, secrets, buried memories, and unrecognized talents. As we draw upon the wisdom of Al-Anon's Steps, principles, and tools, we learn to overcome obstacles to personal growth, such as the effects of alcoholism and a variety of defects of character.

We are guided on this journey by a Power greater than ourselves, but the steps we take must be our own. Only by facing the darkness can we receive the treasure—the light and joy of emerging released from all that has held us back.

Today's reminder

Self-knowledge is the path to personal freedom. The Steps give me directions and help me to cope with anything I encounter along the way.

> "The world cannot be discovered by a journey of miles . . . only by a spiritual journey . . . by which we arrive at the ground at our feet, and learn to be at home."
>
> Wendell Berry

A long-time member says, "An expectation is a premeditated resentment." I take this statement to suggest that when I have a resentment I can look to my expectations for a probable source.

Here's an example: I have a brother who is less attentive to being prompt than I am. When I make a plan with him that involves meeting at a certain time, I am co-operating in establishing conditions that encourage me to nurse a resentment. On the other hand, when I make a plan with my brother that is based on no expectation of promptness, I feel no resentment.

Today's reminder

I have the right to choose my own standards of conduct, but I do not have the right or the power to impose those standards on others.

"I have accepted myself and I'm beginning to accept other people the way they are each day. Now I have fewer resentments."

Living With Sobriety

One gift of being a long-time Al-Anon member is that I have accumulated a large supply of healthy, positive experiences which remind me that my Higher Power is worthy of my trust. Although I have faced many challenges and difficulties over the years, my Higher Power has never let me down. This hasn't prevented me from having problems; if that had been the case, I would have missed out on life-changing lessons I might not have learned any other way. Instead, I was given challenges and opportunities—but never more than I could handle. Even when I feared that my circumstances were too much for me, help, guidance, and comfort were always there.

Today when I encounter a crisis, I have no need to fear. My own experience teaches me that I can rely on a Power greater than myself to help me through whatever happens. At first I had to "act as if" I believed that I'd be cared for. But each time I took this risk, I observed the results. Again and again, my Higher Power stepped in to help. I have never once regretted my decision to trust.

Today's reminder

Each day is an opportunity to build a supply of positive spiritual experiences. Today I will take note of what happens when I trust my Higher Power.

"By far the best proof is experience."

Francis Bacon

In order to keep family and friends from interfering with their drinking, alcoholics sometimes create diversions by accusing or provoking. At such a time, we who have been affected by someone else's drinking tend to react, to argue, and to defend ourselves. As a result, nobody has to look at the alcoholism, for we are too busy focusing on the particular point being argued—any topic will do. And unfortunately, what we defend against we make real.

When we take Step One, we admit that we are powerless over this disease. We do not have the strength necessary to fight it. Defending ourselves by engaging in arguments with actively drinking or otherwise irrational people is as fruitless as donning armor to protect ourselves from a nuclear explosion. Only a Power greater than ourselves can restore us to sanity.

Today's reminder

I am responsible for taking the actions necessary to keep myself safe. But when my safety is not at risk, I can take time to make choices about my responses. I don't have to react instantly to provocation, and I am not obligated to justify myself to anyone. By turning to my Higher Power for protection, rather than my wits or my will, I avail myself of the best possible defense.

"Once we learned to see our situation as it really was, we understood why it was necessary for us to turn to a Power greater than ourselves."

Al-Anon's Twelve Steps & Twelve Traditions

The Second Step is about possibility, about hope. With this Step, we come to believe that a Power greater than ourselves *could* restore us to sanity. We are asked to open our minds to the possibility that help is available. Perhaps there is a source of assistance that can do for us what we have been unable to do for ourselves. We don't have to believe that it *will* happen, only that it could.

This little bit of hope, this chink in the armor of despair, is enough to show that we are willing to move in the direction of healing. Once we recognize that the possibility of help exists, it seems worthwhile to explore a relationship with a Higher Power. A little willingness can go a long way toward making hope and faith an ongoing part of our lives. In the hands of a Higher Power, sanity and serenity become realistic hopes.

Today's reminder

Our literature speaks of the possibility of finding contentment and even happiness through recovery in Al-Anon. Today I will take the Second Step in that process and open my mind to hope.

"Finding inner strength is looking beyond the visible and focusing life's search on the unseen."

As We Understood . . .

The Third Step talks about placing my will and my life in the *care* of a Higher Power. For me, this Power is a presence that loves me as I am, that accepts me with compassion on the bad days as well as the good. Once I have accepted that the destructive presence of another's alcoholism has affected my life, I need the benevolent influence of a Power untouched by this disease. What I do in turning over my will and my life is to become receptive to guidance; I become willing to accept the care of a Power greater than myself.

I think of this care as a source of love and support that surrounds me in my daily life. I do not need to earn it or to work for it; I need only be receptive to it. I continue to have a will to exercise and a life to live, but I do so bathed in a light of love and understanding.

Today's reminder

When I open my heart to a Power that fills me with love and acceptance, I can begin to extend those qualities to others. I may not do it perfectly or even consistently, but I can recognize my progress one day at a time.

"God's gifts put man's best dreams to shame."

Elizabeth Barrett Browning

How easy it can be to justify our own unacceptable behavior! Perhaps we excuse ourselves, claiming that we were provoked or had no choice. Or we dismiss our actions by telling ourselves that everyone does the same thing. With these and other justifications, we pretend that our wrongs don't count. This denial must be overcome when we take the Fourth Step.

With this Step we take a searching and fearless moral inventory of ourselves. It is fearless because of the strong spiritual foundation we have established by taking the first three Steps. It is moral because we list what we feel has been right or wrong about our conduct. And it is searching. The only way we can take this Step thoroughly, searchingly, is to resist the desire to justify and excuse what we uncover. It may demand courage and self-discipline, but by freely acknowledging who we have been, we can make positive changes about who we are becoming.

Today's reminder

I am a human being with strengths and weaknesses, capable of achievements and mistakes. Because I accept this, I can look closely at myself. Today I will find something to appreciate and something to improve.

"You never find yourself until you face the truth."

Pearl Bailey

When I took Step Five I looked carefully at the words, "Admitted to God, to myself, and to another human being . . ." The order of these words, placing God first, then myself, and then someone else, struck me. So often I have been vaguely aware of some truth in my life that I was unwilling to admit to myself. Yet my Higher Power had already placed that thought in my mind. He must have—if I'm trying to ignore it, I surely didn't put it there.

I try to use this when making decisions about my life. When I assume that my Higher Power has already put the answer in my mind, I can then be willing to acknowledge that answer— whether I think I'll like it or not. It may rise up into my awareness right away, or it may take some time and patience, but I can trust that the answer is within me and when the time is right, it will become clear. Then I share my thoughts with another person I trust. This process helps me to take action on the answers I receive and to move forward with my life.

Today's reminder

There is nothing in life that need confound me. With my Higher Power's help, I can find the answer to any problem I face. This knowledge gives me courage to follow through with action. I need only be willing to accept the answer I receive.

"Look within! . . . The secret is inside you."

Hui-neng

Step Six speaks of being entirely ready to have God remove all my defects of character. Yet I find that I often cling to my defects because they give me a certain amount of pleasure.

What defects could possibly give me pleasure? Revenge, for one. I spend lots of time creating mental scenarios in which I punish those who have hurt me. I also get a great deal of enjoyment from thinking that I am never wrong; in other words, I cling to my pride. Yet these characteristics are defects that get in the way of living the kind of life I want to live and prevent me from treating myself and others with love and respect. There is abundant reason to let them go, but to do so, I have to become willing to lose the enjoyment they sometimes deliver.

My recovery will have a giant void as long as I am unwilling to give up my shortcomings. If I want healing, I must turn over my will, my life, and my character defects to God.

Today's reminder

Are the small, temporary pleasures I get from my defects of character worth the price I am paying to keep them? If not, I may be entirely ready to let some of them go today.

"I know that help is waiting only for my acceptance, waiting for me to say, 'Not my will but Thine be done.'"

The Dilemma of the Alcoholic Marriage

When my study of the Steps reached Step Seven ("Humbly asked Him to remove our shortcomings"), I stumbled on the very first word. "Humble!" I thought. "The last thing I need is to be more humble." Hadn't I been humble all my life, putting everyone's needs ahead of my own? What had it ever brought me except abuse?

But Al-Anon suggested that perhaps I had confused humility with humiliation. Humility does not mean begging for mercy. Real humility, I discovered, is the ability to see my true relationship to God and to my fellow human beings.

The second word wasn't much easier. I had learned not to ask anyone for anything. Al-Anon showed that my knowledge and experience are limited. I don't know all the answers—and I don't have to know them! I can ask for help.

My concept of the last word has also changed. I used to think of shortcomings as crimes, faults, sins, or mistakes. Now I think of them as blocks within me that prevent me from reaching my full potential and distance me from my Higher Power.

Today's reminder

There are many things that I can do to improve my life and to further my recovery, but I cannot heal myself. Today I can ask for help in becoming free of all that blocks me from my true self.

"If my problems have brought me to prayer, then they have served a purpose."

As We Understood . . .

When it came time to actively pursue the Eighth Step ("Made a list of all persons we had harmed and became willing to make amends to them all"), I stopped dead in my tracks! I knew of quite a few people I had harmed, but I was absolutely unwilling to even consider making amends to some of them!

My sponsor suggested I divide my list into three categories: those to whom I was willing to make amends; those to whom I *might* make amends; and those to whom I would absolutely *not ever* make amends. When I finished, I started Step Nine by making amends to those on the first list.

The amazing thing was that, as I proceeded, I found some of the names from my "maybe" list shifting to my "willing" list. In time, even some "absolutely not" people appeared on my "maybe" list. Eventually it became easier to make amends, even to "absolutely not" people. My reward? Some renewed friendships and family ties; more importantly, an ability to face the new day without guilt, because I had owned up to my responsibilities.

Today's reminder
I will not let myself be stopped from taking Step Eight or Step Nine because I can't do it perfectly overnight. I will let myself be where I am today, and do what I am able to do.

"It does not matter how slowly you go
So long as you do not stop."

Confucius

Step Nine says I need not make direct amends to those I have injured if, in doing so, I might cause further injury. How do I know whether or not to take action?

If direct amends are inappropriate, I can trust my Higher Power to let me know. Otherwise, if I have worked the Eighth Step and become truly willing to make amends, I believe the opportunities will arise when I am ready.

For example, I was unable to discuss my personal life with my mother. Fearing her rejection, I rejected her instead. An upcoming visit presented an opportunity to make amends, but I wasn't sure I was ready. Would making amends at this time injure *me*?

After my mother arrived, I had the feeling that this was "the time." I prayed for courage and asked my Higher Power to help me find the words. My mother sat down with me in a quiet moment and, to my amazement, brought up every subject I had wanted to discuss. I realized that the opportunity to be close to her had always existed, but I hadn't been willing, until then, to take part in it.

Today's reminder

My Higher Power does not put any challenges before me that I am unable to face. The comfort I find in that knowledge can overcome my fears.

"The lure of the distant and the difficult is deceptive. The great opportunity is where you are."

John Burroughs

Since the Tenth Step is part of my daily routine, I try to think of it as a gentle, warm, and loving way to take care of myself. By continuing to take my own inventory and promptly admitting when I am wrong, I clear out many unwanted attitudes that might otherwise clutter my day.

This Step has helped me to learn that living "One day at a time" involves more than pulling my attention back from fears about the future. It also means leaving yesterday's baggage in the past. Each day I ask myself if carrying this extra weight will in any way help me today. If not, I can drop it here and now and walk away from unwanted negativity with a lightness of spirit.

Today's reminder

On this new day, let me quietly reflect and search out any negative feelings that are left over from yesterday. Old resentments will interfere with my serenity today. Perhaps it is time to let them go.

"Each day, each new moment can be an opportunity to clear the air and start again, fresh and free."

. . . In All Our Affairs

In Step Eleven I seek to improve my conscious contact with God through prayer and meditation. How I do this is completely up to me. Perhaps I become more conscious of a Higher Power when I look for signs of guidance in the people around me, or in the events and unexplained coincidences of my life. Or perhaps I seek this Power further away from the world of logic and reason: I might look for answers through my feelings, or my instincts, or my dreams. Maybe I pursue a more traditional spiritual path. Or I can decide to keep myself open to all of these possibilities. Whatever path I choose, I know I must keep trying as often as I can to follow the course offered to me by my Higher Power. Only in this way can I be confident of my actions; only in this way can I find the courage to change.

Today's reminder

I will take time to clear my mind of unnecessary, hurried thoughts. There seems to be a limited amount of space in my mind until I do. But when I clear this clutter away, the space becomes limitless and the guidance I am truly willing to accept comes through.

> "The spiritual exercise suggested by the Eleventh Step is a powerful force for good in our lives. Let me not ever think I have no time for it."
>
> *The Dilemma of the Alcoholic Marriage*

Slowly, as I began to recover, I realized what a wonderful gift the Al-Anon program was. It gave me an understanding of this disease, the tools to change my life, the courage to use them, and a place to talk about my secrets and to hear others share theirs. I wanted my family and friends to have all of these things as well.

Then I read the Twelfth Step, about carrying the message to others, and began my missionary work. I dragged people to meetings. I preached what I'd learned to anyone who would listen— and even those who wouldn't. Of course, I made a fool of myself and none of this worked.

Then I read the Twelfth Step again. This time I noticed the part about practicing these principles in all my affairs. Slowly I came to understand that in living these principles I would carry the message by example.

Today's reminder

It's only natural to want to share what works for me with those I love. But when I *must* share it *now*, I may be more interested in changing others than in sharing my experience, strength, and hope. If I am insistent on carrying the message, I can work on improving the message my own example conveys.

"We ought not to insist on everyone following in our footsteps, nor to take upon ourselves to give instructions in spirituality when, perhaps, we do not even know what it is."

Teresa of Avila

"Many have fallen by the edge of the sword, but more have fallen by the tongue." This quotation calls attention to a weapon many of us have been known to use: sarcasm. The cutting remark, the snide innuendo, the scornful sneer.

If I could see myself uttering these verbal assaults I would not be proud of the picture. So why do it? When I am angry or frustrated I may get momentary satisfaction in scoring a hit, but does sarcasm get me what I truly desire? Will attacking someone else help to solve the problems between us? Is this really the way I wish to behave? Of course not.

Sometimes I feel helpless and angry. When that happens, I might try calling an Al-Anon friend or going to a meeting where I can get some perspective. I might write down every nasty word I want to say and then read it to my sponsor. Sometimes it feels good to let it out. But I need to do it appropriately and not hurt others needlessly in doing so. Afterward, I'll be better able to behave constructively and communicate in a way I can be proud of.

Today's reminder

Most of us carry more than our share of shame. I will not add to the problem by using cruel, clever words to humiliate a fellow human being. In doing so, I would be shaming myself.

> "*Everyone* in an alcoholic situation deserves and needs extra loving care."
>
> *Living With Sobriety*

In Al-Anon we talk a lot about the need to let others experience the consequences of their actions. We know that most alcoholics have to hit a "bottom" and become uncomfortable with their own behavior before they can effectively do something about it. Those of us who love alcoholics often have to learn to get out of the way of this bottom. We learn to detach with love.

Another reason for detachment with love may be equally important in building healthy, loving, respectful relationships. Many of us have interfered not only with a loved one's problems but also with their achievements. I may have the best of intentions, but if I take over other people's responsibilities, I may rob them of the chance to accomplish something and to feel good about what they've done. Although I am trying to help, my actions may be communicating a lack of respect for my loved ones' abilities. When I detach with love, I offer support by freeing those I care about to experience both their own satisfactions and disappointments.

Today's reminder

I am learning the difference between help and interference. Today I will examine the way I offer support.

> "Detachment did not mean disinterest . . . I considered detachment 'respect for another's personhood.'"
>
> *Al-Anon Faces Alcoholism*

Al-Anon helps many of us to cope with crises that we simply could not have managed on our own. We learn to lean on a Power greater than ourselves, and through the faith and support that surround us, we discover that we can live and even grow through terribly difficult times. For most of us, the situation eventually alters, or we learn to find peace with it.

But some of us continue to worry. What if crises return? Al-Anon has helped before, but will it work for me if I need it again? What if some other misfortune comes to pass?

I cannot know what the future will bring. My best hope is every bit as likely to occur as my worst fear, so I have no reason to give more weight to my negative assumptions. All I can do is make the most of this day. Today I can choose to trust my recovery, the tools of the program, and my Higher Power, and to recognize how very far I have come.

Today's reminder

Today I will take a few minutes to acknowledge my growth. I am not perfect, but I certainly have made progress.

". . . we may not recognize our progress right away, but the effects of working the Al-Anon program are profound and lasting."

. . . In All Our Affairs

By the time we reach Al-Anon, many of us resent others whose lives appear less troubled, envying what we think they have. But in time we discover that each of us is special. I have a unique set of skills, interests, and opportunities. I'm assured that I have everything I need to do what I am here to do today. That doesn't mean I have everything I want, but I can trust that my Higher Power has a better grasp of what's good for me than I do.

To envy someone else because I want what I think they have is a waste of time. We are on different paths. They have what they need, I have what I need. Resentment will only put a wedge between me and another human being.

I am no one's victim. I am where I belong. Envy is nothing more than a hostile form of self-pity. I will not succumb to it today. Instead, I will be grateful for the many gifts, talents, and opportunities I have been given. When I appreciate what I *have* instead of dwelling on what I *lack*, I feel good about my life. This allows me to be happy for another person's abundance.

Today's reminder

Another person's bounty reminds me that wonderful things can happen at any time to anybody. I will appreciate the many gifts I have been given.

"Whatever hour God has blessed you with, take it with grateful hand."

Horace

When I'm troubled by another person's behavior, a complicated situation, or a disappointing turn of events, Al-Anon reminds me that I don't have to take it personally. I'm not a victim of everything that happens unless I choose to see myself that way. Though things don't always go my way, I can accept what I cannot change, and change what I can.

Perhaps I can take a different view of my problems. If I accept them at face value without taking them personally, I may find that they are not problems at all, only things that have not gone as I would have liked. This change of attitude can help free me to evaluate the situation realistically and move forward constructively.

Today's reminder

Blaming my discomfort on outside events can be a way to avoid facing the real cause—my own attitudes. I can see myself as a victim, or I can accept what is happening in my life and take responsibility for my response. I may be guided to take action or to sit still, but when I listen to the guidance of my Higher Power I will no longer be the victim of my circumstances.

"God asks no man whether he will accept life. That is not the choice. You must take it. The only choice is how."

Henry Ward Beecher

Fear was a daily part of my experience of alcoholism, and I learned certain ways to cope with it. I often catch myself reacting to my fears in the same way today, even though my circumstances have changed. For example, I often keep quiet when confronted, instead of speaking my mind. This might be a legitimate response, except that I don't consciously make the choice. This is not responding, it's reacting, giving up my self-respect out of fear and out of habit.

My best alternative is to admit that I have a problem, accept my reactions, and turn them over to my Higher Power. I've often heard that courage is fear that has said its prayers. I must recognize my fear, I must say those prayers, and I must have faith as I wait for healing.

In the meantime, there are important ways in which I can help myself. The first step in learning to respond more effectively to others is to learn to respond more effectively to myself. I can learn to respond with love, caring, and respect for myself, even for those parts of me that experience fear, confusion, and anger.

Today's reminder

Today I'll try to become more aware of alternatives that I haven't yet recognized.

". . . Al-Anon helped me to accept the fact that, although I have no control over other people's reactions or thoughts, I can change the way I react."

. . . In All Our Affairs

What exactly is meditation? Is it something hypnotic, strange, and beyond my capabilities? The dictionary tells me it means, "to think contemplatively." When I look up "contemplate" it says, "to view thoughtfully."

In every quiet moment I can find to calm my mind and think through the day ahead of me, I am meditating. During these moments, by clearing my mind and asking my Higher Power to guide me, I find answers to my concerns. I don't always expect or enjoy the answers I get, but to turn away from them causes even greater turmoil.

I have spent too much of the past working against my better instincts. God gave me instincts as a help, not a hindrance. The more I am quiet enough to discover and follow these instincts, the stronger they become.

Today's reminder

I will take time to clear my mind and focus on what is essential for today. I will release any unimportant thoughts. I will then allow myself to be guided toward the best action I can take for today. Regardless of how simple the answers may seem, I will listen without judgment. I will not take my thoughts for granted, for they may be my only guide.

"Go to your bosom:
Knock there, and ask your heart what it doth know."

                                    William Shakespeare

My sharing at early Al-Anon meetings went something like this: "She makes me so mad," and "I'm a nervous wreck because of him." Thank God for a sponsor who always brought the focus back to me and encouraged me to look at what my words really said. When I blamed others for how I felt, I was giving them power over my feelings, power that rightly belonged to me. Nobody can make me feel anything without my consent. I had a lot of attitude-changing to do.

Today, by being aware of the words I use, I am learning to communicate more responsibly. I not only share in a more straightforward manner, but I also argue in a healthier way. There are better ways to express myself than to say, "You did such and such to me." I can talk about myself and my feelings. I can explain the way I experienced something rather than telling the other person how he or she *made me* feel. I can talk about what I want. I am no longer a victim.

Today's reminder

What do my words communicate? Do they express what I am trying to say? Today I will listen more closely to what my words have to say.

> "We learn in time that it is not subjects which are controversial, but the manner in which we communicate about them and the elements of personal blame we add to them in anger."
>
> *The Dilemma of the Alcoholic Marriage*

The courage to be honest with ourselves is one quality we can cultivate to help our spiritual growth. It takes a commitment to honesty to admit that someone we love has a drinking problem, that alcoholism and many other things are beyond our control, that there is a source of help greater than ourselves, and that we need the care of that Higher Power.

Honesty allows us to look at ourselves, to share our discoveries with God and others, to admit that we need spiritual help in moving forward, and to free ourselves by making amends for past wrongs.

We need to be truthful with ourselves as we continue to review our attitudes and actions each day. This allows us to be humble enough to reach out to others as equals, and to continue to grow in every area of our lives. Where do we find the courage to be so honest with ourselves? The courage to change the things we can is found in our continuously-developing relationship with a Power greater than ourselves.

Today's reminder

I know that honesty is an essential part of the Twelve Steps. I am willing to be more honest with myself today.

"Where is there dignity unless there is honesty?"

Marcus Tullius Cicero

A farmer found a magical flute. Hoping to charm his hens into laying extra eggs, he played the flute to them all day, but at nightfall he had no more eggs than usual. Later, when asked if he'd had any success, the farmer replied, "I sure did. It wasn't much of a day for egg-laying, but it was a great day for music!"

In Al-Anon, as in this fable, we learn that success and failure are a matter of perspective. Before coming to Al-Anon, many of us had known great disappointment because we couldn't cure alcoholism in someone we loved. In time, we began to doubt our ability to take *any* effective action. We didn't realize that we achieve many successes every day.

Our program helps us to recognize how much we have accomplished simply by being willing to walk through the doors of an Al-Anon meeting to ask for help. In spite of difficult circumstances, we now have the opportunity to change long-held behavior and beliefs. That is a great achievement.

Today's reminder

The finest gift I can give to ensure my continued recovery is willingness. Each demonstration of willingness, each meeting attended, each Al-Anon tool used, is a mark of my success.

> "Every good thought you think is contributing its share to the ultimate result of your life."
>
> Grenville Kleiser

In Step Six I become entirely ready for God to remove my defects of character—those roadblocks that keep me stranded, unable to freely travel life's magnificent boulevard. Take for example self-pity: the hours I have languished thinking there was nothing in life for me, that I could never make a dream come to reality! To an extent I was right, for in focusing all my time on self-pity, I was assuring that I would not spend time growing. How could my dreams come true under those conditions?

My Higher Power removes my defects by helping me see them at work, getting in the way of my everyday life. Today I can recognize self-pity when it creeps into my thinking. I can't wipe out this defect by myself, but I can see it for what it is—a waste of time. Then I can humbly turn to my Higher Power, who gives me joy and confidence to put in its place.

Today's reminder

I am not perfect. The character defects I have carried around for so many years will not vanish instantly. But with faith and hope I can work my way through them one at a time, one day at a time.

"God seldom delivers . . . virtues all wrapped in a package and ready for use. Rather He puts us in situations where by His help we can develop those virtues."

C.R. Findley

Forgiveness can be just a change of attitude. I came to Al-Anon full of bitterness toward the alcoholic in my life. When I realized that my bitterness hurt me more than anyone else, I began to search for another way to view my situation.

In time, I came to believe that my alcoholic loved one might be the messenger my Higher Power used to let me know that I needed to get help. It is not fair to shackle her with credit or blame for the amount of time it took for me to pay attention to that message. I chose to tolerate a great deal of unacceptable behavior because I was unwilling to admit that *I* needed help. I did the best I could with the tools and knowledge I had at hand, and I believe that she did too. Eventually the message got through. I made it to the rooms of Al-Anon, and my life changed in miraculous ways. I don't deny that hurtful things were said and done along the way, but I refuse to carry the burden of bitterness any further. Instead, I am grateful for what I have learned.

Today's reminder

I will not allow old resentments to drag me down any longer. I am building a better and more loving life today.

"Forgiving is not forgetting, it's letting go of the hurt."

Mary McLeod Bethune

One day I received a call from a newcomer to Al-Anon. We chatted for a while, and then he asked if I would consider being his sponsor. I was shocked! I never expected anyone to ask me! I felt deeply humbled and ecstatically grateful at the same time.

But had I grown sufficiently to offer help to someone else? Did I have anything to give? Could I be there for someone else without losing myself? Fear took over for a minute, but then I remembered that he was not asking me to be his savior, only his helper, whose example and experience might lead him to his own recovery.

I know that my Higher Power brings people into my life who can help me to grow. So I said a quick prayer, asking to be worthy, and answered that I would be honored to be his sponsor.

Today's reminder

Being a sponsor is as much a commitment to myself as it is to someone else. It is not a favor. Sponsorship gives me a chance to share intimately, to care, to practice detaching with love, and to apply the Al-Anon principles more consciously than ever. And, if I listen to my own words, I find that I usually tell those whom I sponsor exactly what I myself need to hear.

"Give what you have. To someone, it may be better than you dare to think."

Henry Wadsworth Longfellow

I always felt that my loved one's drinking was a terrible reflection on me, and I worried about what people thought. One day he told me he wanted to get sober. I was elated for a day, until his next binge. Then I was devastated.

Some months later, my loved one finally did go to AA. Two days later, the drinking began again.

The most important thing I've learned in Al-Anon since then is that my well-being cannot depend upon whether or not the alcoholic drinks. His behavior is not a reflection of me, it's a reflection of his disease. However, *my* behavior is a reflection of me, and I owe it to myself to pay attention to what it has to tell me. I have to take care of myself. I have to accept that alcoholism is a disease which can be arrested but not cured. Many alcoholics make a number of attempts at sobriety before actually getting sober; others never do. My life is too important to waste waiting for someone else's choices, even when it's someone I dearly love.

Today's reminder

No matter whether the alcoholic in my life is drunk or sober, the time to put energy into my own recovery is right now.

"Al-Anon helped me to focus my attention on what I could do about my situation, instead of concentrating all my attention on what I thought the alcoholic should do. I was the one who had to take a stand."

. . . *In All Our Affairs*

After some time in recovery, I picked up a *Blueprint for Progress*, Al-Anon's guide to taking a searching and fearless moral inventory (Step Four). I was well aware of many character defects, and I was eager to be free of their hold on me. But I didn't expect so many questions about my character assets!

Again and again I was asked to recognize positive qualities about myself. It was frustrating! Why waste time on things that already worked? These assets hadn't kept my life from becoming unmanageable; obviously they weren't worth much. My sponsor suggested that my resistance to this part of the Step might have something to teach me. He was right.

Eventually I realized that my assets are the foundation upon which my new, healthier life is being built. Refusing to recognize them just holds down my self-esteem. As long as I see myself as pitiful, hopeless, and sick, I don't have to change.

I knew I was ready to feel better about myself, so I gathered up my willingness and listed all the positive attributes I could find about myself. I've felt much better about myself ever since.

Today's reminder

Today I will acknowledge that I have many positive qualities, and I will share one or two of these with a friend.

"All progress must grow from a seed of self-appreciation..."

The Dilemma of the Alcoholic Marriage

"While walking through the woods one day, I was surprised to hear a child's voice. I followed the sound, trying in vain to understand the child's words. When I spotted a boy perched on a rock, I realized why his words had made no sense: he was repeating the alphabet. 'Why are you saying your ABC's so many times?' I asked him. The child replied, 'I'm saying my prayers.' I couldn't help but laugh. 'Prayers? All I hear is the alphabet.' Patiently the child explained, 'Well, I don't know all the words, so I give God the letters. God knows what I'm trying to say.'"

Years ago, when my grandmother told me this story, it meant little to me, but the spiritual life I've found in Al-Anon has given it new meaning. Today the story reminds me that prayer is for me, not for God, who knows what I'm going through without explanation. With prayer I say I am willing to be helped. The meaning behind my prayers comes from my heart, not from my words.

Today's reminder

Prayer is my most personal form of communication. I can pray by consciously thinking, writing, creating, feeling, and hoping. Whether I reach deep inside myself or turn outward toward the majesty of nature, it is the spirit of prayer rather than its form that matters. Today I will let my heart speak.

"God meets me where I am . . . If I am just willing, He will come to me."

As We Understood . . .

Most of us have spent far too much time feeling badly about who we are and what we have done. We may have been harshly criticized by others or we may have simply lost perspective and become overly hard on ourselves. Today we have an opportunity to stop that kind of self-destructive thinking. Isn't it about time we allowed ourselves to feel good about ourselves?

It takes time for old doubts to fade and wounds to heal. Self-confidence comes slowly, but it grows with practice. We can begin by acknowledging that we do have positive qualities. For those of us who have negative, self-critical thoughts running through our heads all day long, we can make an extra effort to counteract them with positive thoughts. For every defect we identify, we can also try to name an asset. Some of us find it helpful to list five or ten things about our day that we have a right to feel good about before we go to sleep.

With practice, we learn to treat ourselves with gentleness and compassion. We all have many admirable qualities, and we owe it to ourselves to let them shine.

Today's reminder

Today I will make an effort to remember that I am a terrific human being.

> "Ever'thing there is but lovin' leaves a rust on yo' soul."
>
> Langston Hughes

Al-Anon helps many of us to identify and change self-destructive behavior. In my case, procrastination was the source of a great deal of needless anxiety, but with Al-Anon's help I have managed to recognize and change that pattern.

As I learned to focus on myself, I began to pay attention to my own thoughts and feelings. When I felt anxious, I took the time to find out what was causing my discomfort. I realized that I had a habit of postponing unpleasant tasks until the last possible moment. Knowing I would have to perform the task eventually, I found it hard to relax until it was done. I came to see that if I took care of the task right away, I could usually let go of anxiety and appreciate the rest of the day. Old habits can be hard to break. It didn't happen overnight, but as I became more willing to let go of procrastination, my life became more manageable and more enjoyable.

Today's reminder

If I am getting in the way of my own best interests, a closer look at my behavior can lead to positive changes. By focusing on myself, I move toward freedom and serenity today.

"Do not look where you fell, but where you slipped."

Liberian proverb

Normally, our group welcomes newcomers in a particular way—we share what Al-Anon has done for us, introduce our literature, and offer a few Al-Anon slogans before getting on with the meeting. No one ever took a group conscience about this procedure, it's just the way we've done it for some time.

One evening, the chairperson departed from the usual procedure. I completely forgot why I was at the meeting and spent the rest of the evening worrying about the newcomers. They weren't hearing what they were supposed to hear! Would they be all right? Would they come back?

At the very end of the meeting, one of the newcomers timidly spoke up. I was on the edge of my seat with concern until he said how grateful he was to have heard the words the chairperson spoke, because they were exactly what he needed to hear. Once again I was reminded that God works through our groups to make sure that we all get what we need. I certainly got what I needed that night.

Today's reminder

I do not know what is best for other people. Today I will remember that newcomers, and everyone else, are in the hands of a Power greater than myself.

"When I stopped dwelling on how things would probably work out, I was better able to pay attention to what I was doing."

Living With Sobriety

Tradition Three reminds me of two aspects of Al-Anon that I cherish. First, I know that I can go to a meeting anywhere in the world and expect to find no other affiliation promoted by the group. The members will not try to sell me a religion, a treatment program, a therapy, a political platform, or anything else. Should any individual in the fellowship discuss any of these with me, I am free to take what I like and leave the rest.

Second, I know that I meet the sole requirement for membership in Al-Anon: I have encountered a problem of alcoholism in a relative or friend. I do not have to dress, act, feel, speak, or work a certain way to belong. I do not have to believe or disbelieve. I am free to be myself. This is a come-as-you-are program.

Today's reminder

Al-Anon has come to my support—undiluted and with no strings attached—when I have needed it. I hope to pass it on in the same spirit.

"Tradition Three explains two ways in which my Al-Anon friends and I can 'Keep it simple.' One is to avoid being diverted from our program by others, and two is to welcome into Al-Anon anyone who is suffering from the effects of another's alcoholism."

Al-Anon's Twelve Steps & Twelve Traditions

I think the word detachment is often misunderstood. For me, detachment is the freedom to own what is mine and to allow others to own what is theirs.

This freedom allows me to keep my own identity and still love, care about, and identify with the feelings of others. In fact, I believe that the degree of our humanity can be measured by our ability to know another person's pain and joy. I have been practicing the principles of Al-Anon to the best of my abilities for a long time. But when someone in the fellowship shares about having a difficult time, I can go right back to day one. I no longer live with that type of emotional pain, but I can feel theirs. I can identify without needing to remove their pain. To me, that is an Al-Anon success story.

Today I don't have to like everything my alcoholic loved one says or does, and I don't have to change her, even when I think she's wrong. I continue to learn how to care without taking everything personally.

Today's reminder

I can detach and still love, still feel. I can learn to take care of my own business while allowing others to tend to theirs. Today I can detach without losing compassion.

"Love your neighbor, yet pull not down your hedge."

George Herbert

So many of us come to Al-Anon feeling that we've gotten a raw deal from life. "It isn't fair!" we complain. "Don't I deserve better after all I've been through?" The prayer quoted in our "Just For Today" pamphlet may shed some light on this subject when it says, "Grant that I may not so much seek to be consoled as to console; to be loved, as to love; for it is in giving that we receive." Instead of questioning what life is giving us, perhaps we might profit more by asking what we ourselves can give.

By reaching out to help others in a healthy way, we move beyond our problems and learn to give unconditionally. Every moment can be an opportunity to serve, an opportunity to change our lives. Al-Anon offers us many good places to start— setting up chairs, welcoming newcomers, leading a meeting. When we discover that we really can make a positive contribution, many of us find that self-esteem has replaced self-pity.

Today's reminder

Today I seek to be an instrument of the peace of God. I know that it is the most loving and generous commitment I can possibly make—to myself.

"When people are serving, life is no longer meaningless."

John Gardner

I thought that in every conflict, in every confrontation, someone was invariably at fault. It was essential to assign blame and I would stew for hours weighing the evidence. I became a chronic scorekeeper. Because I approached every situation with this attitude, I was consumed by guilt and anger. Defensive and anxious, I made sure my own back was always covered.

Al-Anon helps me understand that disputes come up even when everyone is doing their best. Obsessively reviewing everyone's behavior focuses my attention where it doesn't belong and keeps me too busy to have any serenity. Instead, I can consider the part *I* have played. If I have made mistakes, I am free to make amends.

Today I know that conflict is not necessarily an indication that someone is wrong. Difficulties may just arise. Sometimes people simply disagree.

Today's reminder

Today I accept that each life has its share of conflict. It is not my job to document every such incident. Instead of wringing my hands and pointing my finger, I can consider the possibility that everything is happening exactly as it should. Sometimes, blame is just an excuse to keep busy so that I don't have to feel the discomfort of my powerlessness.

"The mind grows by what it feeds on."

Josiah G. Holland

I remember, as a child, climbing trees to better observe a nest of baby birds, and lying on my back wondering what it would be like to fall into a sky full of clouds. I still have deeply spiritual feelings when I am out in nature, and today I think I know why.

One of Al-Anon's basic principles is living "One day at a time," and nature surrounds me with wonderful role models.

Trees don't sit around and worry about forest fires. The water in the pond doesn't fret over turbulence it encountered a few miles upstream. And I have never seen a butterfly pry into the affairs of its fellows. All of creation is going about the business of living. If I keep my eyes open, I can learn to do the same.

Today's reminder

A great deal can be learned as a result of painful circumstances, but they are not my only teachers. I live in a world full of wonders. Today I will pay attention to their gentle wisdom.

"I discovered the secret of the sea in meditation upon a dewdrop."

                                      Kahlil Gibran

Life is a package deal. It is not enough to look only at the parts we like. It is necessary to face the whole picture so that we can make realistic choices for ourselves and stop setting ourselves up for disappointment.

Living with alcoholics, many of us coped with an ever-shifting situation in which our sense of reality changed from one minute to the next. We adapted by taking whatever part of reality suited us and ignoring the rest. Again and again we were devastated because reality didn't go away just because it was ignored.

Our lives will remain unmanageable as long as we pretend that only half of the truth is real. That's why sharing is such an important Al-Anon tool. When we share with other members about what is really going on, we cut through our denial and anchor ourselves in reality. While it may be difficult to face certain facts, when we allow ourselves to confront them, we cease to give our own denial the power to devastate us at every turn.

Today's reminder

I can't cope with something unless I acknowledge its reality. When I am willing to look at the whole picture, I take the first step toward a more manageable life.

> "If you have built castles in the air, your work need not be lost; that is where they should be. Now put foundations under them."
>
> Henry David Thoreau

As a result of our exposure to alcoholism, many of us lose perspective on who we are and what we can and cannot do. We accept ideas about our own limitations that have no basis in reality. Al-Anon helps us to sort out the truth from the falsehoods by encouraging us to take a fresh, objective look at ourselves.

I had always been told that I had a weak constitution and had to avoid excitement and overexertion. Believing this, I avoided exercise, sports, certain jobs, and even dancing, sure that my poor weak body couldn't handle the strain. My most frequent response to any invitation was, "I can't."

In Al-Anon I realized that I had a distorted self-image. I had never thought to question my beliefs, but when I took a good look, I discovered that they were untrue. I am as fit as anyone I know. I began to wonder how many other false assumptions were limiting me. A whole new way of life opened up because I had the support and encouragement to take a fresh look at myself.

Today's reminder

I won't let old, limiting ideas and doubts go unchallenged. I may discover strengths and talents that never had the chance to come to light. Today, by letting go of obsolete ideas, I have an opportunity to learn something wonderful about myself.

"Argue for your limitations, and sure enough, they're yours."

Richard Bach

It seems to me that many of us deal with our anger in inappropriate ways. Denying it, we stuff it, or we go off in fury, directing the feelings outward. I, for one, opt for avoidance of any conflict, and then I turn into a doormat.

The Al-Anon program encourages me to acknowledge my feelings and to be responsible for how I express them. The problem is not that I get angry, but that I do not know how to direct my anger appropriately.

Lately, when I feel like hitting somebody, I take my pillow and beat the daylights out of my bed. When I want to wipe someone out, I attack my dirty oven. I try to release my anger as soon as I can so that I won't build resentments that will be harder to get rid of later.

I'm learning to communicate my anger too. I may not do it gracefully, and my words may not be well received. It means facing the awful discomfort called conflict, but I can't run away any more.

Today's reminder

Feeling our feelings is one important part of the recovery process. Learning how to balance feelings with appropriate action is another.

> "When angry, count ten before you speak; if very angry, an hundred."
>
>   Thomas Jefferson

Tradition Five talks about "encouraging and understanding our alcoholic relatives." This puzzled me at first. After all, doesn't Al-Anon teach us to focus on ourselves? It seemed to be a contradiction.

Maybe the reason for my confusion is that I tended to think in extremes. Either I focused on myself and separated myself completely from the lives of others, or I wrapped myself around those others until I lost myself. Al-Anon helps me to come back to center.

I can focus on myself and still be a loving, caring person. I can have compassion for loved ones who suffer from the disease of alcoholism, or its effects, without losing my sense of self. Encouraging and being kind to others is one way of being good to myself, and I don't have to sacrifice myself in the process.

Today's reminder

I am learning how to have saner and more loving relationships. Today I will offer support for those I love and still take care of myself.

"If you would be loved, love, and be loveable."

Benjamin Franklin

How many days of my life have I wasted? I missed the joys of my children's early years because I was preoccupied with the alcoholic. I rejected overtures of friendship from co-workers so that I could fret uninterrupted about what was bothering me. Not once during those days did I think about my right to enjoy the day.

Al-Anon has led me to see that I have choices, especially about my attitudes. I don't have to see my life as a tragedy or torment myself with past mistakes or future worries. Today can be the focus of my life. It is filled with interesting activities if I allow myself to see it with a spirit of wonder. When my worries and sorrows cloak me, the laughter and sunshine of the everyday world seem inappropriate to the way I feel. Who is out of sync—the rest of the world or me?

Today's reminder

Today I will live in the present and find what I can to enjoy there. If there is pain, I will accept that too. But my pain does not have to completely overshadow the enjoyable parts of my reality. I will participate in making more of my joy: I may join in a conversation at work or at a meeting, tell a joke at the dinner table, or laugh with a friend. Just for today, I might even allow myself to sing.

"Look to this Day!
For it is Life, the very Life of Life."

From the Sanskrit Salutation of the Dawn

I didn't know how great a burden my guilt was until I made amends and gained release from it. I never wanted to face the harm I'd done in the past. Consequently, without knowing it, I carried guilt with me most of the time. Making amends has helped me to put the past behind me and move on with a clear conscience. My self-esteem has grown ever since, and I feel much better about myself.

But I had a problem. The person I felt I owed the most amends to is no longer living. Deep in my heart I knew she had understood and forgiven me, but I could not forgive myself for the harm I had done. How could I make amends?

After much prayer and thought, I realized that I couldn't change the past. All I could do was to change my present behavior. Now, when I feel tempted to shirk a responsibility, I can remember my friend and reconsider my choice. Each time I talk to a newcomer, chair a meeting, or share my story, I am making amends to my friend.

Today's reminder

I can't make past wrongs disappear, but I can take actions that will help me to let them go. When I make amends, I do what I can to correct the situation. Then I can put the past in its rightful place and leave it there.

"Let me remember that the reason for making amends is to free my own mind of uneasiness."

The Dilemma of the Alcoholic Marriage

Each of us puts the Al-Anon program into practice in our lives as best we can, moving at the
pace that is right for us. That is why I avoid
speaking harshly, using phrases such as "get off
the pity-pot" or "quit feeling sorry for yourself."
Perhaps someone needs more time to work
through a painful situation than I do. Their story
may sound repetitious to me, but who am I to
judge?

When I'm struggling with my difficulties, I am
so grateful that no one in Al-Anon stands over
me with a stopwatch, telling me that I am taking
too long when I learn my lessons slowly. A non-
judgmental, listening ear can be a great blessing,
and I'm learning to offer it more freely.

Today's reminder

Today I will try to extend to my fellow members the respect, patience, and courtesy that I want
for myself.

> "Great Spirit, help me never to judge another un-
> til I have walked in his moccasins."
>
>   Sioux Indian Prayer

One of the wonderful, but unexpected, benefits of working the Al-Anon program is learning how to relax. Until now, most of my life sped by in a frenzy of activity. School, work, projects, obligations, all helped me focus outward. That way I didn't have to rest long enough to feel how frightful my home life was.

There is nothing wrong with working hard and producing results, but I was abusing these activities. They were socially acceptable ways to deny my feelings. Both family and society supported my hiding behind them until, beaten down and exhausted, I reached the doors of Al-Anon. By that time I couldn't have relaxed if I had wanted to—I didn't know how it was done.

In Al-Anon it was suggested that I would not treat anyone as harshly as I treated myself. I would never ask someone I loved to go without rest, never letting up, and never having any fun. But that was exactly what I asked of myself. My sponsor helped me to learn what gave me pleasure and how to take it easy. Now, relaxation is part of my daily routine.

Today's reminder

Hard work can be terrific, and my activities can be highly rewarding. But I am striving for some balance. Today I will look at how I spend my time, and set some of that time aside to relax.

"The time you enjoy wasting is not wasted time."

Bertrand Russell

Two of those closest to me were newly-recovering alcoholics. During the drinking years, I had become so enmeshed with them and their self-destructive behavior that I lost sight of the idea that I could be happy even if they were depressed; I could live a serene life even if they went back to drinking. The turning point in my Al-Anon recovery came when someone said to me, "You'll have to learn to make it whether the alcoholics do or not."

From that day on I tried to keep in mind that I had my own life and my own destiny. Once I began to separate my welfare from that of the alcoholics, I found it easier to detach from the decisions they made about how and where, and when and with whom to conduct their lives. Because my fate—my very life—was no longer tied directly to theirs, I was able to accept them for who they were and to listen to their ideas and concerns without trying to exercise control. Thanks to Al-Anon, I can concentrate my energy where I *do* have some control—over my own life.

Today's reminder

My time is too precious to waste living in the future or worrying about something over which I have no power. I am building a wonderful life for myself today.

> "As I continue to practice putting the focus on myself, it is a relief to see I can let go of others' problems instead of trying to solve them."

> *Al-Anon is for Adult Children of Alcoholics*

We often come to Al-Anon with the philosophy that if something works, it will work even better and faster if we try harder. But Al-Anon involves a long-term process of growth and change. Our efforts to speed up this process are more likely to interfere with it, leaving us frustrated and depressed. In Al-Anon we learn that "Easy does it." The work often gets done when we stop pushing.

When I first came to Al-Anon I heard that, although we learn to entrust our lives and our future to a Power greater than ourselves, we must do our part as well. With my usual fervor I threw myself into doing "footwork." I made at least ten Al-Anon calls every day and began a frantic effort to practice all Twelve Steps at once. No wonder I was soon overwhelmed—and exhausted.

Today I know that I can plant a seed in fertile soil, but I don't help the plant to grow by tugging at the seed in hope that it will sprout. I have to let the process unfold at its own pace.

Today's reminder

I take my commitment to recovery seriously, but I can't expect to recover overnight. When I approach my life with an "Easy does it" attitude, I treat myself and the world around me gently and lovingly.

"When we try to absorb too much too quickly in Al-Anon, we may be discouraged . . . We would be wise to take it slowly, concentrating on one idea at a time."

One Day at a Time in Al-Anon

Al-Anon taught me the difference between walls and boundaries. Walls are solid and rigid; they keep others out, and they keep me trapped inside. Boundaries are flexible, changeable, removable, so it's up to me how open or closed I'll be at any given time. They let me decide what behavior is acceptable, not only from others but from myself. Today I can say, "No," with love instead of hostility, so it doesn't put an end to my relationships.

I've learned about boundaries from Al-Anon's own set of boundaries: the Twelve Traditions. Although their purpose is to protect Al-Anon, they actually encourage the growth of the fellowship. This is true of my personal boundaries as well. As I decide what is and isn't acceptable for me, I learn to live protected without walls.

Today's reminder

Do my defenses keep me safe, or do they isolate me? Today I can love myself enough to look for healthier ways to protect myself, ways that don't close everyone out.

"People are lonely because they build walls instead of bridges."

                                    Joseph Fort Newton

In the past, joy was a rare visitor to many of us. Al-Anon recovery often leads us to find it more frequently. But instead of sitting back and enjoying these pleasant moments, we tend to cling desperately to happiness, trying to freeze time and hold change at bay, as if our joy will be snatched away forever the moment our guard is down. We can become too busy avoiding change to enjoy the gifts we fear to lose. By clutching at what we most want to keep, we lose it all the more rapidly.

Change is inevitable. We can depend on that. When we become willing to accept change, we make room for a loving God. By letting go of our efforts to influence the future, we become freer to experience the present, to feel all of our feelings while they are happening, and to more fully enjoy those precious moments of joy with which we are blessed.

Today's reminder

Today I will try to open myself to receive the abundance God holds out to me by experiencing what is and allowing God to decide what will be.

> "The harder we try to catch hold of the moment, to seize a pleasant sensation . . . the more elusive it becomes . . . It is like trying to clutch water in one's hands—the harder one grips, the faster it slips through one's fingers."
>
> Alan Watts

"The people I love won't take care of themselves, so I have to do it. How will they survive unless I . . . ?" This was my thinking when I came to Al-Anon, my excuse for interfering in everyone's business. My needs seemed so unimportant compared to the constant crises all around me. Al-Anon told me that I had other options, one of which was to "Let go and let God."

When I think of letting go I remind myself that there is a natural order to life—a chain of events that a Higher Power has in mind. When I let go of a situation, I allow life to unfold according to that plan. I open my mind and let other ways of thinking or behaving enter in. When I let go of another person, I am affirming their right to live their own life, to make their own choices, and to grow as they experience the results of their actions. A Higher Power exists for others, as well. My obsessive interference disrupts not only my connection with them but also my connection with my own spiritual self.

Today's reminder

I am my top priority. By keeping the focus on myself, I let go of other people's problems and can better cope with my own. What can I do for myself today?

"I will remind myself . . . that I am powerless over anyone else, that I can live no life but my own. Changing *myself* for the better is the only way I can find peace and serenity."

The Dilemma of the Alcoholic Marriage

Al-Anon's Suggested Closing says that "though you may not like all of us, you'll love us in a very special way—the same way we already love you." In other words, every Al-Anon meeting can be an opportunity to practice placing principles above personalities. Most of us are highly aware of the personalities of people around us. Instead of getting lost in petty likes and dislikes, it is important to remember why we come to meetings. We all need each other in order to recover.

I don't have to like everybody, but I want to look deeper to find the spirit that we share in common. Perhaps I can find peace with each person by reminding myself of those things that draw us together—a common interest, a common belief, a common goal. I will then have a resource for strength rather than a target for negative thinking. I will have placed principles above personalities.

Today's reminder

I will keep an open mind toward each person I encounter today. If I am ready to learn, anyone can be my teacher.

> "The open door to helpful answers is communication based on love. Such communication depends on awareness of and respect for each other's well-being and willingness to accept in another what may not measure up to our own standards and expectations."

> *The Dilemma of the Alcoholic Marriage*

A miraculous change has come about because of my commitment to the Al-Anon program: I have discovered that I have a sense of humor. When I came to these rooms, I never cracked a smile and resented anyone who did. I couldn't understand all the laughter during meetings; I didn't hear anything funny! Life was tragic and serious.

Recently, I was sharing about a series of events that I had found extremely difficult. It had been one of those weeks in which everything seemed to go wrong. The odd part was that now that it was over, I found my traumatic tale incredibly funny, and so did most of the others at the meeting.

More than any other change I have observed in myself, I find this the most glorious. It tells me that I see myself and my life in a more realistic way. I am no longer a victim, full of self-pity and bent on control of every aspect of my life. Today I can take myself and my circumstances more lightly. I can even allow joy and laughter to be a part of a difficult experience.

Today's reminder

If I take a step back and look at this day as if I were watching a movie, I am sure to find at least a moment where I can enjoy some comic relief.

"You grow up the day you have the first real laugh—at yourself."

Ethel Barrymore

Every day I pray for knowledge of God's will and the power to carry it out (Step Eleven). Then I try to trust that my prayer has been heard and will be answered. In other words, I trust that at some point in my day I will do God's will.

To me, doing God's will doesn't mean that I perform heroic acts on a daily basis; it means that, at any given time, smelling a rose or emptying waste baskets or washing the car may be exactly what is needed.

I have a Higher Power that loves me as I am. When I learn to love myself as my Higher Power loves me, I believe I am doing God's will.

Today's reminder

What loving action can I take today? Maybe I will make some time for nothing more practical than simple pleasure—a movie, a good book, or a breath of fresh air. Or perhaps I'll deal with paper work that I've been avoiding. I could make a commitment to eat well and get the rest I need, or make amends for something that's been on my mind. A simple gesture can be the beginning of a lifelong habit of self-love.

> "God alone knows the secret plan
> Of the things he will do for the world
> Using my hand."
>
> Toyohiko Kagawa

After years of letting people take advantage of me, I had built up quite a store of anger, resentment, and guilt by the time I found Al-Anon. So many times I wanted to bite off my tongue after saying, "Yes," when I really wanted to say, "No." Why did I continue to deny my own feelings just to gain someone's approval?

As I worked the Al-Anon program, the answer became apparent: What I lacked was courage. In the Serenity Prayer I learn that courage is granted by my Higher Power, so that is where I turned first. Then it was up to me to do my part. Was I willing to try to learn to say, "No," when I meant no? Was I willing to accept that not everyone would be thrilled with this change? Was I willing to face the real me behind the people-pleasing image? Fed up with volunteering to be treated like a doormat, I squared my shoulders and answered, "Yes."

Today's reminder

It is not always appropriate to reveal my every thought, especially when dealing with an active alcoholic. But do I make a conscious choice about what I say? And when it *is* appropriate, do I say what I mean and mean what I say? If not, why not? All I have to offer anyone is my own experience of the truth.

> "There is a price that is too great to pay for peace. . . . One cannot pay the price of self-respect."
>
> Woodrow Wilson

I'm learning to identify illusions that make my life unmanageable. For example, I wanted to stop controlling people and situations, but the harder I tried, the more I felt as if I were knocking my head against a wall. Then someone mentioned that I couldn't give up something I didn't have. Perhaps I could try giving up the *illusion* of control. Once I saw that my attempts to exercise power were based on illusions, it was easier to "Let go and let God."

Another illusion is that I have a big hole inside and I must fill it with something from outside myself. Compulsively shopping, obsessing about relationships, trying to fix everyone else's problems—these are some of the ways I've tried to fill this hole. Yet the problem is spiritual emptiness and must be filled from within. It wasn't until I saw through the illusion that I was deficient and needed to look outside myself for wholeness, that I began to heal.

Today's reminder

Today, if I hear myself thinking that I am not good enough or that I need something outside myself to make me whole, I'll know that I am listening to illusions. Today I can call an Al-Anon friend and come back to reality.

". . . Human beings, by changing the inner attitudes of their minds, can change the outer aspects of their lives."

William James

I take to heart the words in the Suggested Closing that say, "let there be no gossip or criticism of one another." I try to leave my judgmental attitude at the door. Unfortunately, I pick it up again the instant I get into my car after the meeting.

Nobody drives well enough to suit me. The car ahead of me goes too slowly, and I am *forced* to get very close and push it along. The driver behind me does the same to me. Not to be intimidated, I swear at him and drive even slower. Don't they know my rules of the road? In other words, through constant criticism and expectations of others, I isolate myself and act like a victim.

Whatever happened to practicing the Al-Anon principles in all my affairs? Do I really think I can fully reap the benefits of the program by practicing unconditional love for a single hour two or three times a week? It may be a start, but only a start.

Today's reminder

I can't keep thoughts from coming into my head, but I have a choice about whether or not to entertain those thoughts for the next hour. Am I making the choices I want to make, or is habit making my choices for me? A change of attitude means a change in my thinking. I will look at the principles I am practicing today.

> "We must alter our lives in order to alter our hearts, for it is impossible to live one way and pray another."
>
> William Law

A stonecutter may strike a rock ninety-nine times with no apparent effect, not even a crack on the surface. Yet with the hundredth blow, the rock splits in two. It was not the final blow that did the trick, but all that had gone before.

The same is true of Al-Anon recovery. Perhaps I am working on accepting that alcoholism is a disease, or learning to detach, or struggling with self-pity. I may pursue a goal for months without obvious results and become convinced that I am wasting my time. But if I continue going to meetings, sharing about my struggle, taking it one day at a time, and being patient with myself, I may awaken to find that I have changed, seemingly overnight. Suddenly I have the acceptance, detachment, or serenity I've been seeking. The results may have revealed themselves abruptly, but I know that all those months of faith and hard work made the changes possible.

Today's reminder

We are often reminded to "Keep coming back." Today I will remember that this not only applies to meetings, but to learning the new attitudes and behavior that are the long-term benefits of Al-Anon recovery. I may not see the results today, but I can trust that I am making progress.

> "Try to be patient with yourself and your family. It took a long time for the disease of alcoholism to affect each and every one and it may take a long time for everyone to recover."

> *Youth and the Alcoholic Parent*

Al-Anon is a spiritual program based on no particular religion, and no religious belief is required. To those of us who have had less than wonderful experiences with religion in the past, this freedom is important. Spirituality doesn't have to imply a particular philosophy or moral code; it simply means that there is a Power greater than ourselves upon which we can come to rely. Whether we call this a Higher Power, God, good orderly direction, Allah, the universe, or another name, it is vital to our recovery that we come to believe in a Power greater than ourselves (Step Two). Until we do, the rest of the Steps will not make much sense.

This Higher Power might be likened to the electricity that operates the lights and machinery of our recovery. It's not necessary to understand what electricity actually is to enjoy its use—all we need to do is turn on the switch!

Today's reminder

I may be seeking a more loving God in whom I can place my trust, or facing a challenge that puts my long-established beliefs to a test, or struggling with the very idea of a Higher Power. Whatever I believe, I can pray for greater faith today. Just that little act of willingness can work miracles.

"When I have at last realized that my problems are too big to solve by myself . . . I need not be alone with them if I am willing to accept help from a Higher Power."

Al-Anon's Twelve Steps & Twelve Traditions

I've often heard that happiness is an inside job, and, much of the time, I can be as happy as I decide to be. Yet I've often found happiness fleeting. I know it's unrealistic to expect to be happy all the time, but I think I might achieve this goal much more often if I made a firmer commitment to my decision to be happy. Instead, I choose happiness and then abandon my choice at the first sign of trouble. How deep can my commitment be if I allow even slight obstacles to rob me of my sense of well-being?

Commitment takes work; it is a discipline. When I make a decision, I must ask myself what I really want and if I am willing to work for it. Old habits are hard to break. If I have a long-standing habit of responding to problems by feeling like a helpless victim, it may not be easy to stand by my decision to be happy. A change of attitude sometimes helps: Perhaps I can look at problems as opportunities to commit more deeply to my choices. In other words, every obstacle can prompt me to assert that I really mean it—I do want to be happy.

Today's reminder

When I make a choice and then stick with it, I teach myself that my choices do have meaning and I am worthy of trust. I have an opportunity to make a commitment to one of my choices today.

"Our very life depends on everything's
Recurring till we answer from within."

                                    Robert Frost

A source of friction between my alcoholic loved one and myself has always been housekeeping. I usually feel so overwhelmed by all the things that need doing that I am not able to get organized. So when he drinks, he rages about whatever needs dusting, scrubbing, or picking up.

Recently we were cleaning up the kitchen after a big breakfast. Without thinking, I moved the containers on one refrigerator shelf and wiped up a spill. No big deal, but one part of the refrigerator was now clean. I thought, "Maybe that's all there is to cleaning house. If I'd do one small task at a time, I'd get something accomplished." Then the light went on inside my head. That's what "One day at a time" is all about! When I take one day, one moment, one task at a time and really concentrate on it, a lot more gets done.

Today's reminder

When I catch myself feeling overwhelmed, or not being able to get anything done because there is so much to do that I don't know where to start, I'll stop for a moment and remind myself to take it one step, one task, one day at a time.

> "Remembering that we can live only one day at a time removes the burdens of the past from our backs and keeps us from dreading the future, which none of us can know anyway."
>
> *This Is Al-Anon*

I came to Al-Anon to discover how to get a loved one to stop drinking, hoping that my life would then return to normal. In Al-Anon I came to understand that I did not cause alcoholism, I can't control it, and I can't cure it. But I can apply the Twelve Steps to my own life so that I can find sanity and contentment whether the alcoholic is still drinking or not. This is why, in Al-Anon, the focus must be on me.

I soon discovered that I had problems of my own that needed attention: I had undergone some unhealthy changes as I attempted to cope with the disease of alcoholism. These changes had occurred so slowly and subtly that I had not been aware of them. I shared openly about this in Al-Anon meetings and became willing to let go of attitudes that no longer seemed appropriate. With the help of my Higher Power, I began to shed self-destructive habits. In time I felt I had regained my true self. I began to grow again.

Today's reminder

I do not respond well when someone tries to impose their will on me; why have I tried to impose my will on those around me? There is only one person I am responsible for, and that is me. There is only one person who can make my life as full as possible—that, too, is me.

"Today I will keep hands off and keep my focus where it belongs, on me."

. . . *In All Our Affairs*

My overwhelming desire for control becomes glaringly obvious when I am tempted to control my group. I decide that I know what is best for all of us, or that I am the only one who truly understands the Traditions, or that I know what newcomers need to hear and I alone must make sure they hear it. I may view this as a finely-developed sense of responsibility, but my attitudes and actions still amount to a form of dominance.

The Second Tradition says that "For our group purpose there is but one authority—a loving God as He may express himself in our group conscience. Our leaders are but trusted servants; they do not govern." We strive to conduct our meetings as a fellowship of equals and to practice rotation of leadership. No single member has the right to take charge.

When I insist upon having my way, I am tampering with the spiritual nature of Al-Anon as a whole. Just as my Higher Power guides me in my daily life, a Power greater than myself is working within my group through the voices of its members.

Today's reminder

I am only one voice in a thriving worldwide fellowship. When in doubt, I will defer to the wisdom of the group conscience.

"Any attempt to manage or direct is likely to have disastrous consequences for group harmony."

Alcoholism, The Family Disease

There was a time in my life when I furiously insisted that alcoholism did not exist in my family. We were normal; everything was fine! Today I know that alcoholism is a family disease that affects not only the drinkers but those around them as well. Denial is a symptom of this family disease.

When I began to recognize the alcoholism in my family, my unfortunate past became the topic of all my conversations. Then an Al-Anon member shared about having learned to look back without staring. She pointed out how easy it can be to lose perspective, to feel trapped, to stop living in the present. Unlocking the secrets of the past can offer many gifts, but the purpose of this search is to recover from the effects of alcoholism and get on with our lives here and now.

Today, with the love, support, and encouragement of Al-Anon members, I am able to face the reality of the past, not to place blame or wallow in self-pity but to learn from it.

Today's reminder

There is much to learn from the past, but I cannot allow past hurts to smolder and destroy today. Instead, I can ask my Higher Power to help me use my experiences to move forward and to make healthier, more loving choices than ever before.

"Experience is not what happens to you, it is what you do with what happens to you."

Aldous Huxley

I can certainly learn from criticism, and I want to remain open to hearing what others have to say, but neither my popularity nor my ability to please those I live and work with are legitimate measures of my worth as an individual. Al-Anon helps me to recognize that I have value simply because I breathe the breath of humanity. As I gain self-esteem, I find it easier to evaluate my behavior more realistically.

The support I get in Al-Anon helps me find the courage to learn about myself. As I come to feel at home with myself and my values, my likes and dislikes, my dreams and choices, I am increasingly able to risk other people's disapproval. I am equally able to honor others when they choose to be themselves, whether or not I like what I see.

Today's reminder

With the help of a loving sponsor and the support of my fellow Al-Anon members, I am learning to find my place in this world—a place where I can live with dignity and self-respect.

> "I exist as I am, that is enough, if no other in the world be aware I sit content, and if each and all be aware I sit content."
>
> Walt Whitman

Resentments poisoned most of my waking hours before I found Al-Anon. I could keep a fire under a resentment for days, or years, by constantly justifying why I felt the way I did. Today, although it is important to notice my feelings, I don't have to continually rehearse and re-rehearse my grievances. It's not necessary to keep reviewing how I have been hurt, to assign blame, or to determine damages.

Ultimately, I may not resolve everything with the person in question—though that might be pleasant if it came to pass. I just want to be rid of the resentment because it prevents me from experiencing joy. I try to shift my energy to where it will do some good. I apply Steps Six and Seven because, to me, the way to let go of resentment is to turn to my Higher Power. I want to become entirely ready to have my Higher Power lift it, and I humbly ask for help.

Today's reminder

If I am holding a resentment, I can simply ask for relief, for peace of mind in the present moment. I will remind myself that this relief will come in God's time. Then I can grow quiet, be patient, and wait.

"No man can think clearly when his fists are clenched."

George Jean Nathan

I dreamt that I was trapped in a burning room. Thick smoke filled the air, and the only exit door was blocked by fire. As I gasped for breath, a hand appeared behind the flames, beckoning me to come. I knew that freedom, light, and air were on the other side of that door, and that certain death awaited me if I remained. Still, I hesitated. How could I walk through the fire?

Sometimes I feel the same way about the challenges I face in my waking life. Even when my position is hopeless and my Higher Power beckons, urging me to take a risk, I still hesitate, hoping for a miracle. I forget that the miracle is already here. Today, thanks to Al-Anon, I have a Higher Power who is always there for me, helping me to cope with my fears and find new, effective solutions to my problems. Thus, I am taken beyond the problems that once held me hostage. I am free to act or not to act, to take a chance, to hold off on a decision, to make choices that feel right.

Today's reminder

It takes courage to step beyond what is comfortable, predictable, and known. Courage is a gift from my Higher Power that I find in the rooms of Al-Anon and in the hearts of its members.

"Courage faces fear and thereby masters it."

Martin Luther King, Jr.

I've heard my Al-Anon friends refer to Steps Ten, Eleven, and Twelve as "maintenance" Steps. But I don't want to merely maintain where I was when I completed Step Nine. This is no time to stagnate! Instead, I call them "growth" Steps. No matter how old I get, these last three Steps let me continue to challenge myself.

I tested this theory of mine when my spouse and I retired. I have more time now to meddle in others' affairs, worry about our health, worry about finances, worry about world conditions, or to put it bluntly, just more time to go back to my old "stinking thinking." But with the help of these Steps, I find I also have more time to be aware of the extraordinary benefits of personal growth, with my Higher Power ever there to guide me and give me strength. Only with this increasing conscious contact with my God, can I live as I want to today.

The icing on the cake has been that I have more time to carry the message of this beautiful way of life. Some of my most pleasant memories, not to mention the times of greatest growth, have come from this sharing with others and in giving service to my group and to Al-Anon as a whole.

Today's reminder

With the help of the Steps, I need never be stuck again.

"Be not afraid of growing slowly,
Be afraid only of standing still."

Chinese proverb

In Step Six I contemplate my life undergoing change—tremendous change. The great fear is this: If I shed many characteristics that stand in my way, what will be left? It is as though I face a great void, a terrifying unknown. Yet when I acknowledge how far I have come, I can see how much I *want* to change. The desire to grow and to heal has brought me to this uncomfortable point, because I am tired of the way I have been. My Higher Power is there to guide me when I am ready.

I find solace in the fact that in Step Six I need not change anything; I must simply prepare myself for change. I can take all the time I need. Such manageability is what I set out to find in the first place. Now it is a part of my life.

Today's reminder

I need not judge the rate at which I change old habits or ways of thinking. If I am uncomfortable with old behavior, then on some level I am already moving toward changing it. Change will not be effective unless I am ready for it. I need only trust that, when the time comes to move forward, I will know it.

> "Remind me each day that the race is not always to the swift; that there is more to life than increasing its speed. Let me look upward into the towering oak and know that it grew great and strong because it grew slowly and well."
>
> Orin L. Crain

Before coming to Al-Anon, I never felt I could be myself around other people. I was too busy trying to be what I thought others wanted me to be, afraid people wouldn't accept me the way I am.

But with my first Al-Anon meeting I felt at ease. Members talked about common characteristics that I recognized in myself. "They're talking about themselves, but they're describing me!" I thought. "I'm not crazy after all!" Meetings helped me to realize that there were many people in this world like me—people who had been affected by another's alcoholism. I didn't have to lie to people in these meetings, and eventually I learned that I didn't have to lie to anyone anywhere. I came to see that I can live my life for inner peace and not for outward appearances.

Today's reminder

Living with joys and problems affirms my membership in the human race. What sets me apart is the path on which I have been placed to walk. No one can walk it for me, nor can I change my path to suit anyone else.

> "The shell that had enclosed my life, that had prevented me from living and loving, has cracked, and the power of the Al-Anon program is filling the void that for years kept me at a distance from life."
>
> *As We Understood . . .*

At an Al-Anon meeting we discussed the way our housekeeping habits reflected the effects of alcoholism. One person shared that his life felt completely unmanageable unless his house was perfectly neat. Tidiness gave him an illusion of control.

Others, including me, spoke of floors so strewn with clothes, books, and papers that we could not cross the room without stepping on, or tripping over, something. I had always considered this just a bad habit until I heard someone share that this clutter was her way of keeping people at a distance—isolating.

Then I remembered that in the house where I grew up, clutter had served just this function: I was always afraid to invite friends over because everything was too messy. It was uncomfortable to realize that I was doing the same thing in adulthood that had kept me isolated as a child.

Today's reminder

By taking a fresh look at what I thought of as just a bad habit, I can free my life of some clutter today. I can consider hidden motives for that habit without condemning myself or my family. Clutter doesn't have to be physical; I may also find areas of my mental, spiritual, or emotional life that are in disarray. I can heal without making moral judgments about myself or others.

". . . the Al-Anon program can give me a new view of my world by helping me to see myself more clearly . . ."

One Day at a Time in Al-Anon

When I feel I just can't face the world and want nothing more than to bury my head under the covers and hide, I know I need an Al-Anon meeting! I may have to push myself out the door, but I always feel better—and saner—when I break the isolation and reach out for help. I usually feel relief the minute I walk into an Al-Anon room, even if it's a meeting I've never attended before. I find a healing, comforting Power in these rooms, a Power greater than myself. And because my Higher Power speaks through other people, I often hear exactly what I need.

We all go through periods of sadness, lethargy, and grief—that's part of life. But depression can become a habit that perpetuates itself, unless I intercede by acting on my own behalf. Al-Anon cannot solve every problem, and if depression lingers, I may want to consider seeking professional help. But more often than not, what I need to do is bring my body to an Al-Anon meeting. I know that no matter how I feel, when I take an action to get some help, I make myself available to the Higher Power in these rooms.

Today's reminder

When in doubt, I will go to an Al-Anon meeting and invite my Higher Power to do for me what I cannot do for myself.

> "There are times when I have to hurt through a situation and when this happens, the choice is not whether to hurt or not to hurt, but what to do while I am hurting."

> ... *In All Our Affairs*

A particular incident reminds me of the sense of surrender that I feel when I truly take the Third Step and turn my will and my life over to God's care. Some years ago my sister discovered that she had a brain tumor. Her initial diagnosis was dire—also, fortunately, inaccurate. When I heard about my sister's choices for treatment, I felt that she should pursue certain avenues that she had ruled out. I grew increasingly impatient with her choices until I read a commentary by a person I respect, suggesting that the avenues I had been championing could do more harm than good.

That's when I realized the limits of my own understanding. I saw that my sense of urgency stemmed not from certainty but from fear. I discovered that my only honest course of action was to turn my fear and my love over to the care of my Higher Power. I could no longer pretend to know what was best.

Today's reminder

I am not a rocket scientist, a philosopher, or a wizard. Even if I were all three, I would still find myself looking off the edge of my understanding into a vast unknown. As I recognize my own limitations, I am more grateful than ever for a Higher Power who is free from such restrictions.

> ". . . Time will change and even reverse many of your present opinions. Refrain, therefore, awhile from setting yourself up as a judge of the highest matters."
>
> Plato

I put my sponsor on a pedestal. I looked to her for all the answers and saw her as my mother, friend, mentor—a goddess. She appeared to be more than I could ever be; she was perfect.

One day she made a mistake and fell from the pedestal on which I had placed her. How could she be so human? How dare she display such imperfection? At first I felt frightened and abandoned. But my sponsor's slide from grace led me to see that I was responsible for my own Al-Anon program.

I found that the "answers" she had given me were simply her own experience, strength, and hope, along with her understanding of the Twelve Steps of recovery. I learned that the tools of the program are available to me too. And I learned that, although she was my sponsor, we were both changing, stumbling, growing members of Al-Anon. Most importantly, I learned that setting a human being up to be perfect creates inevitable failure.

Today's reminder

Have I put someone on a pedestal? Am I encouraging anyone to have an exaggerated view of me? Al-Anon helps me see that while we offer mutual support, we must learn to rely on ourselves. Today I will remember that my answers lie within me.

> "Sponsorship is a friendship made up of two members learning from one another, two people learning a new way to live—one day at a time."
>
> *Sponsorship—What It's All About*

Since coming to Al-Anon, I have become aware of certain choices that I never knew I had. If I am uncomfortable about doing something, I have learned that I don't necessarily have to do it. I can look into my heart and try to discover my true feelings before making that decision. What freedom!

Does this mean that I should never do anything unless I feel comfortable doing it? Of course not. If I waited for inspiration, my taxes might never be paid, my work might not get done, and my teeth might not get brushed. Sometimes I have to feel the feelings and then act anyway.

I believe that is why our "Just For Today" suggests doing two things each day that I don't want to do, just for practice. To create a balanced life, I must exercise some self-discipline. That way I can pay attention to my feelings without being tyrannized by them.

Today's reminder

Today I will do something that is good for me even if it feels uncomfortable.

"Self-discipline is self-caring."

M. Scott Peck

After living in the chaos of an alcoholic relationship, it can be hard to know the difference between a minor inconvenience and a major crisis. Al-Anon's slogan, "How important is it?" helps many of us to regain some sense of proportion.

When plans fall through, when unexpected bills arrive, when I am disappointed in someone's response, I can ask myself, "How important is it?" Most of the time I find that what I might have viewed as a disaster is really insignificant. If I try to keep my attention on this day instead of worrying about possible future consequences, I can take my disappointment or irritation at face value and refuse to dramatize it.

Because of this simple slogan, many days that I would once have seen as tragic are now filled with serenity and confidence.

Today's reminder

Today, if I encounter an upsetting situation, I will ask myself, "How important is it?" before I react. I may find that it is not important enough to sacrifice my serenity.

"It is almost as important to know what is not serious as to know what is."

John Kenneth Galbraith

During stressful periods it can be tempting to skip a meal, push ourselves until we are totally exhausted, and generally ignore our basic needs. In the midst of crisis, taking time out for an Al-Anon meeting, a call to a sponsor, or a breath of fresh air may seem like a waste of all-too-precious moments. There don't seem to be enough hours in a day, and something has to go. But are we choosing wisely?

At the very time we most need to take good care of ourselves, we are likely to do the opposite. If we decide that our needs are unimportant or that we're too busy, we sabotage our own best interests. In times of crisis, we need to be at our best. By making an extra effort to get nutritious food, sleep, Al-Anon support, relaxation, and quiet time with our Higher Power, we strengthen ourselves physically, emotionally, and spiritually. This can make a difficult situation a little easier.

Today's reminder

I am the only one who can make my well-being my top priority. I owe it to myself to pay attention to the needs of my body, mind, and spirit.

> "Putting 'First things first' in troubled times means finding whatever way I can to set aside my burdens, even if just for a moment, to make time for myself."
>
>   . . . *In All Our Affairs*

Some of us believe that most defects of character are merely traits that we no longer need. Many of us develop clever methods of surviving in an alcoholic situation, such as denial or secrecy. But once we have the support of the Al-Anon program, we may find that our old methods do more harm than good. What once allowed us to function in a nearly impossible situation is now an obstacle to further growth. An asset has become a deficit.

Others define defects of character as assets that have lost proportion. For example, a genuine desire to help a loved one can be exaggerated into a desperate need to fix another person.

From this perspective, we aren't facing the daunting task of rooting out every shred of the defect; we are only turning it over to our Higher Power so that it can be brought into balance or dropped because it is no longer serving our needs.

Today's reminder

Instead of condemning myself when I become aware of a defect of character, I can acknowledge my growth. I've recognized that a characteristic that once allowed me to survive is no longer necessary, or that an asset that has lost its proportion makes my life unmanageable. Instead of proving sickness, this shows a willingness to face reality and a readiness to choose health.

"Sometimes we must accept ourselves, defects and all, before those defects are removed."

. . . *In All Our Affairs*

Tradition Six tells us that "Our Al-Anon Family Groups ought never endorse, finance, or lend our name to any outside enterprise, lest problems of money, property and prestige divert us from our primary spiritual aim."

I've had occasion to refer to this Tradition many times while doing service work at our local Al-Anon information office. I often receive requests for Al-Anon's endorsement from various research projects, charities, and treatment programs. These requests always pique my interest, and many appear to have merit.

As an individual, I am free to participate in any cause I support. As an Al-Anon member, I am free to send information about our fellowship to outside organizations. But I cannot consider affiliating my group with these outside enterprises, no matter how worthy they may be. Doing so could divert us from the primary spiritual aim of our program, which is to help families and friends of alcoholics recover from the effects of alcoholism.

Today's reminder

I come to Al-Anon to receive the spiritual benefit of the meetings, principles, and fellowship. I wish to do my part to see that we are not diverted from our primary aim.

"We must always remember why we are here, and never use the group to promote our pet projects, or our personal interests in outside causes."

Twelve Steps & Twelve Traditions for Alateen

There was a piece of reality that I never wanted to see: I loved someone who couldn't be trusted. Again and again I suffered the disappointment of broken promises, contradictions, and outright lies. Each time, I felt crushed, betrayed, outraged. Nevertheless, hours or sometimes days later, I put the incident out of my mind. When the next promise was made, I trusted without hesitation and with my whole heart.

I continue to find it hard to accept that I can't trust the promises of someone I love. Yet I see that most of my heartache has come from my own refusal to accept reality. Al-Anon helps me to trust my experiences more than the inconsistent words of others.

I'm learning not to depend on someone who has been consistently untrustworthy, but at the same time realizing that that is no excuse to give up on the whole human race. Facing reality means accepting that many of my experiences in Al-Anon demonstrate that there *are* people upon whom I can rely.

Today's reminder

Today I make a commitment to be honest with myself. By facing reality, I become someone I can depend upon.

> "Awareness is so much better for me than closing out all feelings, shutting out people, withdrawing from living. No matter how hard the truth is or what the facts are, I prefer to know, look at, and accept this day."
>
> *As We Understood . . .*

A billboard in my town reads, "Some come to the fountain of knowledge to drink. Some come to gargle." My pre-Al-Anon self would have chuckled at this message, but I would have felt some anxiety about whether I was a drinker or a gargler. Life was either black or white, and in order to feel comfortable, I had to know which extreme applied. But whichever label I pinned on myself would leave me feeling wrong, so I would scramble to fix myself.

Now, thanks to Al-Anon, I accept more easily the thought that sometimes I drink, sometimes I gargle, and sometimes I stub my toe on the fountain as I stumble by. I don't *have* to do better or differently. The best that I can do is good enough. I can relax and enjoy the joke.

Today's reminder

Al-Anon encourages me to examine my thoughts and actions, but this is meant as an act of self-love, not as a weapon to use against myself. When I begin to accept myself exactly as I am, life will feel a lot more gentle.

"Sometimes we try so hard that we fail to see that the light we are seeking is within us."

As We Understood . . .

Some Al-Anon suggestions, such as getting a sponsor, were easy for me because I'm good at following specific instructions. But I didn't know what to do with the slogan, "Live and let live." Al-Anon helped me to "let live" by teaching me about detachment and helping me to see that many of my problems stemmed from minding everyone's business but my own. But how do you turn your eyes on yourself and *"live"* for the first time in your life?

When I put this question to my sponsor, she asked me one in turn—what had I done earlier that day? Although I'd had a very busy day, I could barely remember what I had been doing. My sponsor suggested that I begin learning how to live by becoming more aware of my life as I was already living it. Then I would be better able to make choices about how I would like to live.

Searching for the real me, living according to my needs, and loving myself as a new-found friend have been the most rewarding benefits of the Al-Anon program. Strangely, they're the last ones I would have imagined receiving when I began.

Today's reminder

Today I can choose to take responsibility for my own life. If I stay out of others' affairs and become more aware of my own, I have a good chance of finding some serenity.

"Each man's life represents a road toward himself."

Hermann Hesse

My Al-Anon recovery involves becoming aware of what motivates my choices. I was appalled to discover that fear ruled my life! I seemed to be afraid of everything! I was afraid to say, "No," to show hurt or anger, to be confused. With clenched teeth and a painted-on smile, I'd say, "Oh no, everything's OK," while thinking, "There'll come a day when I'll get even." Even that scared me because I was afraid of my own anger!

Many of my Al-Anon friends used the slogans to deal with their fears, but when fear engulfed me, all I could think of was "Came to believe . . ." I couldn't finish the rest of the Second Step, but that one phrase was enough. So when the telephone rang and I was startled and beginning to imagine the worst, I would take a deep breath and say to myself, "Came to believe . . ." Then it became possible to pick up the phone. And I always hung up feeling so much lighter because *we* had handled it!

Today's reminder

Before taking any action, I need only remind myself that I am in the care of a Higher Power. Whether the words I use say, "Help!" or "Let go and let God," or "Came to believe," I know that my Higher Power and I can deal with whatever we are facing.

> "We turn our will and our life over to the *care* of God as we understand Him. A Higher Power is like a friend who really cares about us and wants to share our problems."
>
> *Alateen—A Day at a Time*

I developed a tremendous fear of making mistakes. It seemed crucial to cover every possible outcome, because mistakes often led to an avalanche of accusations and abuse from the alcoholic—and eventually from myself. My self-esteem diminished because the slightest error felt huge and I couldn't let it go. So I began to cover up and rationalize my mistakes, all the while desperately trying to maintain an appearance of perfect self-control.

In Al-Anon I learned to take down that rigid wall of seeming perfection, to honestly admit mistakes, and to open myself for growth. Step Ten, in which I continue taking my inventory and promptly admit when I am wrong, has been liberating because it challenges me daily to be honest. Sometimes it makes me squirm, but I know that when I tell the truth, I am free of the lies that held me back. As Mark Twain put it, "If you tell the truth, you don't have to remember anything."

Today's reminder

I will probably make a mistake of some sort every day of my life. If I view this as a personal failing or pretend that no mistakes have occurred, I make my life unmanageable. When I stop struggling to be perfect and admit when I am wrong, I can let go of guilt and shame. That is cause for rejoicing.

"Help them to take failure, not as a measure of their worth, but as a chance for a new start."

Book of Common Prayer

I'm usually such a gentle, easy-going person that you'd never believe what happens when I get angry. I fly into a rage, my blood pressure seems to double, and I unleash a torrent of profanity. After years in Al-Anon, my anger is still a problem, but my behavior has greatly improved.

Some time ago my dog got its feet tangled in an extension cord and broke a beautiful vase. My temper flared, and angry words cut like sharp swords. What helped me to change this behavior was the look of hurt and bewilderment on my pet's face at the sudden, violent change in me. If a little animal could respond this way, what were my outbursts doing to the people in my life who understood every nasty word?

Today's reminder

I am human and I get angry, but I don't have to act out my anger in destructive ways. I do not have the right to take it out on others. Whether my usual response is to scream, sulk in cold silence, or lash out with cruel words, today I can look at what I do when I get mad. Maybe next time I will try something new.

"We can pave the way for calm, reasonable communication only if we first find healthy outlets for our own negative feelings."

The Dilemma of the Alcoholic Marriage

When students first learn to play the piano, they are usually taught to use only one hand and include very few keys. Then they move on to using two hands, eventually learning to play all the keys, the high ones as well as the low. In fact, part of the pleasure of playing lies in hearing the rumble of the lowest bass notes and the light chiming of the high treble.

Today in Al-Anon I am learning to play a new instrument—myself. I am a person with the capability to experience a wide range of emotions, from love to joy to wonder. I am profoundly grateful for laughter and light spirits—and also for anger and fear, because all of these feelings are part of what makes me whole. I believe that my Higher Power wants me to be fully alive and fully aware of all my feelings: The crashing crescendo of great anger, the soft chant of serenity, the heights of wonder, and the new insights that stretch my heart and mind just as my fingers stretch to reach all the keys in a challenging chord. I am learning to play richer sounds than I ever thought possible.

Today's reminder

Today I will appreciate the full range of feelings available to me. They make my experience of life full indeed.

> "I have sometimes been wildly, despairingly, acutely miserable . . . but through it all I still know quite certainly that just to *be alive* is a grand thing."
>
> Agatha Christie

Looking back, I have often reproached myself, "How could you not have known what was happening?" Alcoholism left messy tracks all over my life, yet I didn't see them. How could that be?

Denial is one of the chief symptoms of this family disease of alcoholism. Some of us deny that the drinker has a problem; others are all too willing to blame him or her for all our problems, denying our own participation. Why? Because we alone can't defeat this disease, so we invent ways to survive the constant crises, broken promises, lost hopes, and embarrassments. One way to cope is to deny the unpleasant or terrifying reality.

In Al-Anon we learn more productive ways in which to cope with alcoholism, ways that don't cost so much in loss of self. With the support of other members, and with tools and principles that offer direction, we become able to face what is really going on. We go beyond mere survival and begin to live again.

Today's reminder

At all times, I have done the best I was able to do. If my only way to cope with a difficult situation was to deny it, I can look back with compassion to that person who saw no better option at the time. I can forgive myself and count my blessings for having come so far since then.

> "Regret is an appalling waste of energy; you can't build on it; it's only good for wallowing in."
>
> Katherine Mansfield

At my first Al-Anon meeting, I was disappointed when I was given the Twelve Steps instead of a "do's and don't's" list for changing the alcoholic. Nevertheless, I was desperate enough to give the Steps a try, anyway.

At my second Al-Anon meeting I thought I had those first three Steps down pretty well—I knew I was powerless, I believed in God, and I was willing to dump my problems onto anyone who would take them. As I continued to attend meetings I began to see that I wasn't really admitting my powerlessness or I wouldn't keep trying to control everyone and everything around me. OK, so I skipped the part about letting go and letting God.

Today I am so glad to have a patient God, so that when I finally say, "Not my will but Your will," God steps in and sorts things out in ways I never would have imagined. The first three Steps aren't as easy as I once thought, but in Al-Anon I've learned to aim for progress, not perfection.

Today's reminder

When I was dealing with alcoholism without the help of Al-Anon, I developed coping skills. These are no longer enough. Al-Anon is teaching me a new and better set of skills. I will try to be patient with myself. I'm doing fine.

"As long as you live, keep learning how to live."

Seneca

I had never dared to trust another person the way I trusted my first Al-Anon sponsor. With faltering self-confidence I had asked her to sponsor me: I was a mess, would she have me? I was sure she would turn me down because I thought I was not worth saving. Her positive response really took me by surprise.

Gently, she guided me through the Steps. I was so desperate to feel better that I was willing to try whatever Al-Anon tool or idea she suggested. I lived, breathed, and ate Al-Anon.

One lonely day I phoned her, crying out in despair that I'd never get the hang of feeling better. What she said at that critical time was, "I don't know anyone who is as willing to work the program as you are." My spirits soared! She had said to me what I couldn't say to myself, but I knew that it was true—I *was* very willing. In that moment of acknowledgment I knew I'd be OK, because I had what it took. In time, her example helped me learn to give that kind of acknowledgment to myself.

I had taken a chance. I had trusted. And as a result, I learned that I was worth saving!

Today's reminder

Learning to value myself can begin by having the courage to find, and use, a sponsor.

> "Nothing we do, however virtuous, can be accomplished alone; therefore, we are saved by love."
>
> Reinhold Niebuhr

Since childhood I have been nagged by those moments when I said or did something that brought pain to another person. These are ugly memories that I never believed would go away. With Step Eight, however, I discover a means to release myself from unrelenting guilt.

This Step says to make a list of all people I have harmed and to become willing to make amends to them all. Finally, I can put down in words all the memories and all the pain. When I see them written in front of me, they seem almost manageable, and I feel hopeful about freeing myself from their weight as I become willing to make amends. I need not take any further action at this point. All I am concerned with now is the harm I have caused others, the guilt I have brought on myself, and the desire to do what I can to clear it all away.

Today's reminder

Guilt is a burden that keeps me from giving myself fully and freely to the present. I can begin to rid my mind of guilt by quietly admitting where and when I have done wrong to people, including myself.

"Al-Anon has shown me another way of living, and I like it. Life can either be a burden and a chore or a challenge and a joy. One day at a time I can meet the challenges of life head-on instead of head-down."

As We Understood . . .

Normally my sponsor would recommend a gratitude list when I felt low, but one day, when I complained about a family situation, he suggested that I list all the things I was unhappy about. Several days later my depression had passed, and when I told my sponsor about the terrific day I was having, he suggested a gratitude list. He thought it might help me to refer to it the next time I felt blue. That made sense to me, so I complied.

When I went to put this new list in the drawer where I keep my papers, I noticed the earlier list and read it once more. To my surprise, my list of grievances was almost identical to my gratitude list—the same people, same house, same life. Nothing about my circumstances had changed except the way I felt about them. For the first time I truly understood how much my attitude dictates the way I experience the world.

Today's reminder

Today I recognize how powerful my mind can be. I can't always feel good, and I have no interest in whitewashing my difficulties by pasting a smile on my face. But I can recognize that I am constantly making choices about how I perceive my world. With the help of Al-Anon and my friends in the fellowship, I can make those choices more consciously and more actively than ever before.

"Change your thoughts and you change your world."

Norman Vincent Peale

I have often tried to change other people to suit my own desires. I knew what I needed, and if those needs weren't met, the problem was with the other person. I was looking for someone who would always be there for me but would not impose on me very much. Looking back, it's almost as if I were looking for a pet rather than a human being. Naturally, this outlook put a strain on my relationships.

In Al-Anon I have learned there is a difference between what I expect and what I need. No one person can be *all* things to me.

Once again I'm faced with examining my own attitudes. What do I expect, and is that expectation realistic? Do I respect other people's individuality—or only the parts that suit my fancy? Do I appreciate what I do receive?

Today's reminder

Trying to change other people is futile, foolish, and certainly not loving. Today, instead of assuming that they are the problem, I can look at myself to see what needs changing within.

> "The beginning of love is to let those we love be perfectly themselves and not to twist them to fit our own image."
>
> *One Day at a Time in Al-Anon*

After taking a good look within itself, our very small home group discovered we had gotten into a rut without realizing it. It had been a long time since we'd had new members, new input. And all of our meetings, which were either round-table discussions, or based solely on the *One Day at a Time in Al-Anon (ODAT)* book, seemed to cover the same ground with little change.

We took a group conscience and decided to try some meetings using other Al-Anon literature. We began a series of speaker exchanges with other local groups. It was not long before things began improving. Our membership tripled within a year. We soon had so many newcomers that we set up a series of beginners meetings as an extension of our group. Each of us has personally benefited because of our willingness to take an inventory as a group.

Today's reminder

Each group, like each individual, goes through changes. But we don't have to face those changes alone. The Second Tradition reminds us that a loving God expresses himself through our group conscience. When each of us is willing to grow, we all benefit.

> "There is a comfortable feeling in knowing that guidance for the group comes not through individuals, but from the willingness of the group to follow whatever wisdom may be expressed through the membership."

Al-Anon Faces Alcoholism

During my years in Al-Anon I have done lots of thinking about the First Step; lately I have done lots of feeling about it, too. The feeling work can be described mostly in one word: Grief. Recalling a friend's rapid progression through alcoholism, from reasonable health and apparent happiness to cirrhosis and death, I feel grief.

I don't necessarily hate this disease today, but I do feel fiercely its crippling, powerful presence in my life. I have memories of the damage done to my family, my friends, and myself. I grieve for the loss of love and life that alcoholism has caused. I grieve for the lost years I have spent jumping through the hoops of this disease. I admit that I am powerless over alcohol and that my life has been utterly unmanageable whenever I have grappled with it.

Today's reminder

I have suffered many losses as the result of alcoholism. Part of admitting the effects of this disease in my life is admitting my grief. By facing alcoholism's impact on my life, I begin to move out of its grip and into a life of great promise and hope.

> "It's not easy to admit defeat and give in to that powerful foe, alcoholism. Yet, this surrender is absolutely necessary if we are ever to have sane, happy lives again . . ."
>
> *Al-Anon IS For Men*

Before coming to Al-Anon, I had built a life-time of dreams and promises that were reserved for that one special day called, "Someday." Some-day I'll begin—or end—that project. Someday I'll call that friend with whom I've lost touch. Some-day I'll let them know how I feel. Someday I'll be happy. I'm going to take that trip, find that job, speak my mind... Someday. Just wait and see.

Wait—just as I waited for the alcoholic to come in from a binge, and for inspiration to bring in-teresting friends and career opportunities to my doorstep, and for everybody else to change. But Al-Anon has helped me to see that *today* can be the Someday I've always wanted. There isn't enough time in these twenty-four hours to do ev-erything I've ever hoped to do, but there is time to start making my dreams come true. By asking my Higher Power for guidance and by taking some small step in the direction of my choice, I will be able to accomplish more than I would ever have thought possible.

Today's reminder

Today I will not wait for a blue moon, a rainy day, the 366th day of the year, or Someday to accomplish good things in my life.

> "Each indecision brings its own delays and days are lost lamenting over lost days . . . What you can do or think you can do, begin it. For bold-ness has Magic, Power, and Genius in it."
>
> Johann Wolfgang von Goethe

As we let go of obsession, worry, and focusing on everyone but ourselves, many of us were bewildered by the increasing calmness of our minds. We knew how to live in a state of crisis, but it often took a bit of adjustment to become comfortable with stillness. The price of serenity was the quieting of the constant mental chatter that had taken up so much time; suddenly we had lots of time on our hands and we wondered how to fill it.

Having become more and more serene as a result of working the Al-Anon program, I was surprised to find myself still grabbing for old fears as if I wanted to remain in crisis. I realized that I didn't know how to feel safe unless I was mentally busy. When I worried, I felt involved—and therefore somewhat in control.

As an exercise, my sponsor suggested that I try to maintain my inner stillness even when I felt scared or doubtful. As I did so, I reassured myself again and again that I was safely in the care of a Power greater than myself. Today I know that sanity and serenity are the gifts I have received for my efforts and my faith. With practice, I am learning to trust the peace.

Today's reminder

Today I will relish my serenity. I know that it is safe to enjoy it.

"Be still and know that I am with you."

                                             English prayer

When I began studying the Seventh Step, which says, "Humbly asked Him to remove our shortcomings," my list of shortcomings included an extensive catalogue of feelings. I humbly asked God to remove my anger, fear, and guilt. I looked forward to the day when I would never experience any of these emotions again.

Of course, that day never arrived. Instead, I have learned that feelings aren't shortcomings. The true nature of my problem was my stubborn refusal to acknowledge feelings, to accept them, *and* to let them go. I have very little power over what feelings arise, but what I choose to do about them is my responsibility.

Today I can accept my feelings, share about them with others, recognize that they are feelings, not facts, and then let them go. I'm no longer stuck in a state of seemingly endless rage or self-pity, for when I give myself permission to feel whatever I feel, the feelings pass. My emotions have not been removed; instead, I have been relieved of shortcomings that blocked my self-acceptance.

Today's reminder

When I take the Seventh Step, I pray that whatever interferes with my Higher Power's will for me may be removed. I don't have to have all the answers. I need only be willing.

> "We didn't necessarily get the results we wanted, but somehow we always seemed to get what we needed."
>
> *. . . In All Our Affairs*

A writer for a local newspaper recently maintained that most people spend more time planning vacations than they do thinking about what is really important in their lives. Of course a vacation has a certain importance, but as our slogan asks, "How important is it?"

In my case, the main focus of my mental activity usually is whatever problem, grievance, or irritation I am entertaining at the moment. "Now," I tell myself, "I'm concentrating on what's really important!" But, "How important is it?" When I look back on this two years from now, or next month, will it matter?

Al-Anon helps me to address the larger concerns in my life. For example, how can I make better contact with my Higher Power? Am I taking time to enjoy the present moment? Am I becoming the person I want to be? What can I give thanks for today?

Today's reminder

Are my priorities in order? Am I so busy with smaller, less meaningful concerns that I run out of time for the really important considerations? Today I will make room to think about what really matters.

"Today I'll use the slogan, 'How important is it?' It will help me think things through before I act and it will give me a better picture of just what *is* important in my life."

Alateen—A Day at a Time

I never thought much about Tradition Seven, which says that every group ought to be fully self-supporting. I thought it referred only to paying the rent. But recently I was involved with a group that maintained itself financially and still was not fully self-supporting because no one would commit to service. I already held several positions, and when my various terms expired, no one was willing to take my place. I made what felt like the responsible choice for myself and stepped down anyway. The meeting closed. In my opinion, a group that cannot fill its service positions is not fully self-supporting.

Today, in other, more flourishing groups, I have a greater appreciation of my responsibility to this Tradition. I believe that as we nurture our groups, we nurture and empower ourselves. We *can* make a contribution; we *can* make choices that help us to allow healing in ourselves and others.

Today's reminder

There's more to maintaining a fully self-supporting Al-Anon group than just paying the rent. Continuity of service is important to our common welfare. Today I will think about the contribution I am making to my home group.

> "I can support my group in a number of ways. When the basket is passed, I can give what I can. Just as important, I can give my time and moral support to help make ours the kind of group I *want* to belong to."

> *Alateen—A Day at a Time*

Is there anything that stands in the way of my trusting in a Higher Power? What obstacles block me from turning over my will and my life to God? In my case, the answer is obvious: I want guarantees. I hold out, thinking that I'll come up with a new solution to my problems even though I've tried and failed, again and again. The risk of faith seems so great. If I turn a situation over, I won't be in control. I can't be sure I'll get my way.

Yet I want recovery. If I continue to do what I have always done, I will continue to get what I have always gotten. I want the benefits that this spiritual program has to offer. Therefore, I must take the risk and "Let go and let God."

Maybe faith will bring me the results I seek, maybe not. Although there are no guarantees, the benefits of building a strong relationship with a Higher Power can help me to grow confident, strong, and capable of coping with whatever comes to pass long after this particular crisis has been resolved.

Today's reminder

Today I will make a contribution to my spiritual development. I will try to identify the obstacles that block my faith.

> "Understanding is the reward of faith. Therefore, seek not to understand that thou mayest believe, but believe that thou mayest understand."
>
> Aurelius Augustinus

Sometimes I sit in a meeting and I don't know how to ask for help. I can get trapped inside my pain. Some nameless thing seems to tear at my insides. I freeze, thinking that if I don't move, it will go away. So I don't ask, I don't talk, and the pain grows.

Does my face look calm? Don't be fooled. I'm just afraid to let you see the truth. You might think I'm foolish or weak. You might reject me. So I don't talk, and the pain remains.

But I listen. And through other people, my Higher Power does for me what I can't do for myself. Someone in the meeting shares and expresses the very feelings I am afraid to describe. My world suddenly widens, and I feel a little safer. I am no longer alone.

Today's reminder

One of the miracles I have found in Al-Anon is that help often comes when I most need it. When I can't bring myself to reach out for help, it sometimes comes to me. When I don't know what to say, I am given the words I require. And when I share what is in my heart, I may be giving a voice to someone who cannot find his own. Today I have a Higher Power who knows my needs.

> "As I walk, As I walk,
> The universe is walking with me."
>
> —from the Navajo rain dance ceremony

My denial was so thick when I came to Al-Anon that I didn't even know there were alcoholics in my life. Al-Anon helped me feel safe enough to look at the truth. As my denial began to lift, I was horrified at the lies I had told myself and others.

But I went from one extreme to the other and became a compulsive truth teller. It became my mission to inform anyone who would listen about what was *really* happening. I labeled this "honesty," but I was actually expressing my anger and scorn for the alcoholic—and crying out for help.

Al-Anon has shown me that my view of a situation is only the "truth" as seen from my tiny corner of the universe. I can't undo past denial by blaming the alcoholic for having a disease that has affected both our lives, or by bitterly insisting that I now know the *real* truth. But I can forgive my extreme responses to extreme situations, knowing that I did the best I could at the time. Today I can be honest and still be gentle with myself.

Today's reminder

When I stop worrying about how others see things and focus on myself, I gain more serenity than I have ever known. I cannot control the disease of alcoholism, but I can step away from its grip by honestly examining my motives and feelings.

"Whoever fights monsters should see to it that in the process he does not become a monster."

Friedrich Nietzsche

During the entire process of working on my Fourth Step (making a searching and fearless moral inventory of myself), I felt a nagging suspicion that I wasn't doing it right. With my Higher Power's help, I finally realized that the problem wasn't that I had done my Fourth Step wrong; the fact was that I had the same sense of inadequacy about my whole life. *Whatever* I'm doing, I'm inclined to feel that I'm doing it wrong, that my best is not good enough. And that is simply not true. I am doing just fine.

The awareness that I have developed through Step Four puts my self-doubt into perspective. It's just an effect of years of living with problem drinkers. So when the feeling comes up, I recognize it, share about it, accept that I feel it, and then set it aside. I no longer assume that it has any validity.

Today's reminder

Step Four offers me a chance to find some balance. It helps me to identify the things I've been telling myself about myself, and to learn whether or not those things are true. Today I will take one of my assumptions about myself and hold it up to the light. I may find that it stems from habit rather than reality.

"Let me realize . . . that self-doubt and self-hate are defects of character that hinder my growth."

The Dilemma of the Alcoholic Marriage

In dealing with a change, a problem, or a discovery, awareness is often followed by a period of acceptance before we can take action. This process is sometimes referred to as the "Three A's" — Awareness, Acceptance, and Action.

Coping with a new awareness can be extremely awkward, and most of us are eager to spare ourselves pain or discomfort. Yet, until we accept the reality with which we have been faced, we probably won't be capable of taking effective action with confidence.

Still, we may hesitate to accept an unpleasant reality because we feel that by accepting, we condone something that is intolerable. But this is not the case. As it says so eloquently in *One Day at a Time in Al-Anon (ODAT)*, "Acceptance does not mean submission to a degrading situation. It means accepting the fact of a situation, then deciding what we will do about it." Acceptance can be empowering because it makes choice possible.

Today's reminder

I will give myself time to accept my situation before I act. Unforeseen options can become available when I accept what is.

> "For here we are not afraid to follow truth wherever it may lead."
>
> Thomas Jefferson

Each moment of this day is precious, and I will make it count. I will use this time to enrich my life and to improve my relationship with my Higher Power, other people, and myself. Each of the Twelve Steps can help me to pursue this goal regardless of my circumstances. Meetings, Al-Anon telephone calls, and Al-Anon literature all help me to apply the Steps to what is happening in my life here and now. In this moment, I can make a positive change.

Perhaps I will think of time as a special kind of checking account. I have twenty-four hours to spend. By putting Al-Anon's principles to work in my life today, I am choosing to use these hours to grow, enjoy, and improve. I even have an opportunity to learn from my mistakes, since a brand new twenty-four hours can begin at any moment.

Today's reminder

This day offers me a chance to make a new start at living. How can I make the best use of it?

> "We start with gifts. Merit comes from what we make of them."
>
> Jean Toomer

Living with alcoholism taught me that it was best not to hope for anything. The lessons were too painful—I would get excited about something, only to have my hopes shattered. As time passed and hope diminished, I fell deeper into despair. Eventually I shut down my feelings and refused to care or to hope for anything at all.

Through Al-Anon's Twelve Steps, I am discovering a spirituality that allows me to believe that there is every reason to hope. With my Higher Power's help, regardless of my circumstances, I can feel fully alive in the moment and enjoy this feeling. The painful lessons of a lifetime are not unlearned overnight, but Al-Anon is helping me to learn that it is safe to feel, to hope, even to dream.

Today's reminder

It is risky to care—I may be disappointed. But in trying to protect myself from pain, I could cut myself off from the many delights that life has to offer. I will live more fully today.

"Years may wrinkle the skin, but to give up enthusiasm wrinkles the soul."

Samuel Ullman

Night after sleepless night, I tossed and turned and worried. Why couldn't I sleep? What was the matter with me? My life was stressful, but no more so than usual. I'd tried hot milk, reading in bed, soft music, even a visit to the doctor, but still I couldn't get more than a few hours sleep. I was in a panic!

I spoke about my concerns in an Al-Anon meeting, and another member related a similar problem. What had helped him was to accept the situation fully and admit that he was powerless to make himself sleep. In retrospect, he said, his sleeplessness had been a blessing; it had kept him too tired to get into trouble.

I realized that the same was true for me. Instead of worrying compulsively about a loved one's sobriety, watchful and nosy despite many attempts to mind my own business, lately I've been too tired to be overly involved in *anything* that wasn't my concern. I had often prayed to be released from my obsessive worry, and now, in an unexpected way, my prayers seem to have been answered.

Today's reminder

My Higher Power's gifts sometimes take unusual forms. Perhaps something I regard as a problem is really a form of assistance.

"Nothing is either good or bad. It's thinking that makes it so."

Benjamin Franklin

In the face of seemingly impossible problems, it is easy to believe that our most negative thoughts reflect the truth. They plead the worst case scenario in a very convincing way, until it almost seems frivolous to consider a positive outcome. Yet the loudest voice is not necessarily the truest.

No matter how insistent a feeling may be, it is just a feeling, not a prophecy. We don't get to know today what will happen tomorrow. Counting on any particular outcome can lead to disappointment, but sometimes it helps to remember that a positive outcome is just as likely as a negative one.

We are powerless over the results of our actions. We can try to make wise choices today, but what will happen in the future is out of our hands. Since we can't know what to expect, why not trust that a Higher Power can use whatever happens to further our growth?

Today's reminder

Today I will place the future in my Higher Power's hands. I trust that by turning it over, it can be used for my good.

> "This time, like all times, is a very good one, if we but know what to do with it."
>
>   Ralph Waldo Emerson

Most human beings have an instinctive need to fit in. The urge to belong, to keep the peace, helps us to get along with others and be a part of society. This instinct has allowed many civilizations to survive, and is not harmful unless I lose my sense of balance.

People-pleasing becomes destructive when I ignore my own needs and continually sacrifice my well-being for the sake of others. Al-Anon helps me find a compromise that allows me to respond to my feelings, including my desire to belong, and still take care of myself.

The best way to maintain this balance is to build my self-esteem. When I treat myself with kindness and respect, I become better able to get along with others.

Today's reminder

I will appreciate that all of my instincts and feelings exist for a reason. Today, instead of trying to banish these feelings, I will strive to find a balance.

> "If I am not for myself, who will be for me? And if I am only for myself, what am I? And if not now—when?"
>
> Hillel

When I am troubled about what lies ahead, I look back to see where I've been. When I was very new to the program, I would say, "I'm better off now than I was before I came to Al-Anon. I'll keep coming back." When I grew frustrated because of all the changes I wanted to make in myself, I said, "At least I'm aware of the problems. Now I know what I'm dealing with." And recently I found myself saying, "If someone had told me a year ago that I would be where I am today, I wouldn't have believed it possible."

Time offers me evidence that the Al-Anon program works—I can see the growth in my life. The longer I live by these principles, the more evidence I have. This reinforcement provides strong support in times of doubt and helps boost my courage in times of fear.

Today's reminder

When I feel unable to move, or when I am filled with fear, I have a wonderful gift to help clear my way—the gift of memory. Too often my memory has given me sadness, bringing back past hurt and shame. But now I can use my memory to see the progress I have made and to know the joy of gratitude. My own experience is teaching me to trust this wonderful recovery process. All I have to do is pay attention.

"God gave us memories so that we might have roses in December."

                                        James M. Barrie

In making a list of all the people we have harmed (Step Eight), some names come to mind at once, while others require more thought. Our Fourth Step inventory can help to refresh our memories. We can ask ourselves about situations in which each character defect might have led us to act in a harmful manner and add the names of those concerned to our Eighth Step list.

We can also look at names already on the list and ask ourselves if we have behaved in similar fashion toward others. Many of us discover previously hidden patterns of destructive behavior as a result of putting this list in writing. Even when our defects were not involved, we may have harmed others despite the most honorable intentions. Their names also belong on the list.

Once we are clear about the harm we have done, it becomes possible to make changes and amends so that we can feel better about our behavior and about the way we relate to others.

Today's reminder

An Eighth Step list helps me to let go of guilt and regret I may be carrying from the past. I will approach this Step with love and gentleness because I take it for my own freedom.

". . . Our actions have consequences, and sometimes other people get hurt. By taking Step Eight, we acknowledge this fact and become willing to make amends."

. . . In All Our Affairs

Trying to follow a suggestion I heard in Al-Anon meetings, I dutifully wrote lists of things for which I was grateful. I listed such things as my health, my job, and food on my table. When I was finished, I didn't *feel* very grateful; my mind was still weighted down with the negative thinking that had resulted from living with alcoholism. But I had made a gesture, and the seed of gratitude was planted.

I gradually learned to appreciate the small accomplishments of my daily life. Perhaps I was able to avoid a pointless argument by reciting the Serenity Prayer, or my sharing helped a newcomer, or I finished something I had been neglecting. I was beginning to change. I made a point of recognizing small changes, and my self-esteem grew. The daily application of Al-Anon principles helped me to deepen my sense of gratitude and replace those nagging, negative thoughts. Eventually I was able to go back to my original list and be truly grateful for those things I had taken for granted.

Today's reminder

I need to nurture myself with gratitude. Today I can practice appreciating myself, my world, and my Higher Power.

> "I would lie in bed at night and say the alphabet, counting all the things I had to be grateful for, starting with the letter A . . . This made a great change in my life."
>
> *As We Understood . . .*

In living with the disease of alcoholism, I became a fearful person who dreaded change. Although my life was full of chaos, it was familiar chaos, which gave me the feeling that I had some control over it. This was an illusion. I have learned in Al-Anon that I am powerless over alcoholism and many other things. I've also learned that change is inevitable.

I no longer have to assume that change is bad because I can look back at changes that have had a very positive effect on me, such as coming into Al-Anon.

I still have many fears, but the Al-Anon program has shown me that my Higher Power will help me walk through them. I believe that there is a Power greater than myself, and I choose to trust this Power to know exactly what I need and when I need it.

Today's reminder

Today I can accept the changes occurring in my life and live more comfortably with them. I will trust in the God of my understanding, and my fears will diminish. I relax in this knowledge, knowing that I am always taken care of when I listen to my inner voice.

"We may wonder how we are going to get through all the stages and phases, the levels of growth and recovery . . . Knowing we are not alone often quiets our fears and helps us gain perspective."

Living With Sobriety

The Fifth Step ("Admitted to God, to ourselves, and to another human being the exact nature of our wrongs") is a very intimate experience in which we share our private thoughts and experiences with another person. Much has been said about the freedom this Step offers to the person who is doing the talking, but it can be extremely rewarding to the listener as well.

Most of us feel deeply honored to be entrusted to share in such a sensitive and personal experience. It's a wonderful opportunity to practice giving unconditional love and support by simply listening. Many of us hear stories that are similar to our own; others can often identify with the feelings that are expressed. Perhaps we will be reminded of where we have been and how far we have come. We also see that, despite our outward differences, we have a great deal in common with others.

Whether we practice this Step by listening or speaking, we open ourselves as channels for our Higher Power. More often than not, we hear something that sheds light on our own situation.

Today's reminder

When I respond to a request for help with working the Al-Anon program, I help myself as well.

"There is no better way to keep our spiritual benefits than by giving them away with love, free of expectations, and with no strings attached."

... *In All Our Affairs*

One of my character defects is to respond in kind to behavior that is directed at me—to react to insults with more insults, to rudeness with rudeness. I never thought to act any other way until I began travelling to work with a long-time member of Al-Anon. Each day, when my friend would stop to buy the morning paper, the person behind the counter was surly and hostile. No matter how rudely she was treated, my friend consistently behaved with courtesy. I was outraged! Doesn't Al-Anon tell us we don't have to accept unacceptable behavior? Finally I asked her about it.

She told me that, since this is the only newsstand around, she would rather detach from the behavior than do without her morning paper. She explained that she is powerless over other people's attitudes, but she doesn't have to permit them to goad her into lowering her own standards for herself. To the best of her ability, she chooses to treat everyone she meets with courtesy. Other people are free to make whatever choices they prefer.

Today's reminder

Today I will "Let it begin with me." I do not have to accept unacceptable behavior; I can begin by refusing to accept it from myself. I can choose to behave courteously and with dignity.

> "My freedom and independence do not depend on any acts of defiance or confrontation. They depend on my own attitudes and feelings. If I am always reacting, then I am never free."

Al-Anon is for Adult Children of Alcoholics

An Al-Anon friend says, "I have a tendency to think of my experience with alcoholism as an epic, technicolor movie, an extravaganza with my name in lights on the marquee, but it's not really like that. It's really just home movies." From time to time I have shared my friend's exaggerated vision, though of course when I did, the name in lights was my own.

I came to this program with a story to tell that seemed to splash across every inch of a very wide screen. I told it and told it, until one day I noticed that I was sitting in a room with others, showing home movies.

Today I feel happy to be there as part of the show, but my role has changed. I am no longer the martyr, bravely sacrificing myself to the cold, cruel world of melodrama. Realism has taken over. My role is important, but not unique, and I don't expect to see it in lights.

Today's reminder

Al-Anon has given me an opportunity to share my home movies with others. My situation is neither the best nor the worst. Although I am unique in some ways, I am more like others than I ever suspected. I will appreciate this sense of fellowship today.

"... As we learn to place our problem in its true perspective, we find it loses its power to dominate our thoughts and our lives."

Suggested Al-Anon Welcome

I find myself taking Step Three over and over again. Unfortunately, I often wait until a problem starts to overwhelm me before I finally give in and turn it over to my Higher Power. Nevertheless, today I am striving to place my entire will and life in my Higher Power's hands with the willingness to accept His or Her will for me, no matter what.

The awareness I have gained in Al-Anon lets me know that my way has seldom worked in the past. It's only when I let go and trust the inner voice that quietly nudges me in the direction of my Higher Power's choosing that my life becomes fulfilling.

Today's reminder

Is there an area in my life that I treat as though it were too important to turn over to a Higher Power? Are my efforts to control that area making my life better and more manageable? Are they doing any good at all? I can hold on to my will until the situation becomes so painful that I am forced to submit, or I can put my energy where it can do me some good right now, and surrender to my Higher Power's care.

"I have held many things in my hands, and I have lost them all; but whatever I have placed in God's hands, that I still possess."

Martin Luther

When I first came to Al-Anon, I thought that anger, resentment, jealousy, and fear were "bad" feelings. The program has helped me to learn that feelings are neither good nor bad—they are simply a part of who I am.

I have come to realize that good has sometimes come as a result of those feelings. Anger has prompted some constructive changes in my life. Resentment has made me so uncomfortable that I've had to learn to combat it—as a result, I have learned to pray for other people. Jealousy has taught me to keep my mouth shut when I know I will say only irrational, destructive things. And fear has been perhaps my greatest gift, because it forces me to make conscious contact with my Higher Power.

Now that the negative has become the positive, I am better able to accept the whole picture. There is no more need to judge or hate myself just because I experience a human feeling.

Today's reminder

Feelings may not be comfortable, but that doesn't make them bad. With a change of attitude, I have choices about what to do with my feelings. Anything can be used for my good if I allow it. Recognizing this opportunity may take every ounce of imagination I have, but maybe that's why God gave me imagination to begin with.

"My feelings are neither right nor wrong but are important by virtue of being mine."

. . . In All Our Affairs

"If only I had infinite wisdom," I secretly think. "If only I could see everything before me, a clear path, the knowledge of how I must spend each moment of life!" But in meeting after meeting in Al-Anon I am reminded that I can only work with what I have today. I don't know what tomorrow will bring. What's more, I am probably better off not knowing. If I knew what was coming, I suspect that I would spend all my time trying to run from painful experiences instead of living. I would miss out on so much great stuff.

I can trust my Higher Power to lead me through this day so that I will be prepared for the future when it arrives and able to work with whatever it brings. This leaves me time to enjoy the many gifts life has to offer, time that would otherwise be spent worrying.

Today's reminder

An old maxim says, "It'll shine when it shines." If I am willing to listen, I will receive all the information I need when the time is right. "Just for today" I will know that I'm in good hands.

> "Just for today I will try to live through this day only, and not tackle all my problems at once."
>
> *Just For Today*

I received a powerful lesson about letting go one night at an Al-Anon business meeting. It took lots of courage for me to suggest that my home group include the entire Serenity Prayer as part of the meeting opening. Another member suggested that we read the Traditions more regularly.

The group conscience approved the motion about the Traditions, while my pet project, the Serenity Prayer, was shot down. I sat there feeling swollen with offended pride, but something I had learned in Al-Anon kept pounding in my head: "to place principles above personalities." Suddenly it didn't matter that my suggestion had been defeated. We were all together in fellowship, and that was all that mattered.

Within the safety of my Al-Anon group I learn to let go of needing to have my way. With practice, I am able to apply this lesson to all of my relationships.

Today's reminder

It is important to express my ideas. It is also important to accept the outcome. I can acknowledge myself for taking the risk to speak out, knowing that the results of my actions are out of my hands. Today I choose to trust those results to my Higher Power.

> "Your proper concern is alone the *action* of duty, not the *fruits* of the action. Cast then away all desire and fear for the fruits, and perform your duty."
>
> *The Bhagavad Gita*

Some alcoholics become abusive, especially when they drink. How do we handle violence? What can we do about it?

Al-Anon doesn't give specific advice about relationships—we don't advocate ending them or continuing to build them. Those decisions are best left to each individual member to make when he or she feels ready. We do, however, emphasize our personal responsibility to take care of ourselves. If we know that physical danger is a part of our reality, we can admit it and take steps to protect ourselves, at least temporarily. We may arrange for a safe place to go at any hour if we need it. It may be wise to keep money and car keys in easy access. Perhaps we'll also seek counselling or speak with the police about our options.

No one has the right to physically abuse anyone else under any circumstances. We can inventory our own behavior to see if we are contributing to the problem by provoking someone who is drunk, and we can work to change that behavior. But we do not cause another to be violent or abusive.

Today's reminder
I don't have the power to change another person. If I am dealing with violence, I must be the one who changes. I'll start by being honest about what is going on.

"There is hope, there is help, and I have an inalienable right to human dignity."

                                    . . . *In All Our Affairs*

Just for today I can try out new behavior. I can take the point of view that perhaps I have been given a lifetime to learn something about myself. Maybe life is a series of experiments in which some succeed and some fail—and in which the failures, as well as the successes, point the way to fresh experiments.

Just for today I might try slightly changing some pattern of behavior that repeatedly causes me problems, just to see what happens. For example, if I have a habit of responding with a negative attitude to a particular person or situation—getting out of bed, working, requests for help, authority figures—I can try a different, more positive response. I can think of it as research and learn from whatever happens.

This day is all I have to work with. The past is over, and tomorrow is out of my reach. I will try to remember what a great gift this day can be and make full use of it.

Today's reminder

Just for today I will look for ways to enjoy life—stop by a garden, try a new hobby, or call a good friend. I can look for humor. I can savor love. I can explore something new. Maybe just for today, I'll try standing on my head to see if I like the view.

> "Just for today I will find a little time to relax and to realize what life is and can be; time to think about God and get a better perspective on myself."
>
> *Alcoholism, The Family Disease*

Suddenly I am aware of thoughts racing and crashing through my mind at an alarming speed—memories, broken promises, fears about the future, failed expectations of both myself and other people. This is a familiar chaos and one that I can now recognize. It is a signal that my life has, for the time being, become unmanageable.

At such a time, serenity is often just a phone call away. A simple acknowledgement of the chaos immediately diminishes it. I step back, step outside the madness, and all at once it washes away or scatters in all the myriad directions from which it came. The pieces of my chaos return to their proper places, where I can either leave them alone or choose to confront them one at a time.

Today's reminder

If problems arise today, I will try to acknowledge them—and then put a little spiritual space between my problems and myself. If I can share about them with another person, I will further diminish their power. Recognizing that my life is unmanageable is the first step toward managing it.

". . . When we bring things out into the light, they lose their power over us."

. . . In All Our Affairs

It is essential to my recovery to help my Al-Anon group by accepting any of the various responsibilities necessary to keep things running smoothly. Perhaps the principal reason that service is so vital is that it brings me into frequent contact with newcomers. I can get caught up in the trivial problems of everyday life and lose perspective on the many gifts I have received since coming to Al-Anon. Talking with newcomers brings me back to reality. When I set out literature, make coffee, or chair a meeting, I become someone a newcomer might think to approach.

I remember the frustration of struggling with alcoholism by myself. I had no tools, no one to talk to. Al-Anon changed that. Now, no matter how difficult things may seem, I have a fellowship and a way of life that help me to cope. I am no longer alone.

Today I have much for which I am grateful, but I need to remember how far I have come so I don't get lost in negativity over relatively unimportant matters. Service helps me remember.

Today's reminder

The Al-Anon program was there for me when I needed it. I will do what I can to ensure that it continues to thrive. I know that any service I offer will strengthen my own recovery.

> "God did for me what I couldn't do for myself. He got me involved in service work . . . It saved my life, my family, my sanity."

> *. . . In All Our Affairs*

Clearly, I didn't know what compassion was, but I knew what it was not. Compassion was not seeking revenge, holding a grudge, calling names, or screaming and throwing things in anger. Yet that was how I frequently behaved toward this person I claimed to love. For me, the beginning of learning compassion was to eliminate such behavior.

While I still have a hard time defining compassion, I think it starts with the recognition that I am dealing with a sick person who sometimes exhibits symptoms of a disease. I don't have to take it personally when these symptoms, such as verbal abuse, appear, nor do I have the right to punish anyone for being sick.

I am a worthwhile human being. I don't have to sit and take abuse. But I have no right to dish it out, either.

Today's reminder

I will spend more time with myself in this lifetime than with anyone else. Let me learn to be the kind of person I would like to have as a friend.

"He who would have beautiful roses in his garden must have beautiful roses in his heart."

S. R. Hole

I've heard it said that in Al-Anon we try to concentrate on our similarities rather than our differences. This doesn't mean that we don't have differences or that we shouldn't acknowledge these differences. What it does suggest is that, by remembering why we are all here, we need never feel alone.

Like so many others, I came to Al-Anon feeling that my problems set me apart from everyone else. As time passed, I realized that it was my own fear and shame, and not the embarrassing details of my problems, that kept me at a distance. I learned that, when I reached beyond these details, I could clasp the hands of others affected by alcoholism and thus find help.

We are all as unique as our fingerprints, but as our fingers join in the closing prayer, each of us is part of a circle of hope that is greater than any of our individual differences.

Today's reminder

Although we have our unique qualities, all hearts beat the same under the skin. Your heart reaches out to mine as you share your story and your faith. I know that the part of myself which I share with you is taken to your heart. Today I will cherish our collective strength.

> "For the body is one and has many members, but all the members of that one body, being many, are one body."

> *The Bible*

Sometimes I become so bogged down with dissatisfaction that I can't see where I am or where I'm going. When I take time to "Think," I realize that negativity keeps my life at a standstill. Al-Anon has helped me discover that, while it's good to acknowledge whatever I feel, I have a choice about where to focus my attention. I'm challenged to find positive qualities in myself, my circumstances, and other human beings. As I attend meetings, list the things I am grateful for, and talk with other Al-Anon members, these attributes become apparent—if I'm willing to see them.

I believe I have a beautiful spirit that has been created for some purpose. The people and situations I encounter each day also have beauty and purpose. I can begin to look for the positive in everything I do and see. The perspective I've gained by doing so has shown me that some of the most difficult times in my life have produced the most wonderful changes.

Today's reminder

It may be difficult to break a long-established pattern of depression, doom-saying, and complaining, but it's worth the effort. I'll replace a negative attitude with a positive one today.

"Sometimes I go about pitying myself
And all the while I am being carried across
  the sky
By beautiful clouds."

Ojibway Indian saying

Although the crisis that brought us to Al-Anon may be past, there is always something new to learn, even after years of recovery. We change. Opportunities for spiritual growth, as well as new character defects, pop up like weeds in a newly-mown lawn, and we find ourselves turning to the Steps for a fresh look.

I experienced this one day when I noticed that I had begun to be angry much of the time. I thought that other people and situations were to blame, but I decided to concentrate on my own part of the picture. I took a written inventory of my memories, feelings, and behavior whenever I lost my serenity, and then read it aloud to someone I trust. As I read, the common thread—the exact nature of my wrongs—jumped out at me. My problem was my pride and arrogance, not my situation. The need to be right was robbing me of my serenity in all kinds of situations.

No matter how long I work the Al-Anon program, I will never cease finding new ways to apply it to my life. That is a blessing, for it means that my life will continue to get better.

Today's reminder

There is something new for me to learn today. I will open my mind and my heart to the lessons my Higher Power brings me.

"The important thing is not to stop questioning."

Albert Einstein

I felt my life was on hold. I wanted change; I expected it; I even tried to *make* it happen. But it was not within my power to make any of the changes I wanted. I was frustrated. I'm an action-taker, so I feel better when I am busy and industrious. There *is* a time to act. But in Al-Anon I learned that there is also a time to *not* act—to stop and wait. As my sponsor puts it, "Don't just do something, sit there."

How often I still find myself impatient with the pace of life. But today, when things don't happen according to my schedule, I can accept that there may be a reason, and I can learn to adjust to what is. I may be experiencing great change on the inside even though I see little evidence on the outside. I can keep in mind that waiting time doesn't have to mean wasted time. Even times of stillness have lessons to teach me.

Today's reminder

The invitation to live life fully is offered to me each day. I can accept the pace of change today, knowing it will bring both times of active involvement and periods of quiet waiting. I will let the surprises of the day open up before me.

> "Besides the noble art of getting things done, there is the noble art of leaving things undone. The wisdom of life consists in the elimination of non-essentials."
>
> Lin Yutang

My life is a miracle! When I felt alone and far from hope, I was guided to Al-Anon, where I learned that no situation is really hopeless. Others had been through the pain of coping with a loved one's alcoholism. They too had known frustration, anger, disappointment, and anxiety, yet had learned to live serene and even happy lives. Through the program, the tools that lead to serenity and the gift of recovery are mine for the taking, along with the support I need. Just as I was guided to Al-Anon, I am guided through recovery, and I continue to be transformed.

I see that miracles frequently touch my life. Maybe they always have, but I didn't see them. Today I am aware of many gifts and wonders because I am actively practicing gratitude. So I thank my Higher Power for little things as well as big ones. I am grateful for the snooze button on my alarm clock that gives me a few extra minutes of sleep, as well as for the roof over my head, the clothes on my back, and the ability to give and receive love.

Today's reminder

When I take time for gratitude, I perceive a better world. Today I will appreciate the miracles all around me.

> "Even the darkest of moments can be faced with a grateful heart, if not for the crisis itself, at least for the growth it can evoke with the help of our Higher Power."
>
> . . . *In All Our Affairs*

I used to think of God as my adversary. We were engaged in a battle of wills, and I wasn't about to let down my guard. You can imagine how quickly this attitude led me to hit a hard emotional bottom! I came to Al-Anon, but I was reluctant to admit that I was powerless. I knew it was true—I had obviously failed to conquer alcoholism—but I wasn't going to submit to my enemy!

I'm so grateful to Al-Anon for helping me learn to surrender. It took a long time, but I finally realized that surrender does not mean submission— it means I'm willing to stop fighting reality, to stop trying to do God's part, and to do my own.

When I gather flowers, or marvel at nature's wonders, I do not lose face when I concede that I am not in control. So it is with everything in my life. The best way I've found to invite serenity is to recognize that the world is in good hands.

Today's reminder

Today I can be grateful that the earth will continue to revolve without any help from me. I am free to live my own life, safe in the knowledge that a Higher Power is taking care of the world, my loved ones, and myself.

> "The First Step prepares us for a new life, which we can achieve only by letting go of what we cannot control, and by undertaking, one day at a time, the monumental task of setting our world in order through a change in our own thinking."
>
> *One Day at a Time in Al-Anon*

The road to my hometown wound along a steep hillside. As a child, I was often afraid that our car would swerve too widely and go over the edge. I used to take hold of the rear door handle and try to prevent this. I was too young to understand that my actions could not influence the path of the car. Yet I often take a similar approach to my adult fears and persist in futile actions.

Al-Anon helps me to accept what I cannot change and change what I can. Although I can't control the way alcoholism has affected my life, I can't control another person, and I can't make life unfold according to my plans, I can admit my powerlessness and turn to my Higher Power for help.

When I am the driver, the responsibility for steering clear of the road's edge is mine. It is up to me to take my recovery seriously, to work on my attitudes, to take care of my mind, body, and spirit, to make amends when I have done harm— in short, to change the things I can.

Today's reminder

Sometimes the only way I can determine what to accept and what to change is by trial and error. Mistakes can be opportunities to gain the wisdom to know the difference.

> "If a crisis arises, or any problem baffles me, I hold it up to the light of the Serenity Prayer and extract its sting before it can hurt me."
>
> *One Day at a Time in Al-Anon*

When I was a beginner in Al-Anon, it was suggested that I learn about the disease of alcoholism, and I became a voracious reader on the subject. As I read, I began to analyze everything: Was Al-Anon a philosophy or a philosophical system? What would be the logical outcome of believing in a Power greater than myself? And just when was the alcoholic going to have a spiritual awakening?

These questions and others like them kept my mind busy but did not help me to get better. Fortunately, I continued to go to Al-Anon meetings and I read, reread, and rehearsed the Twelve Steps and Twelve Traditions. Gradually I began to catch on. When I stopped trying to analyze and explain everything and started living the principles, actually using them in my everyday situations, the Al-Anon program suddenly made sense—and I started to change.

Today's reminder

Does analyzing my situation provide any useful insights, or is it an attempt to control the uncontrollable? Am I taking inventory or avoiding work that needs to be done by keeping my mind occupied? I have heard that knowledge is power. But sometimes my thirst for knowledge can be an attempt to exercise power where I am powerless. Instead, I can take the First Step.

> "Life can only be understood backwards, but it must be lived forwards."
>
> Soren Kierkegaard

I *needed* my husband to get sober so that we could live happily ever after, because I couldn't face the ugly disease that overshadowed every aspect of our relationship, and I couldn't face the emptiness I felt in my own life. It was so much nicer to think about a future of bliss, if only he'd change.

In Al-Anon I had to unlearn a lot of romantic nonsense in order to find a satisfying life in the here-and-now. When my husband and I separated, my fantasies crashed, but with the support of the program, I learned to look to myself for happiness and to my own real life for enrichment. Two years later, when my husband and I reunited, I had to unlearn a new illusion, this time about recovery. My idea of health was now based on living alone. I had to learn to find a balance between taking care of myself and being there for my partner; I had to learn to love again.

Today's reminder

Recovery can involve as much unlearning as learning. My security cannot be based on learning "the rules," because once I truly learn them, they change. With my Higher Power's help, I will find some security in being exactly where I am today.

> "The Twelve Steps of our program have led me to a faith in God today which is based on acceptance of the world as it is. I no longer agonize over how the world should be."
>
> *As We Understood . . .*

Al-Anon meetings opened my eyes to something I had never thought about before: Shouting and slamming doors were not the best way to handle an already difficult situation. While there may be no harm in occasionally letting off steam with a raised voice, shouting can become a destructive habit. I'd never thought to ask myself if this was how I wanted to behave. Did this behavior get me what I wanted or encourage me to feel good about myself?

When I took a good look, I realized that the answer to this question was, "No." Loud, angry words and actions demonstrated my frustration and pushed away all hope for peaceful solutions to my problems.

The slogan that helps me back to a rational state of mind is "Easy does it." When I use this slogan to quiet myself on the inside, it is easier to quiet the outside as well.

Today's reminder

I am seeking a saner approach to everything I encounter. The slogans can be valuable sources of sanity in chaotic situations. Today, if I am tempted to act out of anger or frustration, I will remember that "Easy does it."

> "I will try to apply "Easy does it" to every incident that might increase the tension and cause an explosion."
>
> *One Day at a Time in Al-Anon*

"Do not search for the truth," said an ancient patriarch, "only cease to cherish opinions." For me, ceasing to cherish opinions is part of the Tenth Step. Much of what I find wrong in my life is related to my opinions—that is, my prejudices, assumptions, self-righteous stances, attitudes.

For example, I continue to assume that I have the inside track on how everything should be done, and that other people are too short-sighted to recognize this great truth. Reality proves me wrong. I also revert to the idea that ignoring my feelings is practical, even desirable. This, too, is wrong. And I act as if I can run my life without trusting in my Higher Power. Wrong again.

I give thanks for Step Ten's reminder that I need to continue taking personal inventory and making frequent corrections, especially in the areas where I tend to repeat my mistakes.

Today's reminder

It is no easy task to change the thinking of a lifetime, even when I am sure that I want to change. The Tenth Step allows me to be aware of sliding back into faulty thinking. I don't have to abuse myself when it happens—that doesn't help at all. By promptly admitting when I'm wrong, I am doing what I can to change.

"No longer must we accumulate burdens of guilt or resentment that will become heavier and more potent over time. Each day, each new moment can be an opportunity to clear the air and start again, fresh and free."

. . . In All Our Affairs

The most loving form of detachment I have found has been forgiveness. Instead of thinking of it as an eraser to wipe another's slate clean or a gavel that I pound to pronounce someone "not guilty," I think of forgiveness as a scissors. I use it to cut the strings of resentment that bind me to a problem or a past hurt. By releasing resentment, I set myself free.

When I am consumed with negativity over another person's behavior, I have lost my focus. I needn't tolerate what I consider unacceptable, but wallowing in negativity will not alter the situation. If there is action to take, I am free to take it. Where I am powerless to change the situation, I will turn it over to my Higher Power. By truly letting go, I detach and forgive.

When my thoughts are full of bitterness, fear, self-pity, and dreams of revenge, there is little room for love or for the quiet voice of guidance within me. I am willing to love myself enough to admit that resentments hold me back, and then I can let them go.

Today's reminder

Every time I try to tighten the noose of resentment around someone's neck, I am really only choking myself. Today I will practice forgiveness instead.

"A part of me wants to cling to old resentments, but I know that the more I forgive, the better my life works."

. . . In All Our Affairs

When I am trying to tackle a tough problem or cope with a stressful situation, and I've done all I can for the moment, what then? I can do something that will nurture my mind, body, or spirit. Perhaps I'll take a walk or listen to music. Maybe I'll meet a friend for coffee and conversation. I could have something nutritious to eat, or sit quietly and meditate, or read a book.

Al-Anon is a program of action in which we recognize that we have choices about what we do with our time. A bubble bath, a massage, an Al-Anon call, a bike ride, or a nap might be constructive ways to fill time that might otherwise be wasted on worry.

Even though I may be powerless to change my circumstances, I certainly am not helpless. I can use my time to do something good for myself. When I treat myself with love and tenderness, I am better able to deal with the challenges that life presents. I have a chance to feel good, even when surrounded by crisis.

Today's reminder

One of my primary responsibilities is to take care of myself. I will find a small way to do something for my mind, body, and spirit today.

". . . part of my recovery is respecting my need and my right to let go and relax."

. . . In All Our Affairs

As newcomers, many of us were surprised by the absence of rules in Al-Anon. Before we found recovery from the effects of alcoholism, a strict sense of order may have been our only way of feeling that we had some control. Naturally we expected a program as successful as Al-Anon to be even more rigid than we were!

Instead, as a newcomer I was told that I was free to work the Steps at my own pace. I could ask questions of anyone as they came up. No one was in charge, yet everyone was in charge. It seemed impossible, yet I could see it working more effectively than any organization with which I'd ever been involved.

As I continue coming to Al-Anon, I'm learning to trust that the group is guided by a Higher Power whose will is expressed in our group conscience. I watch the Traditions in action, guiding us by suggestions rather than rules. And I learn to trust my fellow members, each of whom contributes to the well-being of our fellowship, where no one person is in charge.

Today's reminder

If I take on service responsibilities in my group, it does not mean that I now run the show. Today I will remember that the ultimate authority is a Higher Power who works through all of us.

"Our groups, as such, ought never be organized; but we may create service boards or committees directly responsible to those they serve."

Tradition Nine

As we pursue recovery, we may encounter opportunities to deepen learning we began long ago. Perhaps we once learned to detach from a particular problem. Now, months or years later, when we once again need to detach, it can feel as if we've forgotten everything we knew. It's important to remember at such moments that, although the feelings may be the same, *we* are not the same.

My recovery matters. All of the experience, strength, and hope I have accumulated is within me today, guiding my choices. I may not recognize it right now, but I have made progress, and I continue to make progress with every step I take. Perhaps I am learning something I have learned before; I must need to know it more deeply. I may go through the process this time with greater awareness, or turn to my Higher Power more quickly and easily, or reach out to an Al-Anon friend without hesitation.

Today's reminder

Instead of assuming that I have failed because I am learning a difficult lesson once more, I might embrace the experience as part of a long-term healing process that requires repetition and practice. I can trust that eventually I will learn it so well that it will become an automatic, confident, and healthy response.

"The human mind always makes progress, but it is a progress in spirals."

Madame de Stael

I have recently been reminded that I am not responsible for the workings of the entire universe. An unexpected transfer at my job sent me to a new city, and I had only one week to find a place for my family to live. After three unsuccessful days, I grew frantic. I had been in Al-Anon long enough to know that I needed a meeting. Listening to others share about taking care of our responsibilities and trusting a Higher Power with the rest, I was reminded that I could only do my best. I could do the footwork, but I couldn't force the house to appear. I had to "Let go and let God." On the last day of my search, I found a wonderful place to live.

Struggling and worrying didn't help me to solve my problem. Doing my part and trusting my Higher Power with the rest did.

Today's reminder

What I can't do, my Higher Power can. When I "Let go and let God," I am free to take risks and to make mistakes. I know that I am powerless over many things. Today I can take comfort in knowing that I don't have the power to ruin God's plans.

"Have courage for the great sorrows of life and patience for the small ones; and when you have laboriously accomplished your daily task, go to sleep in peace. God is awake."

Victor Hugo

As a child, I would get down on my hands and
knees for the longest time, just to watch a cater-
pillar crawl around. It never seemed to go very
far, yet I patiently waited just in case it should do
something spectacular. It never did, but I didn't
mind, because simply watching this peculiar-look-
ing creature gave me pleasure.

Remembering this makes me question how
many such precious moments are passing me by
unnoticed because I am so focused on other things.
Before Al-Anon, I spent years ignoring life's
beauty because I was too busy trying to get all
the alcoholics to stop drinking, and in recovery
I've lost many, many hours waiting to solve a
problem or be freed of a character defect. Today I
am learning to make room in my life for the wonders life has to offer.

Today's reminder

I am learning to choose where to focus my attention. Appreciating life's simple gifts may take
some practice, but as I become more aware of the
beauty that is all around me, it gets easier to appreciate the beauty within.

"Just for today I will be unafraid. Especially, I
will not be afraid to enjoy what is beautiful . . ."

                                      Just For Today

Many times I have said, "I wish I had faith." And what I've heard from so many wise Al-Anon members is, "Surrender your lack of faith to your Higher Power, and ask for faith."

I have said, "I know I am powerless, but I feel so helpless, frightened, hopeless," and I have been told I had the option to surrender those feelings and ask for what I need. Powerless does not mean helpless. In fact, it can lead us to a source of enormous power—the power to carry out God's will.

I have also said, "I can't figure out what God wants me to do, though I've prayed for guidance." My loving sponsor always says, "God doesn't speak in code. Ask for clarity, and then trust that you will get it when the time is right."

When in doubt, I am learning that the answer is to ask.

Today's reminder

After years of asking only for a particular solution to a problem, such as, "Please make the alcoholic stop drinking!"—I need to learn a better way to ask for help. Today I will meditate for a few minutes on what I need, and then I will ask a Power greater than myself to help me with it.

"Even if we have struggled with the idea of a Higher Power, we have learned that asking for help works . . ."

. . . In All Our Affairs

When I finally found the courage to speak at an Al-Anon meeting, my sharing was limited to problems I had already solved. I concealed my real feelings by telling funny stories about myself and the alcoholic, because I didn't trust anyone enough to let them see my struggle and my pain. I had a hard enough time facing it by myself. But I didn't seem to be getting better. Only when I was able to stop playing the clown and admit my shortcomings did I begin to enjoy the spiritual growth promised in the Twelve Steps.

The paradox of self-honesty is that I need the help of others to achieve it. I need their support to explore my feelings and motives, and to see that others have benefited from taking this great risk.

Today's reminder

In an alcoholic environment, I had good reasons to hide my feelings, making light of serious situations, overworking, overplaying, managing to focus on everything but myself. Today I have other options. I can begin to listen to what my heart has been trying to tell me, and I can look for someone trustworthy with whom I can share it.

> "It may feel like an enormous risk, but talking honestly about the situation is the key to healing."
>
> *. . . In All Our Affairs*

When the alcoholic I loved got sober I was sure that the nightmare was over! But without the tranquilizing effect of alcohol, she became verbally abusive. She accused, attacked, insulted, and I always defended myself. It seemed crucial that she understand. But that didn't happen, no matter how much I argued, pleaded, or insulted in return. I felt trapped and hopeless.

Sobriety brings change, but it doesn't take away all the problems. Al-Anon helps me learn that I don't have to accept the unacceptable, nor do I have to argue back or convince another person that I'm innocent or right. I can begin to recognize when I am dealing with alcoholism's insanity, and I can detach. I certainly don't have to respond by doubting myself.

Today's reminder

When cruel words fly from the mouth of another person, drunk or sober, Al-Anon helps me remember that I have choices. Perhaps I can say the Serenity Prayer to myself, or refuse to discuss the topic any further. I can listen without taking the words personally; I can leave the room, change the subject, make an Al-Anon call, or explore other alternatives. My sponsor can help me to discover options that seem right for me.

"We may never have the choices we would have if we were writing the script, but we always have choices."

. . . In All Our Affairs

The process of recovery in Al-Anon has been likened to peeling an onion. We peel away a layer at a time, often shedding a few tears as we do.

But recovery always makes me think of the bark of a birch tree. The birch's bark is necessary for protection, yet as the tree grows, the bark peels away gradually of its own accord. If it is removed prematurely—by a deer scraping his antlers or a porcupine searching for food—the tree is wounded and becomes vulnerable to infection, fungus, and insects.

Like the birch tree, I can be wounded if I am prematurely stripped of my defenses. Most of us have spent a significant amount of time trying to cope with these wounds from the past rather than growing and changing. But in Al-Anon I am encouraged to grow at my own pace. As I do, I find some of my defenses and ideas too tight, too limiting. And so I slough them off, just as the birch releases its old skin. They are no longer needed.

Today's reminder

I have an innate ability to heal and to grow. I don't need to force myself to change. All I have to do is show up and be willing. When I am ready, the changes will come easily.

> ". . . We all have our own answers within ourselves and can find them with the help of our Al-Anon program and a Higher Power."
>
> . . . *In All Our Affairs*

One of my defects of character is to make choices passively—letting things happen rather than taking action. For example, I stood by and watched my children suffer abuse because I was unable to make a decision and follow through with it. I had been severely affected by alcoholism, and I was not capable of doing otherwise at the time. It was the best I could do under the circumstances, but harm was done, and I owe amends.

One way to make amends is to stop practicing the defect. In every area of my life I can ask myself: Am I taking responsibility for my choices today? Do I make a positive contribution to my meetings, or do I assume that somebody else will take care of everything? Am I making choices I can be proud of at home, at work, and in my community, or letting the choices be made for me?

Today's reminder

Al-Anon has no opinion on outside issues. It doesn't define my responsibilities or select my values—that is up to me. It does encourage me to define my values, to take responsibility for choices I am already making, and to make amends where I have done harm. I need not think of myself as a victim of unseen forces that make disasters happen. Today I can make active choices.

> "Making amends isn't just saying, 'I'm sorry.' It means responding differently from our new understanding."
>
> *As We Understood . . .*

I remember others' unkind words vividly. Criticism sent me reeling. Snickers crippled me for days. It never occurred to me that I was being abused, or that the harsh words could be untrue. Everyone seemed to know just how wrong I was, and my identity was bound up in a knot of shame. My self-esteem sank lower and lower.

I, in turn, treated others cruelly. I found it great fun to assault someone's character in the company of friends. For a few minutes I felt better about myself—but not for long and only at other people's expense. Gossip never enriched anyone's character. It was only an excuse to avoid focusing on myself.

Today's reminder

Many of us tend to react rather than act. When we hurt, we may want to strike out and hurt someone else. In Al-Anon we learn that we can interrupt this automatic response long enough to decide how we really want to behave.

Someone else's unkindness is no reason for me to lower my standards for my own behavior. When I take responsibility for my actions, regardless of what other people do, I become someone I can be proud of. When I feel good about myself, it's much easier not to take insults personally.

"If one throws salt at thee thou wilt receive no harm unless thou hast sore places."

Latin proverb

One sweltering summer day, I sought escape from the heat at a nearby beach. Lying there with my lemonade, I looked at all the people soaking up the sun. No matter how many people were on that beach, there would be enough sun for everyone. I realized that the same was true of God's love and guidance. No matter how many people seek God's help, there is always enough to go around. To someone who believed that there was never enough time, money, love, or anything else, this was amazing news!

This awareness was tested at an Al-Anon meeting when someone spoke about his Higher Power with a personal love and intensity that matched my own. I felt as if his intimacy with God would leave less love for me. But I think that the opposite is true. I often feel closest to God when I hear others share about how well a Higher Power has taken care of them. Today I try to remember that there is enough love for us all.

Today's reminder

I may not have everything I want, but today I have everything I need. I will look for evidence of abundance and let it remind me that my Higher Power's love is broad enough to touch all who have the courage to place themselves in its presence.

"I can learn to avail myself of the immense, inexhaustible power of God, if I am willing to be *continually* conscious of God's nearness."

One Day at a Time in Al-Anon

It's amazing how my attitude toward others tends to return to me like a basketball rebounding off a backboard. My impatience with other people often generates even more impatience with myself and my world. When I am unkind to someone, I get defensive and expect others to be unkind to me. Likewise, when I accept someone unconditionally, I find that my whole world feels safer.

So it's in my best interest to treat others as I wish to be treated. I try to imagine that my words and actions are being addressed to myself, because in the long run I generally get back what I give out.

If I am unhappy with what I receive, I might try looking for that same behavior in myself. It may not take exactly the same form, but I find that whatever I dislike in another is something that I dislike in myself. The reverse is also true: What I admire in others probably reflects an admirable quality within me.

Today's reminder

There is something for me to learn from every interaction I have with other people. I will make an extra effort today to take note of the attitudes I'm giving and receiving because they both can teach me about myself.

> "Though we travel the world over to find the beautiful, we must carry it with us or we find it not."
>
>   Ralph Waldo Emerson

I recently had an argument with someone I care about. He had made, all too publicly, a few remarks to me about my weight, and I was less than pleased. Later, when I told him that my feelings were hurt, he insisted he had done nothing wrong—that what he had said was true, so I shouldn't take offense.

How often have I justified my own unkindness, or my interfering where I had no business, with that very argument? Too many times, especially during my alcoholic loved one's drinking days. After all, I claimed, I was right: Alcohol was ruining our lives, and it was my duty to say so—again, and again, and again.

I am learning to let go of my certainty about what other people should do. In Al-Anon I heard someone put it this way: "I can be right or I can be happy." I don't have to make anyone over in my image. With help, I can "Live and let live."

Today's reminder

I am not an insensitive person, but at times I have justified insensitive behavior by claiming to be right. I can respect another's right to make his or her own choices, even when I strongly disagree. My relationships will improve if I can love myself enough to let other people be themselves.

> "Lord, when we are wrong, make us willing to change. And when we are right, make us easy to live with."
>
> Peter Marshall

When I was a newcomer to Al-Anon, I remember hearing people say that they were grateful to be involved with an alcoholic. Needless to say, I thought they were crazy! Wasn't the alcoholic the cause of all their grief? I couldn't believe that these people had *anything* to be grateful for. Yet they seemed to be happy despite their problems (which sounded exactly like my own).

Today I find that I am grateful to have found Al-Anon. I too needed to hit a kind of bottom, feel the pain, and reach out for help before I could find any lasting happiness. Because of Al-Anon, I have a relationship with a Higher Power that I never knew existed and friends who give me real support. I have learned that gratitude and forgiveness are necessary to my peace of mind. Now I can truly say that I am a grateful member of Al-Anon.

Today's reminder

Today I will practice gratitude. I will think of some of the things, big or small, for which I am grateful. Maybe I'll even put this list in writing or share it with an Al-Anon friend. Sometimes a tiny action can be a great step toward seeing my life with increasing joy.

"When things look blackest, it is within my power to brighten them with the light of understanding and gratitude."

One Day at a Time in Al-Anon

So many of the choices I've made in my life
have been reactions to fear. Something in my
world changes: a loved one seeks sobriety, a friend
is displeased with something I've said, I'm given
a new task at work, the grocery store runs out of
chicken—and inside I panic. I'm attacked by
thoughts of disaster. I imagine failure, torment,
agony. And then I act. I do something rash or
fruitless in order to put a bandage on the situation, because the one thing I most fear is being
afraid.

Fear can become a power greater than myself.
I may not be able to fix it or make it go away. But
today, with a Higher Power who is greater than
my fears, I don't have to let them run my life or
make my choices for me. I can grab hold of my
Higher Power's hand, face my fears, and move
through them.

Today's reminder

Al-Anon is a program in which we find spiritual solutions to the things we are powerless to
change. Today, instead of seeking relief from fear
by trying to do battle with it, I will turn to my
Higher Power.

"That the birds of worry and care fly above your
head, this you cannot change. But that they build
nests in your hair, this you can prevent."

                                              Chinese proverb

Sometimes a horse refuses to obey the rider's command and races out of control. My thoughts can do this too, when I frantically try, over and over, to solve a difficult problem. Riding lessons have taught me not to continually repeat a command louder, but to stop the horse, get his attention, and begin again.

Likewise, when my thoughts race out of control, I need to stop. I may do this by breathing deeply and looking at my surroundings. It can help to replace the obsessive thoughts with something positive, such as an Al-Anon slogan, the Serenity Prayer, or another comforting topic that has nothing to do with my problem.

Later I may want to think about the problem again in a more serene way with the help of an Al-Anon friend or sponsor. When I put some distance between myself and obsessive thinking, I can better look at my situation without losing all control.

Today's reminder

Sometimes I have to let go of a problem before I can find a solution. My racing thoughts may be making so much noise that I can't hear the guidance my inner voice is offering. Quieting the noise is a skill I can learn with practice. At first I may have to still my thoughts again and again, but in Al-Anon I learn that practice makes progress, one minute, one thought at a time.

"All men's miseries derive from not being able to sit quiet in a room alone."

Blaise Pascal

Step Two states that we "Came to believe that a Power greater than ourselves could restore us to sanity." Recently at a meeting I heard someone paraphrase this Step in a way that perfectly described my own experience: "First I came, then I 'came to,' then I came to believe."

The journey toward a Higher Power has been so gradual for me that I have been unaware of much of it. There has been no burst of light, no burning bush—just a gradual clearing of the fog that I lived in before finding recovery in Al-Anon. Like my fellow member, first I came, bringing my body, if not my faith, to Al-Anon. Then, once I was here, slowly I "came to," and eventually I came to believe that I wasn't alone in the universe. There was and is a force, a drive, an energy that can give me the means to make my life joyous and productive. I need only ask for assistance and keep an open mind.

Today's reminder

The arrival of faith in my life has been a gradual process. This process continues and grows stronger each day I keep myself open to it. Perhaps acknowledging this process will help me when I am impatient with the twists and turns of life.

> "I find the great thing in this world is not so much where we stand as in what direction we are moving."
>
> Oliver Wendell Holmes

By the time we reach Al-Anon, many of us are starving to be heard. We bask in the discovery that the Al-Anon rooms are safe places in which we can talk about the things that have been pent up inside. We share, and the people around us nod with understanding. They talk with us after meetings and mention how much they identify, or they thank us for sharing. Finally we are heard and appreciated by others who have been there too.

This attention can feel so refreshing that we may be tempted to overdo it. Many of us fear to let go of this chance to speak openly, as if it were our last opportunity. But when any member regularly dominates the sharing at meetings, the group suffers.

In keeping with our Traditions, the well-being of the group must come first. That's one reason sponsorship is such a valuable tool. Our needs for self-expression are real and should be addressed. A sponsor can give us the time and attention we need to talk about ourselves and our lives.

Today's reminder

My needs are important. Al-Anon helps me to find appropriate ways in which to meet them. I will take good care of myself today.

"... Very personal details ... are better left to a sponsor who can lend a consistent ear and keep a confidence—someone who knows all about you and accepts you as you are.

Sponsorship—What It's All About

Sometimes I am called upon to accept unpleasant realities. I may wish to avoid disappointments, but I find that the only way to have serenity is to become willing to accept the things I cannot change. Acceptance gives me choices.

For instance, one day I called my sponsor because the alcoholic and I had concert tickets for the evening, and I was afraid he would get drunk and pass out before it was time to leave the house. It had happened many times before: Our tickets would go to waste, and I'd spend the evening in despair.

My sponsor suggested having back-up plans whenever my plans involved someone I couldn't depend on. Plan A was the original night out. Plan B might be to call an Al-Anon friend in advance, explain the situation, and see if he or she would be interested in a last-minute invitation if Plan A fell through. Plan C might be to go by myself and have a good time. This new approach worked like a charm. It was a great way to put acceptance to work in my life.

Today's reminder

I no longer have to depend on any one person or situation in order to get on with my day. Today I have choices.

"Consider the little mouse, how sagacious an animal it is which never entrusts his life to one hole only."

Plautus

Sometimes what I do is less important than why I do it. For instance, if I choose to speak up when something bothers me, my motives for speaking will influence what I say and how I say it. If I speak because I feel it is the right action for me to take and because I have a need to express myself, then the focus is on me. The listener's reactions become far less important.

But if I speak out in order to manipulate or change another person, then their reaction becomes the focus of my attention and the measure by which I evaluate the results.

I may use exactly the same words in both situations, but I am likely to feel much better about the experience if my focus is on myself. Ironically, the results usually seem more favorable that way as well.

Today's reminder

Today, instead of aiming only for the results, I will consider taking actions because they seem to be the right actions for me.

> "Even if I knew that tomorrow the world would go to pieces, I would still plant my apple tree."
>
> Martin Luther

Step Five says, "Admitted to God, to ourselves and to another human being the exact nature of our wrongs." But what is the exact nature of my wrongs? Is it the embarrassing moments, the words spoken in anger, the dishonesty?

For me, the exact nature of my wrongs is the unspoken, self-defeating assumptions that give rise to my thoughts and actions. These include notions that my best is not good enough, that I am not worthy of love, and that I have been hurt too deeply to ever really heal. If I dig deeply enough, I usually find thoughts such as these beneath the things I feel the worst about. I am learning to examine whether or not there is any truth to these assumptions. Then I can begin to build my life around a more realistic, more loving way of seeing myself.

Today's reminder

Living with alcoholism has taken a huge toll on my self-esteem. As a result, I may not recognize how many of my wrongs are built upon a faulty sense of self. That's why the Fifth Step is so enlightening and so cleansing. Together with my Higher Power and another person, I can even change life-long patterns.

"If no one knows us as we really are, we run the risk of making ourselves victims of our own self-hatred. If we can be loved by somebody who sees us as we are, we will then be able to accept ourselves. Others rarely think we're as bad as we think we are."

Alateen—Hope for Children of Alcoholics

Alcoholism is a family disease. It affects not only the drinker but those of us who care about him or her as well. For some of us, much of the thinking that has been passed down from generation to generation has been distorted.

By my presence in Al-Anon, I have committed myself to breaking these unhealthy patterns. As I continue to attend meetings, I begin to heal, to find sanity and peace, and to feel much better about myself. I am no longer playing my old role in the alcoholic system, and so the entire family situation begins to change. Ironically, when I give up worrying about everyone else and focus on my own health, I give others the freedom to consider their own recovery.

Today's reminder

One person's recovery can have a powerful impact on the whole family. When I take care of myself, I may be doing more than I realize to help loved ones who suffer from this family disease.

"If one person gets well, the whole family situation improves."

Living With Sobriety

"Just for today . . . I will do somebody a good turn and not get found out; if anybody knows of it, it will not count." What a terrific exercise! It helps me to break free of the habit of doing kind or generous things in order to get something back. Only when I perform a loving act with no expectations will I reap the true reward of giving.

I am learning that giving doesn't have to take away from me or anyone else—if there are no strings attached, everyone stands to benefit. Every good and loving gesture soothes my soul and contributes to a healthier world. These anonymous, positive actions are the building blocks of a flourishing spiritual well-being. My self-esteem grows because I can feel good about my actions. I am engaged in worthwhile pursuits.

Today's reminder

Today I will put unconditional love into action. When I give freely, without expecting anything in return, I always receive more than I give.

"I was created in love. For that reason nothing can express my beauty nor liberate me except love alone."

Mechtild of Magdeburg

We humans are wonderfully adaptable. We find creative solutions to impossible situations. One coping skill that some of us develop is manipulating other people in order to get what we want. Alcoholism can create such a threatening environment that manipulation seems necessary. Today, with the help of Al-Anon, we are learning to do more than merely survive, and such manipulation becomes unnecessary and unacceptable. In Al-Anon we learn healthier ways to meet our own needs and to behave toward others.

Manipulation had been a normal part of my life for so long that I forgot how to have a discussion or make a straightforward request. If I wanted someone to do the dishes, I tried to make them feel guilty by telling them how much I had done for them, or I complained that they never did their part. It never occurred to me that I could simply and politely ask for what I wanted, or that I could accept my request being turned down! But I'm learning. A day at a time I'm learning.

Today's reminder

Today I am creating a better way of living, free of guilt and deception.

> "We choose to behave with personal integrity, not because it will make someone else feel better, but because it reflects a way of living that enriches and heals us."
>
> . . . *In All Our Affairs*

Al-Anon reminds me that I can only deal with "One day at a time." This allows me to be more realistic about what I can do to improve my situation. It gets rid of the constant urgency.

Today I can see that no problem lasts forever. I used to feel that if I didn't solve a problem immediately, it would remain for all time. Now I know that everything passes eventually, the happy as well as the sad.

Today I can ask myself, "What can I do about this right here, right now?" This question helps me to identify my responsibility more realistically and shows me what part of the situation is beyond my power to control. Reasoning things out with an Al-Anon friend or attending a meeting often helps me to separate today's problems from those belonging to the past or future. Then I do what I can and turn over the rest.

Today's reminder

I can cope more effectively with difficult situations when I am realistic about my responsibilities. I have the tools I need to face today's challenges. I will trust my Higher Power with tomorrow.

"Today is only a small manageable segment of time in which our difficulties need not overwhelm us. This lifts from our hearts and minds the heavy weight of both past and future."

One Day at a Time in Al-Anon

Insanity has been defined as doing something the same way over and over again and expecting different results. In the past I tried to control people, places, and things, believing that my way was the correct way. I knew my track record— my way, based on insisting upon my will, did not work. Yet I kept trying. It was an insane way to live.

Step Three, "Made a decision to turn our will and our lives over to the care of God *as we understood Him,*" was a turning point for me in relinquishing control. It meant choosing between an insane life and a sane one—my will or God's will. Since my will had let me down time and time again, the real question was how long would I continue running around in the same circles before I was willing to admit defeat and turn to a source of genuine help?

Today's reminder

I may find it easy to point to the alcoholic's irrational or self-destructive choices. It is harder to admit that my own behavior has not always been sane. Today I can let go of insisting upon my will. With this simple decision I make a commitment to sanity.

"Though no one can go back and make a brand new start, anyone can start from now and make a brand new end."

                                        As We Understood . . .

I'm not particularly handy with tools. Recently a friend demonstrated to me that oiling a saw before using it makes it work more smoothly, whether it's cutting metal or wood.

Later it occurred to me that learning to oil a saw is a little like learning to apply the Al-Anon program. Though skeptical, I considered learning a new way because I saw it demonstrated. I knew that the program worked when I saw how serenely Al-Anon members in circumstances similar to mine were coping with difficult situations. So I tried their approach—I learned to apply the Steps, Al-Anon literature, slogans, meetings, and sponsorship.

Using this oil doesn't change the raw materials of my life, nor does it provide me with new equipment. It does make what I already have more useful, and that removes many of my frustrations, giving me great satisfaction.

Today's reminder

Building a useful and fulfilling life is not an easy task. Al-Anon helps me learn more effective ways of living so that I can avoid needless difficulty. With the proper tools, progress is just a matter of practice.

> "You learn to speak by speaking, to study by studying, to run by running, to work by working; and just so you learn to love God and man by loving. Begin as a mere apprentice and the very power of love will lead you on to become a master of the art."
>
> Francis de Sales

I read somewhere that the things that are urgent are rarely important, and the things that are important are rarely urgent. I can get so caught up in the nagging, trivial matters of day-to-day life that I forget to make time for more important pursuits. The Al-Anon slogan I find most helpful in getting my priorities in order is "First things first."

Today, maintaining my serenity is my first priority. My connection with my Higher Power is the source of serenity, so maintaining that connection is my "First thing."

If I imagine I am in a dark room and that my Higher Power is my only source of light, then my best hope for navigating around the furniture will be to bring that source of light with me as I move through the room. Otherwise, I may get through the room, but my passage is sure to be slow, confusing, and possibly painful.

Today's reminder

As I think about what to do with this day, I will set some time aside for what is really important. I will put "First things first" today.

> "Let us spend one day as deliberately as Nature, and not be thrown off the track by every nutshell and mosquito's wing that falls on the rails."
>
> Henry David Thoreau

Step Six talks about becoming entirely ready to have God remove all my defects of character. This readiness rarely appears to me in a sudden, blinding flash of enlightenment. Instead, as I struggle to make progress in a positive direction, I become ready a little at a time.

An important part of my Sixth Step work is practicing gratitude. The more I give thanks for my life as it is, the more I can accept the healing that allows me to change and grow. By recognizing and cultivating my abilities, I am increasingly willing to let go of my defects.

This Step is a lesson in patience, but as I see my life opening up before me in new directions, I do finally become ready to have God remove all my defects of character.

Today's reminder

"Progress, not perfection" applies to my readiness to let go of my defects, as well as to other parts of my Al-Anon program. One day at a time, I make progress in readiness.

"Step Six is my chance to cooperate with God. My goal is to make myself ready to let go of my faults and let God take care of the rest."

Alateen—A Day at a Time

I used to feel very hurt if anyone gave me an angry look, spoke in a harsh tone, or didn't speak at all. I've grown enough in Al-Anon to realize that the look, tone, or mood of another person toward me often has nothing to do with me. It generally has more to do with what is going on inside the other person.

So why do my feelings still get hurt? It occurs to me that my extreme sensitivity is a form of conceit—I think I am the focus of everyone's actions. Am I so important that everything that goes on around me must have something to do with me? I suspect that attitude reflects my vanity instead of reality. And vanity is simply a defect of character that I am working on changing.

With Al-Anon's help, my sensitivity to all that happens around me has greatly lessened. I try to ask myself, "How important is it?" When I do carry the hurt, it only hurts and controls me.

Today's reminder

Other people are important to me, and sometimes their opinions matter, but I may be taking something personally that has nothing to do with me. Having opinions of my own about myself lets me accept other people's thoughts without being controlled by them.

> "It was through going to meetings and the daily readings of Al-Anon literature that I awakened to the fact that what other people did and said reflected on *them*; what I did and said reflected on *me*."

Living With Sobriety

For a long time I tried to "Let go and let God," but I couldn't seem to do it. I needed to find a concrete way to let go. I heard someone share at a meeting that she pictured her loved ones on a beautiful ocean beach, basking in the light of a Higher Power.

Al-Anon has taught me to take what I like and leave the rest. I couldn't relate to the beach scene, but I did find comfort in the general idea. Once again, the experience, strength, and hope of another Al-Anon member led me to find my own, personalized answer. I now envision wrapping my loved ones in the kind of blanket that I think they'd like—a down comforter, an army blanket, a patchwork quilt—and gently handing them to my Higher Power. I find it important to be very specific. After all, my fears and worries are specific.

With a clear picture of my loved ones in my Higher Power's care, I am much more able truly to "Let go and let God."

Today's reminder

When I'm anxious about other people, I need my Higher Power's help. Fighting with fear often strengthens its hold over me, but turning my loved ones over to God can free us all.

> "'Let go and let God'. . . teaches us to release problems that trouble and confuse us, because we are not able to solve them by ourselves."
>
> *This Is Al-Anon*

"Keep coming back" is a phrase we often hear in Al-Anon. Why is it so important? Because many of us have grown so hardened in our fights with alcoholics or flights from alcoholics that we literally found it difficult to sit still for the process of recovery. We had to have answers right away or take action right away. Yet we felt just enough relief at our first meeting to come back once more. And then again, and again. Slowly we learned to sit still, to listen, and to heal.

No matter how many years we've been practicing the Al-Anon program, we can use the reminder to keep coming back. Difficult times come and go, even after long-term Al-Anon recovery. With each new challenge, many of us still need reminding that "there is no situation too difficult to be bettered and no unhappiness too great to be lessened."

Today's reminder

If I feel discouraged today, I will turn to the basics of the Al-Anon program. I'll get to a meeting, call my sponsor, go back to the First Step. One day at a time, if I keep coming back, I know my situation will improve.

> "If I really want to learn how to fit easily and happily into my environment and my relations with other people, Al-Anon has something for me."

> *One Day at a Time in Al-Anon*

To me, when the Second Step talks about being restored to sanity, it covers more than the ability to function responsibly and realistically. A sane way of life also includes the willingness to play, to take a break, to cultivate a hobby. I suppose I think of humor as an especially appealing hobby. It takes no special equipment, doesn't require travel, and never falls out of fashion. When I have a good laugh, I know that my Higher Power is restoring some of my sanity.

If I can see nothing but my troubles, I am seeing with limited vision. Dwelling on these troubles allows them to control me. Of course, I need to do whatever footwork is required, but I also need to learn when to let go. When I take time to play, to laugh, and to enjoy, I am taking care of myself and giving my Higher Power some room to take care of the rest.

Today's reminder

A good chuckle or an engrossing activity can lift my spirits and cleanse my mind. I will refresh myself by adding some lightness to this day.

"Now I look for humor in every situation, and my Higher Power is a laughing God who reminds me not to take myself too seriously."

As We Understood . . .

For years I lamented the absence of a label that would identify the soul sickness that brought me to the fellowship. I wanted to say, "I'm a recovering controller, enabler, caretaker, fixer." Although they identify some of my character defects, these labels miss the mark. I'm not simply seeking recovery from one limitation or problem. The goal I'm striving for in Al-Anon is an overall sense of wellness.

My pursuit of this goal began by seeking recovery from the way a loved one's alcoholism has affected my life. But today Al-Anon offers me even more. As I heal and grow, I find that it is no longer enough simply to survive. The principles and tools that brought me this far can help me to create an increasingly rich and fulfilling life.

Today, when I say I'm a grateful member of Al-Anon, I'm not zeroing in on one particular problem but rather participating in a whole host of solutions that can lead to emotional, physical, and spiritual health.

Today's reminder

As I continue on the never-ending path of spiritual progress, I will expand my view of recovery.

"In Al-Anon we believe life is for growth, both mental and spiritual."

The Twelve Steps and Traditions

Although there are many ways to tame a horse, there is general agreement on one point: The important thing is not to break the horse's spirit. Colts, puppies, and little children are full of boundless joy in being alive. What had happened to my joy? Alcoholism, which has touched every generation of my family, had broken my spirit.

Al-Anon gives me a fellowship, a sponsor, and Twelve Steps and Traditions that allow me to heal my broken spirit. My healing started when I quit fighting the God of other people's understanding and found a God who honored the long-forgotten spirit in me. That's the God who can restore me to my true self.

Today I make a sincere effort to roll in the clover, kick up my heels, and celebrate being alive. It is one way in which I touch my God.

Today's reminder

Let me make this day a celebration of the spirit. There is a part of me that retains a childlike sense of curiosity, wonder, enthusiasm, and delight. I may have lost touch with it, but I know it still exists. I will set my problems to the side for a little while and appreciate what it means to be vitally alive.

"Life is no brief candle to me. It is a sort of splendid torch which I have got hold of for the moment, and I want to make it burn as brightly as possible before handing it on to future generations."

George Bernard Shaw

Sometimes I think that, because I've been in Al-Anon for a long time, I shouldn't have any more problems. When difficulties do arise, I feel something is wrong with me or with the program.

Actually, in some ways I have more problems than ever. When I came to Al-Anon, I had only one problem: I didn't know how to fix the alcoholic. (My life was completely in shambles, but I swore that I was fine.) Today I know that I can't fix anyone but myself, and I challenge myself daily to seek a richer, more meaningful life. I'm taking risks, facing fears, making changes, speaking up, making myself available to life.

I'm bound to run into snags here and there. Sometimes life doesn't follow my blueprint. I get overwhelmed and want to crawl under the covers and hide. At such a time it helps to remember that Al-Anon doesn't take away problems, but it does give me the courage and insight to turn stumbling blocks into stepping stones.

Today's reminder

In handling my difficulties, what's important isn't how much time I have in Al-Anon but how willing I am to implement the tools of recovery. While Al-Anon doesn't grant immunity from problems, it does offer a healthy way to deal with them.

"Troubles are often the tools by which God fashions us for better things."

                                                    H.W. Beecher

Al-Anon is a spiritual recovery program. The word "recovery" implies that we are regaining something we once possessed but have lost or set aside.

In the confusion of living with active drinkers, I lost track of my spirit. Life was a survival game, a daily grind of fear and hard work. No matter what I tried, nothing seemed to help. Perhaps that's because I was trying to do it all by myself.

In Al-Anon I have come to know that I have a resource within me and all around me that can guide me through the most overwhelming fears and the most challenging decisions—a Higher Power. Regardless of how I define that Higher Power, it is real to me and has always been here for me. I am so grateful to have recovered that connection to my spirituality, for in doing so, I have regained an essential part of myself. As a result, today my life has a sense of purpose that makes each moment a precious gift.

Today's reminder

I am a spiritual creature, capable of faith, hope, and an appreciation of beauty. I have an unlimited source of strength and comfort at my disposal. Today I will take the time to cultivate that spiritual connection.

"Half an hour's meditation is essential except when you are very busy. Then a full hour is needed."

Francis de Sales

How often have I had a dream I longed to pursue, but quit before I started because it seemed too enormous a task to attempt? Going back to school, moving, taking a trip, changing jobs, all these and many other goals can seem overwhelming at first.

Al-Anon reminds me to "Keep it simple." Instead of approaching the task as a whole, I can simplify it by taking only one step at a time. I can gather information—and do nothing more. Then, when I'm ready, I can take the project further. That takes some of the pressure off having to know all the answers and solve every problem that may arise before I've even begun.

I am also free to try something and then change my mind. I do not have to make a lifetime commitment before I even know whether or not my goal is desirable.

My plans may involve many actions and many risks, but I don't have to tackle them all today. I can take my time and move step by step at my own pace. By focusing on one thing at a time, the impossible can become likely if I "Keep it simple."

Today's reminder

With the help of Al-Anon and my Higher Power, I am capable of many things I could not even have considered before. I may even be capable of pursuing my heart's desire.

"All glory comes from daring to begin."

Eugene F. Ware

I am forever looking at friends and strangers and making little improvements: "She'd look much more attractive if only . . ." or, "He would be a lot easier to deal with if only . . ."

Step Ten is my daily reminder to let go of such thoughts. It reminds me to continue to take my own inventory and to promptly admit when I am wrong.

Every day I can look to myself and decide what improvement I can make. How can I grow today? What can I do by day's end to improve myself? Is there something I can learn? Is there some challenge I can meet? Is there some old, tired fear I can walk through and be rid of? Is there some new happiness I can experience? Step Ten reminds me to be honest with myself, acknowledging my progress, admitting my mistakes, and recognizing opportunities to grow today.

Today's reminder

When I keep track of my inventory on a daily basis, I no longer have to fear that I will fall into that vague, hazy state in which denial so easily takes root. When I turn this inventory over to my Higher Power, I know that I am moving toward freedom.

"A man should never be ashamed to own he has been in the wrong, which is but saying, in other words, that he is wiser today than he was yesterday."

Alexander Pope

When I came to Al-Anon, I knew that a close relative drank too much, and I knew I wasn't happy, but I didn't think I needed much help. I went to a meeting every week unless there was something else to do and I didn't get a sponsor. I grew, but slowly.

A crisis brought my leisurely approach to recovery to an end. When I lost someone very special to me, the pain was almost more than I could stand. I was lucky; I had learned enough to pick up the phone and call someone in Al-Anon. That person helped me to make it through the crisis, but that was only the beginning. I saw how badly I needed the strength and skills that Al-Anon had to offer. I began going to quite a few meetings each week, doing service work, calling Al-Anon friends. My recovery really took off! Today, practicing the program gets top priority in my life, because I know where I would have wound up without that crisis.

Today's reminder

Sometimes the greatest growth comes through pain, but it's not the pain that helps me grow, it's my response to it. Will I suffer through the experience and continue as before or let the pain inspire changes that help me grow? The choice is mine.

"I had learned in Al-Anon to look for opportunities for growth in every situation. This attitude allowed me to gain many spiritual riches from the pain I was experiencing."

. . . In All Our Affairs

Feeling that I don't belong has been a problem all my life. This was especially true when I first came to Al-Anon. My attending seemed wrong because there was no alcohol in my household as a child—it was my grandparents who drank.

At that first meeting, I learned that alcoholism is a family disease. It affects not only the person who drinks, but those who care about him or her. Indeed, the effects of this disease are often passed from one generation to another. When I heard a description of some of those effects, I recognized a profile of myself. For the first time in my life I was with people who knew what I was going through.

Today I see clearly that I have in fact been affected by the family disease of alcoholism. Al-Anon offers me a way to do my part in breaking this family pattern. I can get off the merry-go-round by choosing recovery.

Today's reminder

In Al-Anon I find people who understand as few others can. If I have been affected by the drinking of another, I need not doubt that I belong.

> "No matter what the difficulty, no matter how unique we may feel, somewhere nearby are men and women with similar stories who have found help, comfort, and hope through recovery in Al-Anon."
>
> *. . . In All Our Affairs*

I can be proud of the fact that I am a survivor. I have been brought through many struggles in order to be exactly where I am today. Today I know that I am more than my troubles. I am a human being with dignity. I have a wealth of experience that I can put to use by sharing it with those who are going through similar difficulties. I needn't fear the challenges of the future, because I know that today, with the guidance of my Higher Power and with the strength and knowledge I have gained from Al-Anon, I am capable of facing anything life brings me.

Though I once viewed my life as a tragedy, I now have a different perspective on those experiences. I know that I am a stronger person as a result of what I've been through.

Today's reminder

If I so choose, I can regard everything that happens in my life as a gift from which I can learn and grow. Today I will find something positive hidden within a difficult situation and allow myself to be grateful. I may be surprised at how much a little gratitude can help.

"When it gets dark enough, you can see the stars."

Charles A. Beard

As I worked my way through Step Four, I listed my character traits as honestly and fearlessly as I could. I was struck by a great irony: Many things I had once thought of as virtues—taking care of everyone around me, worrying about other people's lives, sacrificing my own happiness and prosperity—turned out to be the causes of my misery! And those traits I had always ignored—talent, optimism, self-discipline—turned out to be my truly positive qualities. It was as though, through the power of this Step, I had found a way to turn my upside-down personality right-side up.

I still struggle to keep it all from turning over once again. But when I see myself clearly, I have a sense of wholeness and a feeling of pride and peace. I can be happy to be myself now that I know who I am.

Today's reminder

My life is in a constant state of change. Awareness allows me to keep pace with that change. Today let me listen to my words and watch my actions. Only by knowing the person I am can I create the person I want to become.

"Each man must look to himself to teach him the meaning of life. It is not something discovered: it is something molded."

Antoine de Saint-Exupery

Before Al-Anon, I believed that being an adult was to be in control—rigid, cool. Being an adult was looking good on the outside and not feeling what was going on on the inside. Being an adult meant doing for others until I dropped.

Al-Anon has opened up a whole new way of living. The first thing that had to go was the control over others—it simply doesn't work. Trying to be in control is an effective method of keeping loved ones at a distance. Instead, I admitted that I am powerless over others. Then I had to begin to put away the "lookin' good" facade in order to share my feelings at meetings. And one fine day I picked up the *One Day at a Time in Al-Anon (ODAT)* book and read the pages on "martyrdom." I became uncomfortably aware that my "do-gooder" role often masked a martyr.

Becoming more human has been difficult and frightening at times, but being more genuine allows me to have real relationships, real communication, and real happiness.

Today's reminder

Today I can risk being myself. I don't have to live up to anyone's image. All I have to do is be me.

> "As I surrendered my imaginary power over others, I gained a more realistic view of my own life."
>
> *Al-Anon is for Adult Children of Alcoholics*

Everyone who plays a part in our lives offers something we might learn. Other people can be our mirrors, reflecting our better and worse qualities. They can help us to work through conflicts from the past that were never resolved. They can act as catalysts, activating parts of ourselves that need to rise to the surface so that we can attend to them.

Others can learn from us as well. We are all connected. That is our great strength.

So when I grow impatient with someone's sharing in a meeting, or take offense at a loved one's inattention, or feel incapable of coping with another person's choices, I will consider the possibility that my teacher or my mirror stands before me. And I will ask my Higher Power to help me perceive their gifts.

Today's reminder

One reason I come to Al-Anon is to learn to develop healthy, loving relationships with myself and others. I recognize that I need other people. I will welcome those my Higher Power brings to me today.

"Separate reeds are weak and easily broken; but bound together they are strong and hard to tear apart."

The Midrash

Al-Anon was the first place I'd been in a long time where people invited me back even after listening to my woes. I'm so grateful that they did, because Al-Anon was my last hope—I thought that I would kill myself if I didn't do something about the alcoholism in my home. Later, when members of the group asked me to make coffee, I was happy to do *anything* to repay them for their love; yet no payment was required. They loved me whether I was involved in service or not, even when I couldn't love myself.

Al-Anon is the only thing in my life that I've been dedicated to, the only thing I've ever felt consistently good at. As I do service work, I see myself accomplishing things, giving, receiving, growing. I see my progress as I learn to learn, and as the lessons become a part of me, I take them into all areas of my life.

Today I like to think that I get to take an active part in the growth of Al-Anon through service. I'm not doing Al-Anon a favor; Al-Anon is doing me one. It actually thrills me to remember that. I'm allowed to take part! You let me!

Today's reminder

Listening, hearing, thinking, and reading about a spiritual awakening are fine, but if I really want this gift, there is something I can *do* about it: I can get involved.

"What we learn to do we learn by doing."

Aristotle

I can easily itemize my loved one's limitations. Hours pass while I list the ways in which he could stand to change.

But not one thing has ever improved as a result of this mental criticism. All it does is keep my mind on someone other than me. Instead of admitting my powerlessness over another person's choices and attitudes, I flirt with illusions of power. In the end I am a little more bitter, more hopeless, and more frustrated. And nothing about my situation, or the other person, has changed.

What would happen if I took my list of criticisms and applied it, gently, to myself? I may complain about my loved one's verbal abuse— after all, I don't speak to him that way. But at the level of thought, I am just as abusive. The same attitude exists in both of us; we just manifest it differently.

Today's reminder

Al-Anon says, "Let it begin with me." When I identify something I dislike in another, I can look for similar traits within myself and begin to change them. By changing myself, I truly can change the world.

> "Peace of mind depends on recognizing our own shortcomings. An honest personal inventory helps us recognize the faults that so often increase confusion and despair."
>
> *This Is Al-Anon*

What is meditation? Al-Anon leaves that question open for each of us to answer in our own way. Drawing upon the experiences of other Al-Anon members can help us to find our own path. Here are only a few of the ways members of the fellowship have shared:

To me, meditation is a higher spiritual awareness. I practice remembering that every action can serve a spiritual purpose.

I go to a quiet place, close my eyes, and repeat the words of the Serenity Prayer to myself in a gentle voice.

I need to get beyond my thoughts, so I concentrate on my breathing, counting from one to ten over and over as I breathe in and out.

I simply step back and watch my thoughts as if I were watching a play. I try to keep my attention on the present day only, leaving the past and the future alone.

I focus on a flower. When my thoughts stray, I accept that my mind is just doing its job—thinking—and then gently return to my subject.

In my mind, I picture my Higher Power's hands. One by one, I place my problems and worries, my joy and my gratitude, into those hands, and finally, I climb in too.

In the past, many of us learned to make choices strictly on the basis of our feelings, as if feelings were facts. If we were frightened about taking a certain action, for example, then it was best avoided. There was no middle ground and no room for more than one feeling at a time.

Part of Al-Anon recovery involves learning that feelings aren't facts. I am a complex, fascinating human being with a wide range of emotions, experiences, and thoughts. There is more to my identity than one feeling or another, one problem or another. I am a wealth of contradictions. I can value all of my feelings without allowing them to dictate my actions.

Today I can feel anger toward someone and still love them. I can feel afraid of new experiences, yet move forward through them. I can survive being hurt without giving up on love. And I can experience sadness and still be confident that I will be happy again.

Today's reminder

Today I am learning to embrace my complexities and contradictions and to be grateful for the richness they bring.

> "Life, for all its agonies . . . is exciting and beautiful, amusing and artful and endearing . . . and whatever is to come after it—we shall not have this life again."
>
> Rose Macaulay

I was sure there had to be somebody in this world who would understand my every mood, always have time for me, and bring a smile to my face. When that individual appeared, I'd finally have the love I deserved. Until then, I had no choice but to wait. Poor me. What a sad and lonely life I had.

Then someone at an Al-Anon meeting used the word "gratitude," and suddenly this whole scenario began to crumble. When I thought about how much I had to be grateful for, my fantasy showed itself to be no more than a shadow. Reality presented a different picture entirely. There were my friends, the child who comes to me with so much trust, the co-worker who reaches out in friendship, the beloved alcoholic in my life, the Al-Anon members who hug me, talk with me, and encourage me. What was I doing with their love? It seemed to me I was brushing it aside for that one imaginary person or, worse, not noticing it at all.

Today's reminder

If I can't recognize the love that already exists in my life, would I really appreciate receiving more? Let me acknowledge what has already been given to me.

"If the only prayer you said in your whole life was, 'thank you,' that would suffice."

Meister Eckhart

Before Al-Anon, I'd have sworn I didn't have an angry bone in my body. Through working the Steps, however, I discovered that without knowing it I'd often been furious at the alcoholics in my life.

I began to recognize anger while it was happening. At first it felt great to reclaim this suppressed part of myself—I felt more whole, more powerful—but as time went on I began to abuse my new-found sense of power. I blamed all my problems on the alcoholics, pushed everyone away, and felt worse than ever.

Al-Anon has helped me bring the focus back to myself. If I am unhappy with my situation, I can look at my part in it. I am powerless over alcoholism. Sometimes I feel angry about that fact, but anger will not change it. Today I can get angry, express the feelings in the healthiest way I can find, and then let them go.

Today's reminder

Anger can give me an illusion of power. For a little while I may feel I have control over my situation and over other people, but that kind of false security always lets me down. The only real power available to me is that which is mentioned in the Eleventh Step: the power to carry out God's will.

"No one can control the insidious effect of alcohol, or its power to destroy the graces and decencies of life . . . But we do have a power, derived from God, and that is the power to change our own lives."

One Day at a Time in Al-Anon

I used to think that being good to myself meant eating whatever I wanted, buying anything that caught my eye, sleeping only a few hours a night, and avoiding any activity that wasn't fun and exciting. The trouble was that the consequences were very uncomfortable, and when I let myself think about it, I felt I was wasting my life.

Today, being good to myself is far more challenging, but the benefits are absolutely wonderful! I attend two or three Al-Anon meetings each week, read my literature daily, and take time out to talk to God. I try very hard to make my serenity more important than any of the circumstances I encounter.

I now enjoy wholesome food, exercise in a way that I find fun, and handle money in a more conscientious way. I celebrate my growth. I dance, I draw, and I enjoy wonderful friendships. My lifestyle isn't rigid, nor would I want it to be. I still enjoy spontaneous moments, but today I have them by choice.

Today's reminder

I deserve to make choices that let me feel good about myself. It may take a while to see results, but I am building a life that promotes my health and self-esteem. It's worth the wait.

"The strongest principle of growth lies in human choice."

George Eliot

The image of an avalanche helps me to give the drinking alcoholic in my life the dignity to make her own decisions. It is as though her actions are forming a mountain of alcohol-related troubles. A mound of snow cannot indefinitely grow taller without tumbling down; neither can the alcoholic's mountain of problems.

Al-Anon has helped me to refrain from throwing myself in front of the alcoholic to protect her, or from working feverishly to add to the mountain in order to speed its downward slide. I am powerless over her drinking and her pain. The most helpful course of action is for me to stay out of the way!

If the avalanche hits the alcoholic, it must be the result of her own actions. I'll do my best to allow God to care for her, even when painful consequences of her choices hit full force. That way I won't get in the way of her chance to want a better life.

Today's reminder

I will take care to avoid building an avalanche of my own. Am I heaping up resentments, excuses, and regrets that have the potential to destroy me? I don't have to be buried under them before I address my own problems. I can begin today.

> "The suffering you are trying to ease . . . may be the very thing needed to bring the alcoholic to a realization of the seriousness of the situation—literally a blessing in disguise."

> *So You Love an Alcoholic*

When I reflect on Tradition Eleven, in which Al-Anon's public relations policy is described as being based on attraction rather than promotion, I take a fairly personal approach. What this Tradition says to me is that my first responsibility in Al-Anon is to learn to keep the focus on myself and to do my level best to live this program one day at a time.

If I am not walking the walk, there is little point in talking the talk—that is, if I am not demonstrating recovery in my life to the best of my ability, then talking about the program may be nothing more than a substitute for living it.

In this regard, I find that I am very likely to feel most compelled to urge others to attend Al-Anon when I am most in need of a meeting myself.

Today's reminder

Before I start telling people about Al-Anon, I might consider posing this question to myself: "Did they ask?"

"Example is not the main thing in influencing others. It is the only thing."

Albert Schweitzer

Many of us come to Al-Anon confused. We are so focused on our alcoholic loved ones that we may not be able to see where they leave off and we begin. We've lost our sense of what is appropriate. How can we distinguish between acceptable and unacceptable behavior when we don't even know what we want or need?

My Fourth Step inventory helped me discover who I am, what my values are, the behavior I'd like to keep, and the things I'd like to change. With this in mind, I am working to establish new behavior that reflects my integrity and expresses my true values. Where in the past I have allowed unacceptable behavior, I now can choose a different response. I must consistently do what I say I'm going to do. Today I have the courage and faith to be true to myself, whether or not others like or agree with me. I must remember that announcing my new ways to others is not nearly as important as knowing what my own limits are and acting accordingly.

Today's reminder

I will remember that knowing my boundaries does not mean forcing others to change; it means that I know my own limits and take care of myself by respecting them. The focus, today, is on me.

"He that respects himself is safe from others; he wears a coat of mail that none can pierce."

Henry Wadsworth Longfellow

I always figured most of my troubles would be over if I won the lottery. Anything would be possible with that much money! But would it take away the effect alcoholism has had on my family? Would it make the drinkers sober? Could it guarantee happiness? Is money really what I want?

No, of course not. What I really want is to feel better. Nothing will eliminate all problems from my life. Since there are difficulties with which I must live, the only real answer is to seek the serenity to accept the things I cannot change. Today I know that serenity is available to me free of charge when I go to Al-Anon meetings and then apply the principles I learn there to my life.

Money won't buy serenity; in fact, I'd probably have a whole new set of problems and decisions if a fortune ever did fall into my lap. But as an Al-Anon member who can rely on a Higher Power's help with any and every problem that comes along, today I feel like one of life's winners.

Today's reminder

Serenity is always available to me, but it is my job to seek it where it can be found.

"... I now try to take my problems to my Higher Power, but I leave the solutions and the timetable up to Him."

As We Understood ...

Whenever we Alateen members met with Al-Anon, I felt doubtful. I didn't think adults could help me in any way, because they were sure to have the same sick attitudes as my alcoholic parents. I would think to myself, "Oh great, here we go again."

But I was the one with the sick attitude. I had closed my mind, not only to my parents, but to all adults. I brought this attitude to meetings, so I didn't learn a thing. I had to deal with my old resentments before I could recognize the wonderful gift Al-Anon was offering. Here were people who could help me heal the wounds my parents' drinking had left, and help me to know that it is safe to be a part of my world. It took discipline and courage to stop pushing every adult away, but because I made the effort, I began to see that adults are human, too. I have even begun to believe that my parents are doing the best they can, and I can love them the way they are without having to change them or myself.

Today's reminder

Al-Anon helps me to see things as they are. The people in my life aren't the way I sometimes think they should be. With Al-Anon's help I can love them for who they are, instead of who I think they should be.

> "Life truly lived is a risky business, and if one puts up too many fences against risk one ends by shutting out life itself."
>
> Kenneth S. Davis

Flying down a hill on a bicycle, I always feel tremendously alive, in perfect balance. Al-Anon helps me to balance my life as if it were a ride on a bike and to carry that vitality into each day—especially when I apply the slogan, "Live and let live."

I try to embrace whatever life brings, with all its joys and sorrows, for it all has something to offer me. I made that discovery one night in an Al-Anon meeting when someone asked, "What would happen if I started thanking God when problems occurred?" At first I had to force myself to say, "Thank you, God," through clenched teeth. By and by, my teeth unlocked and I replaced self-pity with gratitude. I truly began to live.

When I live my own life to the utmost, it is easier to let others live theirs. Aliveness is mine. I pray others are blessed with it too.

Today's reminder

I want the very best for those I love. I am growing to appreciate the joy of fully participating in life. And I choose to allow others to enjoy this sometimes difficult but rewarding blessing of learning from all of their experiences. Today I will "Live and let live."

> "It is good to have an end to journey towards; but it is the journey that matters in the end."
>
> Ursula LeGuin

There are many forms of loss—divorce, incarceration, illness, death, even emotional change. When I lost the person I loved more than anyone in the world, I was more than devastated, and in my grief, I pushed everyone away. Thank God I had been in Al-Anon long enough to have awakened that part of myself that wanted health, no matter what happened. And so, in time, I once again began to work the program.

With the help of so many wonderful Al-Anon members who held me and let me grieve in my own way and time, I learned to go back to Step One, to admit that I was powerless over this loss and that my life was unmanageable. Once more I saw that the only hope for me lay with a Power greater than myself. And Step by Step I learned to live with loss, with pain, with despair, until eventually I began to feel alive again.

Today's reminder

Pain and loss are part of life. No matter what I do, I will not be able to change that fact. But with the fellowship to support me and the Steps to guide me, I will be able to face, and grow through, anything that comes my way.

> "The foundation I have developed in Al-Anon not only makes me grateful when things are going well, but also makes me realize that the program works especially when things go badly."

> *. . . In All Our Affairs*

For some time Step Three eluded me. How could I turn my will and my life over to the care of a Higher Power? I earnestly tried, but I always took everything right back into my own hands. It felt so scary to think that I was not in control. I found it hard to trust that my Higher Power would be there for me if I let go completely. Again and again, I wondered what absolute surrender would feel like, and how I would know if I was doing it?

A recent speaker at an Al-Anon meeting put it into terms that I could understand. He said that turning our will over is like dancing with a partner. If both try to lead, there is much confusion and little forward movement. As one who has taught many couples how to dance, I know the awkwardness and bucking that result when both partners compete for control. But when the partner who is following can relax and let the other partner do the steering, the couple flows easily across the dance floor.

Today's reminder

If I feel the bucking of uncertainty, despair, or fear, I can take it as a sign that I have gotten out of step. Then I can ask the God of my understanding to help me be a more willing partner.

"There are no guarantees that life will turn out the way we would like, but the program has shown me God's will is the only way; it is up to me to work with Him and turn my life and will over to His care and guidance."

. . . In All Our Affairs

I was convinced that I had to take care of everything and everybody—I had no choice. But with the help of Al-Anon I have learned that, while I do have responsibilities, there are also many things I do *not* have to do:

I don't have to understand everything. Some things are not my business, and others will simply never make sense to me.

I don't have to be reluctant to show my feelings. When I'm happy, I can give in to it! When I'm not, I can turn to my Al-Anon friends who help me to grow through the tough times.

I don't have to feel threatened by the future. I can take life one day at a time.

I don't have to feel guilty about the past. With the help of the Steps, especially Eight and Nine, I can make amends and learn from the mistakes I have made.

I don't have to feel alone. I can go to a meeting, or pick up the phone—there is always somebody to reach out to in Al-Anon.

I don't have to take responsibility for other people's choices. They have their own Higher Power to help them make their decisions.

I don't have to give up on my hopes and dreams— my Higher Power is not limited by my lack of imagination.

Again and again in Al-Anon meetings over the years, I heard the suggestion to pray for those I resented. My early attempts to follow this suggestion did me little good. Over time, however, it has become one of the most effective tools of my recovery.

What made the difference? I stopped praying for other people to change. It used to be, "Please God, let them stop hurting me," or "Show them that I'm right," or "Get them sober, and hurry!" Today I focus on what *I* can change, instead. I ask for a new way of thinking about the situation.

I keep in mind whatever is bothering me when I say the Serenity Prayer. What is it that I need to accept or change? I pray for the wisdom to know the difference, and the serenity and courage to follow through with what I learn. Finally, I pray that the person in question be given the serenity, love, and joy that I want for myself. We all deserve that.

Today's reminder

Resentments mark the places where I see myself as a victim. I want to let them go because they cost me too much self-esteem. I will love myself enough to release myself from the closet in which resentments keep me locked.

> "If we want to stop the vicious cycle of unhappiness, we must learn new ways of living, new ways of relating to each other."
>
> *How Can I Help My Children?*

In places where people depend upon camels for transportation, they have a saying, "Trust in God and tie your camel to a tree." I think of this saying as a colorful way of describing what we in Al-Anon call "doing the footwork."

First we trust in our Higher Power. Trusting is a way of affirming that we are willing to be receptive to whatever the Higher Power chooses for us. We do not resign ourselves to our fate; we meet the day with confident expectation. We expect a miracle, as they say.

But we cannot expect our Higher Power to do for us what we can clearly do for ourselves. We must do *our* part. The Twelve Steps help us to distinguish between our responsibilities and those we can turn over to God.

Today's reminder

Today I give thanks for the guidance of my Higher Power and for the measure of common sense needed to apply this guidance to the details of my daily life.

> "No one else can define our role in the unique partnership we develop with our Higher Power."
>
> *. . . In All Our Affairs*

Alcoholism is a three-fold—physical, emotional, and spiritual—disease. Because I've been affected by another's alcoholism, I check on my own physical, emotional, and spiritual well-being by asking myself:

Is my physical well-being a priority? Do I eat well and get enough sleep? When was the last time I had a check-up or went to a dentist? Do I keep myself clean? Take breaks? Exercise?

Do I ask for or give a hug when I need to? Am I growing more aware of my feelings? Do I have a sponsor and Al-Anon friends to help me through the rough times? Can I celebrate when things go well? Am I taking time to enjoy myself? Is any of the attention I once gave to negative thinking now focused on gratitude?

Do I have a relationship with a Power greater than myself? If not, am I willing to give it a try? Do I make time for prayer and meditation? Am I more willing to ask for help? Do I regularly attend Al-Anon meetings, read Al-Anon literature, and apply the Steps and other tools to my everyday life? Do I recognize and acknowledge my growth?

Today's reminder

By simply taking inventory of my self-care habits, I am beginning to improve them.

"Better keep yourself clean and bright; you are the window through which you must see the world."

George Bernard Shaw

"Each Al-Anon Family Group has but one purpose: to help families of alcoholics." This is part
of our Fifth Tradition, but how do we go about
doing it? "By practicing the Twelve Steps." We
must learn to love ourselves before we can truly
love others. When we tend to our own spiritual
needs, we make it possible for others to see that
special something in us that they may want for
themselves. The best sermon is a good example.

The next part of this Tradition talks of "encouraging and understanding our alcoholic relatives." We can all be more loving. Knowing that
alcoholism is a disease can help us to respond
with compassion rather than hostility.

Finally, "by welcoming and giving comfort to
families of alcoholics," we acknowledge that love
centered only on ourselves and our small family
circle leaves us isolated. We are rich in opportunities to love because we are part of the Al-Anon
family.

Today's reminder
Today I will practice compassion. First I will
be kind and loving to myself, but I will not stop
there. I will extend this compassion to others. I
am one among my fellows. When I offer unconditional love, it eventually comes back to me mul-
tiplied.

"Love is patient and kind, Love is not jealous or
boastful, it is not arrogant or rude, Love does not
insist on its own way."

The Bible

In a meeting I heard someone say of Steps Eight and Nine, "I made the list of people I have harmed—and I put myself at the top of the list." This had not occurred to me. Somewhere in my past I got the message that to think of myself first was wrong, that it was my duty to care for everyone else. As a consequence, I was never ready to take care of myself and so became a burden to those around me.

Have I harmed myself? Of course I have. That is ultimately what I am trying to recover from. In fact, improving myself is the only real action available to me. Now I know that to take responsibility for myself is the first thing I must do to make the world a better place.

Today's reminder

Being true to myself is one of the greatest gifts I can give to those around me. Perhaps I will inspire them to do the same; perhaps not. Why should others bother to follow my example if I can't take care of my own affairs? To give advice to others is to intrude; to give advice to myself is to grow.

"Most of the shadows of this life are caused by standing in one's own sunshine."

Ralph Waldo Emerson

We often concentrate on learning to apply the Al-Anon principles only to a particular family situation. There are, however, many simple ways in which we can keep the Al-Anon program with us wherever we go.

Some of us carry Al-Anon literature in a lunchbox, pocket, or purse, so that we can touch base with the wisdom of the program the minute we lose perspective. Before a difficult situation escalates, we might excuse ourselves and step outside for a moment of privacy. Whether we find ourselves in a shopping center, an office, or a hospital, there will almost always be a restroom available where we can collect ourselves. The telephone numbers of several Al-Anon members and plenty of change for a pay phone can be life-savers. Many of us always keep an Al-Anon meeting list handy.

And prayer is available any time, any place. It is undetectable to outside eyes, but it bears a seed of transformation that can bring the most unmanageable situation into perspective.

Today's reminder

It is good to know about the tools of the Al-Anon program, but it is better to put them to use. Today I will remember that the program is available to me at any time of the day or night.

"... The quality of our lives continues to improve as we apply the Al-Anon program not only to crisis situations but to our everyday lives."

... In All Our Affairs

I went to my first Al-Anon meeting because I wanted to show my support for a close friend who was a member. To my surprise, I found myself identifying with almost everyone who shared. I couldn't understand it—I was positive that I didn't even know any alcoholics! For weeks I kept remembering what I had heard in that meeting, and finally, timidly, I returned, and I stayed.

But I felt like an impostor every time I heard the Third Tradition, which states, "The only requirement for membership is that there be a problem of alcoholism in a relative or friend." This guilt made it almost impossible for me to share in meetings. But I kept coming back, and slowly I began to feel better.

It took me over a year to realize that I was an adult child of alcoholic parents. I am so grateful that I was given the time and the support to come to this awareness when I was ready.

Today's reminder

One of the signs that I have been affected by alcoholism is that I think I know what everyone else should do. As *Al-Anon's Twelve Steps & Twelve Traditions* explains, Tradition Three speaks directly to those of us "who mistakenly feel a newcomer should be rejected when, actually, he or she does meet the condition for membership." I must decide for myself whether I fit the requirement for Al-Anon membership. I will extend the same courtesy to others.

Amidst the constant turmoil and drama that surrounds most alcoholics, many family members and friends stop noticing what is going on with themselves. Something more important and life-threatening always seems to intervene. In Al-Anon we learn to pay attention to our own behavior, thoughts, and feelings. We deserve this attention, and we need it.

But focusing on ourselves doesn't mean that we let other people walk all over us and pretend not to notice, or that whatever others do is acceptable. Nor does it imply that we should stop caring about our loved ones. Focusing on ourselves simply means that when we acknowledge the situation as it is, we look at *our* options instead of looking at the options available to other people. We consider what is within our power to change instead of expecting others to do the changing. As a result, problems have a better chance of getting solved, and we lead more manageable lives.

Today's reminder

Today, if I am troubled, I will assess the situation and consider my options. I will not wait for anyone else to change, but will focus on myself and the part I can play in making the situation a better one.

"Nothing can bring you peace but yourself."

Ralph Waldo Emerson

In Al-Anon we learn to "Think" before we react to angry outbursts and drunken accusations. We learn to hold our tongues when tempted to interfere in something that is clearly none of our business. We learn the value of silence.

But silence can be more cutting than cruel words when it's used to punish. Deliberately ignoring someone's attempts to communicate is no better than engaging in a battle of words. Rage that is expressed non-verbally through cold looks and slammed doors is still rage. When I seek to hurt someone else with silence or any other weapon at my disposal, I always hurt myself.

If I have something I need to say and am as yet unable to say it in a constructive manner, perhaps I can go to an Al-Anon meeting or call my sponsor and release some of the explosive feelings. I will remember that my aim is to heal myself and my relationships. I will try to make choices that support this goal.

Today's reminder

What message does my silence communicate? Today I will try to align the stillness of my tongue with a stillness of spirit.

> ". . . If the silence has in it even a trace of anger or hostility, it loses all its power . . . True quiet has the quality of serenity, acceptance, peace."
>
> *One Day at a Time in Al-Anon*

Here's one of the most useful lessons I've learned in Al-Anon: If I don't want to be a door-mat, I have to get up off the floor. In other words, although I can't control what other people say, do, or think, I am responsible for my choices.

Looking back, I can accept that plenty of unac-ceptable behavior was directed at me, but *I* was the one who sat and took it and often came back for more. I was a willing participant in a dance that required two partners. I felt like a victim, but in many ways I was a volunteer.

Today, as a result of my recovery in Al-Anon, I know that I am not helpless. I have choices. When I get that old feeling that tells me I am a victim, I can regard it as a red flag, a warning that I may be participating (with my thoughts or my actions) in something that is not in my best interest. I can resist the temptation to blame others and look to my own involvement instead. That's where I can make changes.

Today's reminder

It can be very empowering to take responsibil-ity for my own choices. I will act in my own best interest today.

> "I would do well to accept the challenge to look to my own recovery before I spent any more of my precious life wishing the alcoholic would change . . ."
>
> *Living With Sobriety*

Maybe we need many points of view in order to understand life more fully; after all, no one person's view is totally complete. So when my partner, my child, my employer, or an Al-Anon friend takes a position unlike my own, I have a choice. I can assume that one of us is wrong and defend myself, or I can be grateful for the chance to see that there are countless ways of looking at life. An abundance of wisdom is available if I keep an open mind.

I try to practice this attitude when my loved one and I discuss anything, even TV. We often perceive a TV show so differently that it's hard to believe we've been watching the same station! I used to take these disagreements personally. One of us had to be wrong, and my position had to be accepted! Today I don't think there's anything personal about a difference of opinion. If you think the sea is blue and I think it's green, I don't have to spend all day trying to convince you. Al-Anon helps me believe in myself and respect that other people are entitled to do the same.

Today's reminder

I don't have to invalidate anyone else's views in order to validate my own. It's all right to disagree. Today I will respect someone's right to think differently.

"Think for yourself and let others enjoy the privilege of doing so too."

Voltaire

One effect of alcoholism is that many of us are reluctant to get close to people. We have learned that it is not safe to trust, to reveal too much, to care deeply. Yet we often wish we could experience closer, more loving relationships. Al-Anon suggests a gentle way of approaching this goal: sponsorship.

By asking someone to sponsor me, I express a willingness to experience more intimate relationships. When he or she is there for me, returning my calls, offering support, caring, I develop a basis for trust. I realize that my sponsor also has a life and that sometimes he or she will not be available. Because our relationship shows me that people can be reliable, I am better able to reach out to others in the fellowship.

My sponsor helps me learn to receive love, but I also learn about giving. Someone who demonstrates unconditional love and still takes care of his or her own needs and who offers support without telling me what to do can be a wonderful role model. I can best put what I learn into practice by passing it on.

Today's reminder

Intimacy can be one of life's great gifts. I will avail myself of its benefits by reaching out to an Al-Anon friend today.

"The interchange between sponsor and sponsored is a form of communication that will nourish both of you."

Sponsorship—What It's All About

There are times when everything the alcoholic in my life does irritates me. Sometimes he even seems to pour the breakfast cereal wrong! Although it's important for me to learn to recognize and protect myself from unacceptable behavior, that's not always what is going on. When I catch myself watching and criticizing every little detail of his behavior, I can use this as a signal that something is going on with *me* that I've missed or discounted. Am I afraid of an upcoming review at my job? Did something I heard at the meeting stir up unresolved anger from my past? Am I acting this way because of an old resentment I have chosen not to discuss? Making an Al-Anon phone call can help me to sort it out.

Today's reminder

It can be almost as hard for me to give up criticizing as it is for the alcoholic to give up drinking—sometimes it seems so necessary! But though criticism and negative thinking can serve as a steam valve for my pain, they never solve my problems, only distract me from them. In the end, I only avoid getting to know myself.

"A man can detect a speck in another's hair, but can't see the flies on his own nose."

Mendele Mocher Seforim

The unpleasant things other people say or do have no power to destroy my peace of mind or ruin my day unless I permit it. Do I allow myself to respond to the words of a sick person as if they were the ultimate truth? Could I possibly be getting some benefit from accepting humiliation?

Sometimes I wonder. I played the martyr role for a long time. My suffering brought me a lot of attention and pity. I grew accustomed to blaming others for my problems, and I avoided taking responsibility for my own life. In other words, I suspect I may have benefited from my pain. But those benefits are no longer worth the price.

Today I am finding out who I really am with the help of my Higher Power and the Al-Anon program. There is a beautiful person within me who has no need to build an identity around suffering. I am learning to let that person blossom instead of hiding behind a cloak of suffering. I don't want to miss any more of the wonderful opportunities available to me to live, grow, and enjoy.

Today's reminder

There is so much to appreciate in this life. I won't waste another moment feeling sorry for myself.

> ". . . The greater part of our happiness or misery depends on our dispositions and not on our circumstances."
>
> Martha Washington

Now that the year is at an end, I'll take a few minutes to contemplate the progress I've made and to thank my Higher Power for my growth. What did I do to contribute to my success this year? Perhaps it was as simple and as profound as daring to come to my first meeting, or to keep coming even when it was difficult.

How have I reached out to others in the fellowship this year? Did I set out literature, chair a meeting, clean up? Perhaps I welcomed a newcomer or gave them my phone number. Maybe I asked someone to be my sponsor, or opened up more deeply to the sponsor I already had. Have I thanked that person for all they've given me? Have I recognized my growing ability to love and trust others?

Perhaps I finally understood the First Step, or really committed myself to working some of the others. Maybe I had the faith and courage to make some hard decisions.

I am discovering that I do play an important part in my own well-being. I will celebrate my achievements and be grateful for all I have been given. I am not perfect, but I am excellent!

Today's reminder

I'm grateful for the Al-Anon program and all that my Higher Power has given me. I look forward to an even brighter new year.

"I am learning to treat myself as if I am valuable. I find that when I practice long enough, I begin to believe it."

                                    . . . *In All Our Affairs*

Study of these Steps is essential to progress in the Al-Anon program. The principles they embody are universal, applicable to everyone, whatever his personal creed. In Al-Anon, we strive for an ever-deeper understanding of these Steps, and pray for the wisdom to apply them to our lives.

1. We admitted we were powerless over alcohol—that our lives had become unmanageable.
2. Came to believe that a Power greater than ourselves could restore us to sanity.
3. Made a decision to turn our will and our lives over to the care of God *as we understood Him.*
4. Made a searching and fearless moral inventory of ourselves.
5. Admitted to God, to ourselves and to another human being the exact nature of our wrongs.
6. Were entirely ready to have God remove all these defects of character.
7. Humbly asked Him to remove our shortcomings.
8. Made a list of all persons we had harmed, and became willing to make amends to them all.
9. Made direct amends to such people wherever possible, except when to do so would injure them or others.
10. Continued to take personal inventory and when we were wrong promptly admitted it.
11. Sought through prayer and meditation to improve our conscious contact with God *as we understood Him,* praying only for knowledge of His will for us and the power to carry that out.
12. Having had a spiritual awakening as the result of these Steps, we tried to carry this message to others, and to practice these principles in all our affairs.

These guidelines are the means of promoting harmony and growth in Al-Anon groups and in the world-wide fellowship of Al-Anon as a whole. Our group experience suggests that our unity depends upon our adherence to these Traditions:

1. Our common welfare should come first; personal progress for the greatest number depends upon unity.

2. For our group purpose there is but one authority—a loving God as He may express Himself in our group conscience. Our leaders are but trusted servants; they do not govern.

3. The relatives of alcoholics, when gathered together for mutual aid, may call themselves an Al-Anon Family Group, provided that, as a group, they have no other affiliation. The only requirement for membership is that there be a problem of alcoholism in a relative or friend.

4. Each group should be autonomous, except in matters affecting another group or Al-Anon or AA as a whole.

5. Each Al-Anon Family Group has but one purpose: to help families of alcoholics. We do this by practicing the Twelve Steps of AA *ourselves*, by encouraging and understanding our alcoholic relatives, and by welcoming and giving comfort to families of alcoholics.

6. Our Al-Anon Family Groups ought never endorse, finance, or lend our name to any outside enterprise, lest problems of money, property and prestige divert us from our primary spiritual aim. Although a separate entity, we should always cooperate with Alcoholics Anonymous.

7. Every group ought to be fully self-supporting, declining outside contributions.

8. Al-Anon Twelfth Step work should remain forever nonprofessional, but our service centers may employ special workers.

9. Our groups, as such, ought never be organized; but we may create service boards or committees directly responsible to those they serve.

10. The Al-Anon Family Groups have no opinion on outside issues; hence our name ought never be drawn into public controversy.

11. Our public relations policy is based on attraction rather than promotion; we need always maintain personal anonymity at the level of press, radio, TV and films. We need guard with special care the anonymity of all AA members.

12. Anonymity is the spiritual foundation of all our Traditions, ever reminding us to place principles above personalities.

The Twelve Steps and Traditions are guides for personal growth and group unity. The Twelve Concepts are guides for service. They show how Twelfth Step work can be done on a broad scale and how members of a World Service Office can relate to each other and to the groups, through a World Service Conference, to spread Al-Anon's message worldwide.

1. The ultimate responsibility and authority for Al-Anon world services belongs to the Al-Anon groups.

2. The Al-Anon Family Groups have delegated complete administrative and operational authority to their Conference and its service arms.

3. The Right of Decision makes effective leadership possible.

4. Participation is the key to harmony.

5. The Rights of Appeal and Petition protect minorities and assure that they be heard.

6. The Conference acknowledges the primary administrative responsibility of the Trustees.

7. The Trustees have legal rights while the rights of the Conference are traditional.

8. The Board of Trustees delegates full authority for routine management of the Al-Anon Headquarters to its Executive Committees.

9. Good personal leadership at all service levels is a necessity. In the field of world service, the Board of Trustees assumes the primary leadership.

10. Service responsibility is balanced by carefully defined service authority and double-headed management is avoided.

11. The World Service Office is composed of standing committees, executives and staff members.

12. The spiritual foundation for Al-Anon's world services is contained in the General Warranties of the Conference, Article 12 of the Charter.

GENERAL WARRANTIES

In all its proceedings the World Service Conference of Al-Anon shall observe the spirit of the Traditions:

1. *that only sufficient operating funds, including an ample reserve, be its prudent financial principle;*

2. *that no Conference member shall be placed in unqualified authority over other members;*

3. *that all decisions be reached by discussion, vote, and whenever possible, by unanimity;*

4. *that no Conference action ever be personally punitive or an incitement to public controversy;*

5. *that though the Conference serves Al-Anon, it shall never perform any act of government, and that, like the fellowship of Al-Anon Family Groups which it serves, it shall always remain democratic in thought and action.*

Al-Anon books and ISBN listings:

Al-Anon Faces Alcoholism
0-910034-55-9

Alateen—Hope for Children of Alcoholics
0-910034-20-6

The Dilemma of the Alcoholic Marriage
0-910034-18-4

Al-Anon Family Groups
0-910034-54-0

One Day at a Time in Al-Anon *(Original Size)*
0-910034-21-4

Lois Remembers
0-910034-23-0

Al-Anon's Twelve Steps & Twelve Traditions
0-910034-24-9

Forum Favorites Vols. 1, 2 & 3
0-910034-51-6

Alateen—A Day at a Time
0-910034-53-2

As We Understood . . .
0-910034-56-7

First Steps
0-910034-57-5

One Day at a Time in Al-Anon *(Library Edition)*
0-910034-63-X

. . . In All Our Affairs: *Making Crises Work for You*
0-910034-73-7

A

Abuse 51, 106, 167, 273, 297

Acceptance 83, 96, 97, 129, 189, 232, 256, 309

Action 3, 32, 37, 38, 61, 86, 247, 290, 310, 328

Advice 6, 106

Alcoholism, a disease 11, 74, 84, 97, 110, 128, 143, 155, 312, 343

Al-Anon:
  Fellowship 11, 33, 39, 131, 136, 222, 278
  Meetings 68, 224, 253
  Recovery process 19, 28, 46, 50, 76, 82, 102, 135, 152, 210, 262, 280, 286, 292, 298, 317, 324
  Tools 4, 6, 116, 257, 317, 357

Analyzing 61, 285

Anger 167, 193, 237, 280, 287, 341, 360

Anonymity 20, 94

Anxiety 18, 290, 321

Arrogance 268, 280

Asking for help 48, 53, 66, 126, 127, 142, 161, 176, 218, 241, 295, 363

Awareness 105, 121, 191

Awareness, Acceptance, Action (3 A's) 92, 256

B

Balance 54, 227, 261, 286

Belonging 11, 33, 39, 131, 222, 261, 268, 278, 331

Blame 51, 120, 128, 189, 254, 280, 341, 365

Boundaries 201, 345

C

Caretaking 54

Change 3, 32, 50, 77, 96, 147, 202, 221, 230, 245, 265, 274, 286, 298, 330

Changed Attitudes 67, 100, 105, 107, 122, 171, 176, 178, 195, 243, 270, 279, 335, 347

Changing the things I can 4, 35, 58, 214, 336, 352, 353, 359

Character assets and defects 41, 65, 181, 183, 230

Choices 5, 12, 16, 30, 81, 117, 141, 172, 195, 209, 212, 257, 274, 297, 309

Commitment 28, 41, 46, 179, 212, 251, 342, 361

Communication 29, 174, 310

Comparing 44, 140

Compassion 5, 187, 277

Concepts 370

Conflict/disagreements 101, 104, 139, 140, 189, 193, 335, 362

Confusion 45, 69

Controlling 29, 215, 334, 350

Courage 119, 207, 219

Courtesy 104, 267, 302

Crises 15, 47, 139, 154, 169, 229, 248, 330

Criticism 89, 183, 197, 209, 255, 300, 329, 337, 364

D

Decision-making 23, 53, 108, 134, 159, 227

Defensiveness 104, 155, 201, 262, 297

Denial 146, 180, 191, 216, 239, 254

Depression 224, 279

Detachment 12, 22, 43, 72, 100, 124, 168, 180, 187, 199, 289, 320, 343, 365

Disappointment 83, 148, 258

Doubt 69, 133

E

Enabling 5, 32

Envy 170

Expectations 2, 19, 39, 66, 76, 110, 153, 244

F

Facing reality 191, 216, 232

Faith 35, 48, 69, 133, 154, 219, 235, 252, 260, 265, 305, 307

Fantasy/illusions 122, 132, 192, 208, 247, 286, 346

Fear 10, 70, 119, 150, 172, 235, 248, 265, 305

Feelings 83, 96, 114, 227, 238, 249, 270, 320, 339

Focusing on myself 25, 29, 79, 90, 109, 131, 166, 185, 194, 199, 214, 300, 310, 312, 329, 344, 345, 359, 364

Footwork 46, 152, 200, 353

Forcing solutions 37, 68, 115

Forgiveness 75, 178, 289

Freedom 13, 14, 111, 242

G

Gratitude 45, 119, 139, 170, 259, 262, 264, 282, 304, 332, 340, 348, 366

Giving and receiving 90, 136, 188, 302, 313

God of my understanding 13, 117, 133, 156, 165, 211, 307

Gossip 25, 300

Grief 246, 349

Guidance 59, 123, 145, 171

Guilt 120, 144, 242

H

Happiness 107, 148, 212

Helping 18, 137, 168
Higher Power 13, 17, 35, 117, 133, 154, 156, 165, 211,
    301, 307, 318, 327
Honesty 24, 146, 175, 236, 254, 296
Hope 148, 156, 258
Humility 33, 74, 98, 126, 142, 161, 225, 283
Humor 91, 205, 323

I
Intimacy 363
Isolation 223, 278

J
Joy 202, 325
Judgment 33, 44, 197, 209, 270

K
Keep coming back 102, 135, 210, 322

L
Letting go 99, 202, 272
Literature 62, 105
Living fully 41, 238, 257, 274, 281, 294, 325
Living in the present 10, 15, 99, 150, 195, 216, 257
Living with sobriety 8, 96, 297
Loneliness 132
Long-time members 28, 102, 326
Love 2, 42, 136, 301, 313, 340, 355

M
Manipulation 314
Martyrdom 334, 365

Maturity 63
Meditation 7, 173, 338
Memories 99, 190, 216
Mistakes 57, 60, 71, 236, 284
Motives 5, 18, 61, 235, 310, 364

N
Newcomers 185, 240, 276, 291, 304, 358

O
Obsession 141, 306

P
Pain 77, 83, 258, 330
Patience 1, 19, 77, 103, 135, 197, 210, 281
People-pleasing 9, 80, 107, 118, 207, 217, 261
Perspective 27, 91, 111, 176, 192, 228, 243, 259, 268, 332
Pleasure 91, 198, 323
Powerlessness 8, 14, 32, 74, 155, 240, 285
Prayer 48, 182, 352
Priorities 229, 250, 318
Problems 25, 55, 96, 159, 260, 306, 326, 332
Procrastination 184
Progress, not perfection 76, 86, 210, 240, 292, 319, 366

R
Reaching out 6, 66, 116, 123, 253
Relationships 49, 66, 87, 104, 194, 244, 302, 363
Relaxing 7, 198
Resentment 153, 178, 218, 289, 347, 352
Responsibility 85, 101, 293, 299, 351, 361
Risk 70, 86, 148, 219, 252, 328

S

Sanity 17, 134, 316

Sarcasm 167

Secrets 47, 111, 119, 127, 144

Self-acceptance 19, 44, 54, 71, 233

Self-esteem 9, 25, 44, 80, 107, 118, 120, 130, 132, 181, 208, 217, 255, 311, 313

Self-knowledge 24, 125, 152, 192

Self-love 41, 51, 82, 89, 151, 183, 206

Self-pity 170, 177, 188, 279, 348, 365

Self-righteousness 75, 303

Self-will 145

Serenity 28, 34, 129, 248, 318, 346

Serenity Prayer iv, 284, 352

Service 188, 251, 266, 276, 291, 336

Shame 57, 111

Sharing 47, 57, 111, 116, 121, 127, 131, 191, 266, 308

Silence 360

Slips 180

Slogans:

    in general 30, 68

    Easy does it 68, 93, 115, 200, 287

    First things first 107, 229, 318

    How important is it? 228, 250, 320

    Just for today 271, 274

    Keep an open mind 147

    Keep it simple 40, 328

    Let go and let God 8, 88, 203, 208, 252, 293, 321

    Let it begin with me 109, 267, 337

    Listen and learn 21

Live and let live 33, 89, 234, 303, 348
One day at a time 1, 3, 10, 15, 27, 138, 164, 190, 213, 271, 315
Think 16, 64, 279
Spiritual awakening 26, 307, 336
Sponsorship 52, 179, 226, 241, 308, 363
Steps:
    in general 26, 113, 126, 367
    First 8, 14, 32, 74, 155, 240, 275, 283, 285
    Second 17, 149, 156, 211, 235, 240, 307
    Third 23, 59, 157, 225, 240, 252, 269, 316, 350
    Fourth 55, 65, 125, 130, 158, 181, 255, 280, 333, 345
    Fifth 50, 65, 125, 127, 159, 266, 311
    Sixth 31, 65, 160, 177, 221, 319
    Seventh 31, 65, 73, 126, 142, 161, 249, 295
    Eighth 101, 162, 242, 263, 299, 356
    Ninth 163, 196, 299, 356
    Tenth 144, 164, 220, 236, 288, 329
    Eleventh 7, 59, 69, 165, 173, 182, 206, 220, 327, 338
    Twelfth 26, 78, 166, 209, 220, 344, 357
Surrender 59, 103, 145, 225, 269, 283

T

Take what you like and leave the rest 117, 321
Taking care of ourselves 21, 38, 56, 151, 198, 229, 273, 290, 342, 354
Tension relievers 62, 116, 290, 306, 321
This too shall pass 77, 315
Tolerance 49, 197
Three C's 74, 214

Traditions:
    in general 87, 201, 368
    First 108, 308
    Second 215, 245
    Third 186, 358
    Fourth 112
    Fifth 42, 194, 355
    Sixth 231
    Seventh 251
    Eighth 78, 137
    Ninth 291
    Tenth 52
    Eleventh 36, 344
    Twelfth 20, 94, 204, 272
Trust 154, 169, 232, 241

U
Unacceptable behavior 51, 158, 178, 267, 273, 289,
    297, 345, 361, 364

V
Victim role 35, 75, 122, 171, 174, 209, 299, 361
Violence 106, 273

W
Waiting 37, 61, 247, 281
Warranties 371
Wonder 294, 325
Worry 10, 15, 95, 150, 169, 259